Contemporary Religion and Popular Culture

Series Editors
Aaron David Lewis
Arlington, Massachusetts, USA

Eric Michael Mazur
Virginia Wesleyan College
Norfolk, Virginia, USA

Contemporary Religion and Popular Culture (CRPC) invites renewed engagement between religious studies and media studies, anthropology, literary studies, art history, musicology, philosophy, and all manner of high-level systems that under gird the everyday and commercial. Specifically, as a series, CRPC looks to upset the traditional approach to such topics by delivering top-grade scholarly material in smaller, more focused, and more digestible chunks, aiming to be the wide-access niche for scholars to further pursue specific avenues of their study that might not be supported elsewhere.

More information about this series at
http://www.springer.com/series/15420

Martin Lund

Re-Constructing the Man of Steel

Superman 1938–1941, Jewish American History, and the Invention of the Jewish–Comics Connection

palgrave
macmillan

Martin Lund
CUNY Graduate Center
Brooklyn, New York, USA

Contemporary Religion and Popular Culture
ISBN 978-3-319-42959-5   ISBN 978-3-319-42960-1   (eBook)
DOI 10.1007/978-3-319-42960-1

Library of Congress Control Number: 2016958028

Cover illustration: © Przemyslaw Koch / Alamy Stock Photo.

Printed on acid-free paper

This Palgrave Macmillan imprint is published by Springer Nature
The registered company is Springer International Publishing AG
The registered company address is: Gewerbestrasse 11, 6330 Cham, Switzerland

ACKNOWLEDGMENTS

Too many people have helped in the process that led up to this book, in ways big and small, for me to be able to name you all. This does not mean that I do not appreciate you or what you have done for me.

There is one name that towers above all others in my career, one person without whom this project could not have been pulled off: Jonas Otterbeck, supervisor, mentor, friend, and much more. Without him, I would be neither where I am nor who I am today. Thank you for everything you have done for me.

Traveling alongside us on the road to a finished dissertation were two others, without whom also I would not be writing this. Johan Åberg, who first introduced me to the world of Jewish studies, and Hanne Trautner-Kromann, who helped me get started and who stayed behind to make sure I could do this. Thank you both, for opening up the world for me.

I also extend my sincerest thanks to Beth S. Wenger, for a stimulating conversation, and to Pierre Wiktorin, Karin Zetterholm, and Mike Prince, for making me a doctor of philosophy.

Thanks also to David Heith-Stade, Linnéa Gradén, Anthony Fiscella, David Gudmundsson, Ervik Cejvan, and Matz Hammarström, my fellow exiles in that inaccessible wing of our alma mater. Thanks to Anna Minara Ciardi for *everything*. Thanks to Ola Wikander for the long walk-and-talks. Thanks to Bosse for all the procrastination disguised as long conversations. Thanks to the Andreases—Johansson and Gabrielsson—and to Acke, Johan Cato, Simon Stjernholm, Erik Alvstad, and Paul Linjamaa, for their input, support, and friendship in various situations. Thanks also to my doctoral "triplets" Erica and Eva, for helping me keep it together that last summer. Finally, thanks to the many others who, in one way or another, made my time at Centre for Theology and Religious Studies as nice as it was.

Thanks to Chris, Janni, Johan Kullenbok, Hanna Gunnarsson, Niklas and Ida, Ollebär, and the rest of you who helped make my time in Lund so memorable. Thanks to Fredrik Strömberg, Mike Prince (again!), Svenn-Arve, Mikko, A. David Lewis, Julian Chambliss, Ian Gordon, Caitlin McGurk, Julia Round, Steven Bergson and the countless other comics scholars who have made my career in the field rewarding on a personal plane, as well as on an intellectual one. Thanks to Nancy, Ian (again!), Rob Snyder, Suzanne Wasserman, Steph and Josh, and all the rest of you who have showed me New York life. Thanks to Huma for going along on the never-ending mac'n'cheese quest. And thanks to Liz for being Liz— nobody could find a better cousin to be adopted by in their early thirties.

Thanks to Jake, who, while we have only gotten to hang out sporadically since we left Kullen, has remained a constant and palpable presence in my life through the music he introduced me to, and through the music he makes. Thanks to Alex, for being a friend and an enabler. And thanks, with no end, to Martin and Emil, who have always been there, and who I know always will be.

I also thank my family, from the bottom of my heart: mom, Johan, Joakim, and Kent. I love you all.

And last, but by no measure least, thanks to Jordan, for complimenting my taste in books and for making every day better than the one before.

CONTENTS

CHAPTER 1

Introduction: Who Is Superman?

Superman is today probably one of the world's most instantly and widely recognizable pop culture icons.[1] Created at the height of the Great Depression by writer Jerome "Jerry" Siegel and artist Joseph "Joe" Shuster, two young Jewish men living in Cleveland, Ohio, Superman was a near-instant success. He first appeared in *Action Comics* #1, cover dated June 1938, but was on the stands already in April.[2] Each issue of *Action*, which contained one Superman story apiece, soon sold over 900,000 copies a month. His own title, *Superman*, soon sold somewhere between 1,250,000 and 1,300,000 on a bimonthly publication schedule, while most other comic books at the time sold somewhere between 200,000–400,000 copies.[3] Superman has since starred in hundreds, if not thousands of comic books, as well as numerous adaptations into other media. He has featured in radio serials, feature films, live action and animated television series, and even a musical, while his likeness has graced almost every kind of commodity imaginable. Further, he inspired a slew of imitators almost as soon as he appeared. This flurry of superhero publication is now commonly recognized as the beginning of the "Golden Age" of US superhero comics, an era that lasted roughly between 1938 and 1954, and the impact of which still reverberates around the globe.

© The Editor(s) (if applicable) and The Author(s) 2016
M. Lund, *Re-Constructing the Man of Steel*,
DOI 10.1007/978-3-319-42960-1_1

Jerry Siegel was born in Cleveland on October 17, 1914, to Lithuanian Jewish parents. He is often described as a shy loner who spent most of his time in the fantastic worlds of pop culture and dreamed of making a mark in pop culture himself: he wrote for his high school paper; tenaciously tried, and failed, to get published in established pulps; and made several attempts to self-publish his own magazines. In high school, he was introduced to Joe Shuster, born in Toronto on July 14, 1914, to a Dutch Jewish father and Ukrainian Jewish mother. Siegel and Shuster quickly bonded over their love of other worlds and started collaborating on stories and their own science fiction magazine. They even produced a full-length comic book. Despite several false starts, they had moderate success. Their real break, however, came in 1938, when they finally sold a comics story about their superheroic Superman, after years of pitching that character to unreceptive publishers.[4]

Superman first appeared in a story published in *Action* #1, with which any study of Superman and his creators must begin. The story had been created in 1934 as a comic strip, not a comic book feature, and sent to publishers. Accounts vary as to how it was brought to the attention of *Action*'s publishers years later, but either publisher Max Gaines or his assistant Sheldon Mayer was asked by their colleagues at Detective Comics (DC) if they knew of anything that could work as a lead feature for a new comic book. Gaines or Mayer suggested Siegel and Shuster's strip, which they had both seen when the character was making the rounds in the comics business.[5] Siegel and Shuster were sent their old strip and told that if they could quickly adapt it for a comic book, it would be published.[6]

The *Action* #1 story is an arguably haphazard and chaotic narrative that nonetheless proved highly successful. It starts with a one-page origin story, discussed in depth in Chap. 4, before thrusting readers, in medias res, straight into the action: a man in a gaudy red-and-blue costume is seen carrying a woman through the night. He is on his way to a governor's mansion, to bring this woman to justice for a murder and to free another woman, who is about to be wrongfully executed for that same crime. Bursting into the mansion and meeting with the politician, the strange strongman secures the innocent woman's freedom and then, after a change of location, immediately proceeds elsewhere to stop an incident of domestic violence. Next, in the guise of his stuttering alter ego, journalist Clark Kent, he convinces Lois Lane, a coworker, to go out with him. While on their date, the brutish Butch Matson pushes Clark aside and tells Lois that she will dance with him, "and like it!" When Lois refuses, Matson kidnaps her and complains that he let the "yellow" Clark off too easy. Enter Superman again, who hoists the kidnappers' car into the air, shakes them out of it, and overtakes the fleeing Matson, whom he then leaves, disgraced and petrified, dangling from a telephone pole. In a final vignette, Superman turns his attention to the nation's capital. There, he overhears a senator promising Alex Greer, "the slickest lobbyist in Washington," that a bill "will be passed before its full implications are realized. Before any remedial steps can be taken, our country will be embroiled with Europe." In short order, the superhero captures Greer, and Superman's first appearance ends on a cliffhanger, with the hero running along telephone wires with the terrified lobbyist in his arms.[7]

In only 13 short pages, Siegel and Shuster launched what would become a pop culture revolution with Superman, introduced several themes that would accompany the character for years to come—social justice, masculinity, and national politics—and created an icon that has since become the subject of much speculation. Because of Superman's lasting influence and because Siegel and Shuster were Jewish, Superman is nowadays frequently claimed as a "Jewish" character in a popular and academic literature that, I will argue, unintentionally contributes to a forgetting of the complex, and oftentimes fraught, history of identity formation in the USA in the twentieth century, and instead serves to promote Jewish identity in the contemporary USA; indeed, because of his primacy among superheroes, Superman has recently become a linchpin in the discursive creation of a "Jewish–comics connection," a supposed deep and lasting influence of Jewish culture and tradition on superhero comics. Several common tropes recur in this construction, and they have all gained wide traction; as this book will show, however, none of these claims holds up to critical scrutiny, but through their popularity and constant repetition, they have created an "interpretive sedimentation," by means of which a form of Judaizing, or "Judeocentric," reading has become firmly embedded in the commentarial tradition and has caused more and more aspects of that reading to be created and read into the text itself.[8]

Since Superman has been claimed to be so many different things, this book will engage in a critical dialogue with the extant literature about Jews and comics and look at what he, the Man of Steel himself, can say about others' ascribed identifications of him. In what follows, I will present a critical reading of the "Judeocentric" literature on Superman and the so-called Jewish–comics connection, juxtaposed with a contextual revisionist reading of the "original character" as he was represented in his early years. This juxtaposition serves two purposes: first, it aims to provide a corrective to an ongoing diffusion of myth into accepted truth; second, it aims to provide a corrective to the study of Jewish-created superhero characters like Superman, characters whose possible Jewishness has heretofore been largely ignored in the majority of academic comics scholarship.[9] Combined, these perspectives make the argument that critical study, informed by historical formations of American Jewishness, can help further the understanding of these characters' genesis and continued cultural roles for the benefit of both Jewish studies, American studies, cultural studies, and comics studies.

In these pages, Superman will speak for himself, as it were, and is therefore humanized in the choice of pronouns: his characterization under Siegel and Shuster will be read in relation to the context in which he first appeared and analyzed from an intertextual perspective, in an attempt to discern if and how his creators' Jewishness might have played into his creation and characterization. The original Superman's identity, it will be argued, is best read in terms of how it tries to redefine the nation in a slightly more inclusive way that also conforms to a common Americanizing tendency within the Jewish American community at the time. It is also argued that Superman's conformity to common representational conventions caused his stories and creators to perpetuate deracializing and marginalizing US formations of race, class, and gender.

FRAMING SUPERMAN

In one recent formulation, Superman was said to be "seen by pop culture scholars as the ultimate metaphor for the Jewish experience."[10] Others have claimed that Superman should be regarded as a golem,[11] or an extraterrestrial Moses, and his creation has been claimed to be a response to the rise of Nazism in Germany.[12] Alternative interpretations present him as a juvenile power fantasy[13] or a Christ figure in tights.[14] In fact, Superman has been something akin to all of these things, and much more, at one point or another in his long life; indeed, the title of the 1998 series *Superman for all Seasons* is an apt description of the Superman *metatext*, a concept that comics scholar Richard Reynolds defines as "a summation of all existing texts plus all the gaps which those texts have left unspecified."[15] Combined, these elements constitute an eternally incomplete chain of continuity, unknowable in its entirety since, even if someone were to read every single Superman publication to date, the serialized nature of superhero comic books assures that new texts are added every month, each of which can potentially change a series' present and past. The resulting metatextual flow contains myriad versions of the character, similar in many respects and radically different in others, that together provide ample support for a wide variety of interpretations. But no character is static, no characterization eternal, and no series or theme timeless; without clearly defining which parts of the metatext will be used before analyzing Superman, or any other similar character, one risks anachronistically projecting later developments in continuity onto earlier iterations.

Siegel and Shuster's Superman was not the "boy scout" he has been in recent decades, but a tough guy who gleefully dished out his own rough brand of justice. He was stronger than the average man by far, and could famously outrun a speeding train and leap tall buildings, but he was not a godlike character able to move entire planets, which he has since been when it has fit a writer's needs. He had neither X-ray vision nor super-hearing at first. This was a Superman who could not fly. His abilities developed over many years and some, like super-shape-shifting and super-hypnosis, had little staying power. This Superman had no Kansas childhood; until the name Metropolis was introduced in *Action Comics* #16 (September 1939), possibly as a reflection of Siegel's brief move to New York, Superman would live in Cleveland.[16] The elder Kents did not at first play a marked role in his life, and he initially worked for the *Daily Star*—named after *The Toronto Star* of Canadian-born Shuster's childhood[17]—and not the now culturally ingrained *Daily Planet*. There was no Kryptonite and no Fortress of Solitude. Almost everything about this Superman is different from today's character, and much of what is known about him now was introduced by others than Siegel and Shuster, facts that any study must acknowledge.[18]

The Superman discussed in this book is Siegel and Shuster's "original" Superman, introduced in *Action* #1. While Siegel's initial run as writer continued until 1948, the USA's entry into World War II (WWII) on December 8, 1941, has been chosen as the cutoff point for this study.[19] The Great Depression ended that year, and in its stead a time of rapid proliferation of economic as well as social capital began in the USA, resulting in a new national mood that fundamentally changed the socioeconomic backdrop against which the character had initially been projected.[20] Also by that time, from fear that it could endanger the valuable property Superman had become, editorial policy and the introduction of routine script-vetting put a halt to the relatively free rein initially afforded to Siegel and his coworkers.[21]

The explicit social justice focus that characterized early Superman comic books was largely replaced by this time, with high-spirited crime fighting and costumed villains. Just as the Superman that Siegel and Shuster introduced is different from the Superman of today, he was decisively different from the Superman of both the war years and the immediate postwar period.[22] Considering Siegel's entire run would thus make this a study of Superman's development rather than an analysis of the superhero's initial characterization, which is the present purpose. Rather, this book has a dual focus: first, it provides analysis of Superman in his original context, in which focus is on Jewish American and US majority society's cultural and political concerns as they overlapped and diverged; second, it looks at this Superman's new meaning in contemporary Jewish American life, a meaning that, it will be argued, is deeply informed by current cultural and identity political concerns.

Characterizing Superman

In literary critic Shlomith Rimmon-Kenan's definition, character in narrative is a network of character traits that appear in explicit and implicit ways, for which the basic indicators are *direct definition* and *indirect presentation*; the former names the trait explicitly while the latter embodies the trait but leaves the reader to infer it.[23] Direct definition uses simple description, performed by the most authoritative voices in the text, which readers are implicitly called upon to trust.[24] For example, on the first page of *Action* #1, Superman is introduced in the following way: "Early, Clark decided he must turn his titanic strength into channels that would benefit mankind. And so was created... SUPERMAN! Champion of the oppressed, the physical marvel who had sworn to devote his existence to helping those in need."[25] Coming from the omniscient narrator, it constitutes a reliable direct characterization of the protagonist that, adjusting for changes in context and focus, introduces traits that have remained among Superman's most consistent characteristics over the years.

Conversely, indirect presentation is a type of trait indication performed within the story-world through characters' actions, speech, appearance, or in conjunction with their surroundings. An action, whether habitual or one time, can be either an "act of commission (i.e. something performed by the character), [an] act of omission (something the character should, but does not do), [or a] contemplated act (an unrealized plan or intention of the character)."[26] Indirect presentations represent character through a causal relationship which the reader deciphers "in reverse": "X killed the dragon, 'therefore' he is brave; Y uses many foreign words, 'therefore' she is a snob."[27] Thus, in a latter-day Superman story, when a computer deduces that the titular superhero's secret identity is actually that of mild-mannered reporter Clark Kent, his nemesis Lex Luthor refuses to believe it even though the revelation might seem logical. "A *soulless* machine might make that deduction," Luthor says: "But not *Lex Luthor! I* know *better! I* know that no man with the *power of Superman* would ever *pretend* to be a mere *human!* Such power is to be *constantly exploited.* Such power is to be *used!!"*[28] This indirectly (if bluntly) characterizes the speaker: Luthor cannot trust others to not abuse power like he would; "therefore" he is misanthropic and megalomaniacal. By virtue of this characterization, Luthor also enhances Superman's characterization as his own philanthropic and altruistic opposite.

Additionally, appearances have long been used as cues to character; the superhero physique is one example of a character indicator, pointing to the strength of characters' convictions (physically buff does not in itself mean either good or evil, but a muscular physique often symbolized strength, vitality, and heroism during the 1930s and 1940s[29]), just as the fanged and claw-fingered appearances of WWII comic books' "Japanazis" identified them as "subhuman."[30] Finally, environments and landscapes often enhance a character trait through metonymy or analogy, for example, in the way that Superman's clean Cleveland/Metropolis reinforces the essential hopefulness of the character; his fight against injustice has always been invested with a hope for betterment, which is underscored by the bright urban landscape where he pursues his goals.

When contextualized, characterizations provide insight into how comics creators structure their work in conscious and unconscious ways and how they address their audiences, which helps clarify what conceptions of identity their characters stem from. Thus, characterizations can help elucidate whether or not a character like Siegel and Shuster's Superman is Jewish, and in what ways; first, however, we must consider what that means.

IDENTITIES, DISCURSIVE TRADITIONS, AND CULTURAL PRODUCTION

Since at least as far back as the days of biblical authorship, the question of "who is a Jew" has been of considerable consequence to a great many people for a variety of reasons; criteria have included religious adherence, cultural affiliation, race and blood, and whether or not your mother was

Jewish.[31] According to religion-scholar Stuart Charmé, the debate in contemporary Judaism centers on notions of "authenticity," the two main perspectives being "essentialistic authenticities" and "existentialist authenticities."[32] For adherents of the essentialistic model, what matters is depth of personal Jewish knowledge, observance, and commitment, that the identity is "authentically Jewish," rooted in tradition. Existentialists choose instead to understand "authentic" as modifying not the adjective, "Jewish," but rather the noun, "identity." An authentic Jewish identity is here an identity that embraces the individual's sociocultural context wholly, that does so in a way that makes sense to him or her, and that can be internalized but changed according to circumstances, rather than being rooted in an acceptance in "bad faith" of received traditions.[33]

As far as biographical sources suggest, the existentialist model fits Siegel and Shuster best, since they appear to have rejected some traditions and self-identified as Jewish in a way that made sense to them. That does not mean that their Jewishness was a primary determining factor in their creative lives. Ultimately, it cannot be fully known how they privately felt about their Jewish self-identification, wherefore any attempt at studying what ways their Jewish backgrounds affected their work must be anchored in relevant contexts, plausible intertexts, and stated intentions. *If* they were Jewish is not at issue, but *how* they were Jewish and, crucially, *what* that meant for their public creative selves underlies the present argument; what is of interest here, specifically, is how their work textually engaged with contemporaneous hegemonic Jewish and non-Jewish formations of Jewishness and Americanness.[34]

Like Jewishness, Americanness is a fluid concept. It has been articulated and rearticulated many times in the nation's history. One of the most enduring definitions of what makes an American was proposed in 1782 by writer J. Hector St. John de Crèvecœur: "He is an American, who leaving behind him all his ancient prejudices and manners, receives new ones from the new mode of life he has embraced, the new government he obeys, and the new rank he holds."[35] But de Crèvecœur was neither the first nor the last to propose a characterization of the American. A few central concepts recurred time and again; since the time the Puritans disembarked into the Massachusetts Bay, Americans have commonly regarded freedom, progress, and providence as the building blocks of their community. What those concepts represent, however, has rarely been stable and certainly never universally accepted.[36]

When all of this is considered, it becomes evident that, for Siegel and Shuster, as for the many writers who contributed to the 2005 anthology *Who We Are: On Being (and Not Being) a Jewish American Writer*, labels like "Jewish writer" and "Jewish culture" are not straightforward, nor indeed necessarily welcome. Some writers accept them wholly and some in part; others, in literary critic Derek Rubin's words, "scorn" the "Jewish writer" label as a "senseless badge of tribal pride."[37] Author Saul Bellow, for example, writes that "I thought of myself as a Midwesterner and not a Jew. I am often described as a Jewish writer; in much the same way one might be called a Samoan astronomer or an Eskimo cellist or a Zulu Gainsborough expert. [...] My joke is not broad enough to cover the contempt I feel for the opportunists, wise guys, and career types who impose such labels and trade upon them."[38]

Labels like "Jewish writer" and "Jewish culture" can mean many things to those who embrace or reject them, and to those who ascribe them. As men of Jewish heritage practicing a writerly and artistic profession, Siegel and Shuster were Jewish cultural producers by definition. However, in American studies scholar Stephen J. Whitfield's words, such a minimalist definition, common though it may be, lumps together "any activity done by Jews in the United States, whether or not such work bears the traces of Jewish content or specificity."[39] It is difficult to see what such a definition adds to critical understanding. Conversely, a maximalist definition embraces only works that were "conceived not only by Jews but bear directly on their beliefs and experiences as a people." It establishes a consensus about what is Jewish at the cost of full critical appreciation of the creative individual.[40] Further, other influences than a Jewish background help shape Jewish cultural producers, and highlighting Jewishness at the cost of other sociocultural stimuli can lead to "fudging and misjudging" creators' importance and presence in the world of culture.[41]

In discussing writers who are skeptical about the "Jewish writer" label, Rubin notes that some of them subscribe to Isaac Bashevis Singer's dictum that every writer must have an address. For example, Cynthia Ozick, who rejects the label as restrictive, noting that "[n]o writer should be a moral champion or a representative of 'identity'," nonetheless regards herself as a Jewish writer, in the sense that her fiction embodies her connection to the Jewish literary tradition and Jewish history. Similarly, despite some wariness about being pigeonholed, Allegra Goodman welcomes the label insofar as it suggests that she writes for fellow American Jews.[42] Following these characterizations, discussions about the Jewishness of a given writer as a public figure, or of their work, should be framed by considerations about who they address and how.

It can here be countered, rightly, that this analytical framework stacks the deck in favor of an Americanist reading. Superman is not the didactic *Jewish Hero Corps*, the Zionist *Captain Israel*, or any of the Hasidic Chabad movement's numerous educational comics, and he could not be: he was created by two young men who wanted fame fortune, distributed by a publisher that wanted broad appeal, and circulated in a time when overtly ethnic literature was not generally welcome in the USA.[43] That a text primarily addresses one audience, however, does not mean that a secondary, in-group directed or "insider," semiotics cannot parallel, support, or subvert the major tradition employed, signifying a different tradition without necessarily giving it central importance. An ethnically unmarked, American-oriented work can contain marked, Jewish-oriented, signification such as references to Jewish history and culture or Yiddishisms intended as "winks" to the cognoscenti, or even without the producer realizing it. Such signification does not necessarily have to be written in a "Jewish language," but can also be expressed in a language that speaks about or to Jews in other ways. Traces of Jewishness can be found in products that cannot easily be labeled as "Jewish culture," inscribed by people who did not necessarily consider themselves to be "Jewish writers."

Like all identities, Jewishness is fluid. There is no fixed essence that marks Jews throughout history and across the world as being the same. Following what Charmé and other religion-scholars have recently proposed as a more fruitful way of studying Jewish identity, this book regards Jewishness as a contextually based social construction, subject to great variations in expression, instead of attempting to propose a "grand definition" of Jewish identity.[44] Consequently, in attempting to understand Superman's address, this study adapts anthropologist Talal Asad's concept of *discursive traditions*. Asking rhetorically what a tradition is, Asad answers:

> A tradition consists essentially of discourses that seek to instruct practitioners regarding the correct form and purpose of a given practice that, precisely because it is established, has a history. These discourses relate conceptually to *a past* (when the practice was instituted, and from which the knowledge of its point and proper performance has been transmitted) and *a future* (how the point of that practice can best be secured in the long term, or why it should be modified or abandoned), through *a present* (how it is linked to other practices, institutions, and social conditions.)[45]

Much like the Islamic discursive tradition that Asad envisions, a Jewish or American discursive tradition concerns itself with conceptions of the Jewish or American past and future with reference to particular Jewish or American practices in the present. Consequently, not everything Jews say and do, or write and draw, belongs to a Jewish discursive tradition and not everything Americans say and do belongs in an American discursive tradition. This becomes particularly evident when one considers that self-identifying as Jewish does not preclude self-identifying as American, and vice versa. From this perspective, what becomes important in determining to what degree cultural production should be claimed as Jewish or American is to what degree it is oriented toward a notion of Jewishness or Americanness, regardless of whether that notion is conceived of (primarily but not exclusively) in religious, nationalistic, secular, cultural, or ethnic terms.

JEWISHNESS: THE FIGURE OF DIFFERENCE

As will be discussed at length in this book, contemporary writers on Jews and comics use markers and symbols like Moses or the golem to argue for encoded Jewishness in American superhero comics. Often, however, this literature disregards historical context and does not take seriously changing identity formations. Jewishness is a central concern in this book: as the heritage of the comics creators discussed, as presumably an important source of the stories and cultural tools they were raised with, and as essential to how their work is often discussed today. While most people have a concept of Judaism, solidifying it into a workable definition is not easy. Most attempts end up focusing too much, intentionally or not, on one aspect of the religious, cultural, ethnic, and other traditions that comprise its archive of cultural memory, at the expense of others. Likewise, within the communities that the word "Jewishness" denotes, there are no universally agreed-upon understandings of the word. "Jewishness" helps define the imagined Jewish meta-community against other groups, but those defined with the word do not necessarily share a single interpretation of what it means.[46]

Siegel and Shuster, around whose work this book revolves, were individual cultural producers of Jewish heritage, working at a specific historical moment, within and against distinct and contingent understandings of Jewishness in all its ethnic, cultural, religious, linguistic, and American complexity. In order to study this dynamic, a heuristic scheme or catalog of markers and symbols that were part of hegemonic American formations of Jewishness around the time Superman first appeared should be presented. Such a scheme provides an interpretive frame within which it is possible to evaluate in what ways Siegel and Shuster reflected their historical contexts and events that impacted upon American Jewry, and how their representational self-identification and identity politics engaged with the implicit normative Jewish American ethnos of their own time.

Indeed, several large themes run throughout the twentieth-century Jewish American history, the affirmation and rejection of which can be regarded as cultural markers of Jewishness, or at the very least as products of a Jewish experience. Perhaps the most obvious is religious tradition, even if it should be expected that this is also the least represented in these comics, given that mass cultural production is, in the main, a secular undertaking. As already noted, and as will be addressed again, Superman is sometimes claimed to parallel biblical figures such as Moses and Samson. But these figures have long been common in Western culture in general, and thus their possible uses in pop culture must be considered beyond merely pointing to a parallel, based on superficial similarities. The presence and absence of Jewish religious ritual can also be placed within the discursive orbit of religiously based significations of Jewishness.

More likely to appear in the type of material discussed in this book are cultural and ethnic markers of Jewishness. One source of such significations is the Yiddish language. When one discusses Jewish self-identification and representation, the presence or absence of references to history are also significant. Jewish culture has always had a strong sense of its past, although the exact meaning of that relationship changes over time and often differs between communities.[47] As historian of Judaism Beth S. Wenger has convincingly argued, Jewish Americans began a process of creating a distinct American Jewish heritage in the late nineteenth century that culminated in the mid-1900s. Throughout this process, Jewish American leaders and educators attempted to situate Jews within the history of the USA and to identify US history with Jewish American history. In many cases, this argument for convergence highlighted Jewish contributions to the USA and celebrated Jewish specificity.[48] Thus, references to the past can be expected to range from positive or negative representations of the Old World left behind by the creators' families, to national events in the US history that do not bear any particular or obvious Jewish imprint. The uses of history in comics, then, can serve as clues to how writers conceived of their own and of Jews' place in the larger world. There has also been a political thread running through the twentieth-century Jewish American experiences; most obviously, this appears in the disproportionate and persistent identification of Jewish Americans with liberalism and the Democratic Party.[49] This liberalism has often included a dedication to racial liberalism, pluralism, and universal human rights. Activism has been framed in terms both religious and secular, within both Jewish and broad-based US organizational structures.[50]

Finally, one should mention that it is highly likely that the comics will contain explicit and implicit intended or incidental visual cues. Such cues can appear in several ways. First, obvious references, such as the use of a *Magen David*, yarmulkes, ritual or religious objects, and other cultural artifacts, all display a willingness to identify as Jewish, even though that alone should not be regarded as an intention of the creators' to mark the work itself as Jewish. Second, the reproduction of non-Jews' stereotypes of Jews could indicate either anxiety about one's place in American society or a distancing from Jewishness, or that the use of Jewish signification is instrumental or unreflected, rather than an instance of self-identification.[51] Third, American Jews have developed a number of intra-ethnic stereotypes that might appear in texts produced for a mass market, either in their particular Jewish form or in some way adapted for broader consumption. The most easily recognizable examples of the former type are the Jewish Mother and Jewish American Princess, both of which have been widely disseminated in mainstream US culture.[52] Furthermore, when reading is situated within a specific historical context, the very way in which characters are attired might signify reproduction of an ethnic environment or a desire to represent a world that adheres more strictly to majority norms of middle class life and consumption, signifying an attempt to create an ethnically unmarked world. Such avoidance strategies can be a marker of ethnic disidentification that reflects either a desire for or anxiety about Americanization.

Many of the figures of Jewishness discussed above have been articulated and attuned to such concerns. Jewishness in twentieth-century USA was, and in many ways remains, perceived by Jews and non-Jews alike as a type of difference, a divergence from an ostensible norm. By studying comics produced for a mass audience in a time before US popular culture had significantly abandoned the ideal of mass homogeneity, this book seeks to uncover how parallel discourses, concerns, and stereotypes were used, adapted, or eschewed in the creative process of both representation and identity formation, in ways both marked and unmarked. Thus, the current approach, of studying representations of race, ethnicity, class, and gender, and of looking to the course of broader US history, is employed from the belief that the disparate threads can help recount a story that was told not only with words and images, but sometimes also with silences. The history of Siegel and Shuster's Superman, it will be argued, is a history of meaning making, cultural strategies, and coping with the dissonances and tensions experienced by two Jewish American comics creators situated in a changing US and Jewish American world.[53] Before we can delve into this revised history, however, we need to look at how the story has recently been told by others.

Notes

1. The argument in this book is revised and expanded from a version that appeared in my dissertation, "Rethinking the Jewish–Comics Connection," defended at Lund University's Centre for Theology and Religious Studies on November 15, 2013. Part of the argument has also appeared in Lund, "American Golem."
2. Cover dates and dates of publication are rarely the same. At the time discussed, cover dates were usually two or three month ahead of actual publication. According to DC's Jack Liebowitz in United States Circuit Court of Appeals, "Detective vs. Bruns et al.," 5, 26, 92, *Action* #1 was published "on or around April 18th, 1938." See also p. 67: "It is the June issue but published in April."
3. Wright, *Comic Book Nation*, 13; Gordon, *Comic Strips*, 131–32; Tye, *Superman*, 35–39.
4. Ricca, *Super Boys*, 12, 40–118, 125–52; Tye, *Superman*, 12–30; Andrae, Blum, and Coddington, "Supermen and Kids."
5. There are many conflicting versions of Superman's creation that date it as far back as 1931, but it is most likely that the character as it appeared in *Action* #1 was created sometime in 1934. See Jones, *Men of Tomorrow*, 109–15, 122–23; Tye, *Superman*, 16–21.

   In United States Circuit Court of Appeals, "Detective vs. Bruns et al.," 131–137, 140, Max Gaines testifies to having seen drawings that "were rearranged into this page form for use in Action Comics" in January 1936, as does Sheldon Mayer. pp. 68–69 also contain a long back-and-forth between Siegel, the attorneys, and the court. Here, Siegel is asked about "those drawings that you say were made in 1934 and sent to these various people [newspaper syndicates]." Siegel testifies that the 1934 Superman comic strip he and Siegel had made is also the material that appeared in *Action* #1 in 1938: "they are in the magazine. [...] Yes, those drawings were cut up and pasted into magazine form, into page form for magazines. [...] And they were sent in and are now published in Action Comics."

6. Andrae, Blum, and Coddington, "Supermen and Kids," 15; Jones, *Men of Tomorrow*, 121–25; Tye, *Superman*, 28–29; Ricca, *Super Boys*, 148–51; cf. United States Circuit Court of Appeals, "Detective vs. Bruns et al.," 136. See also the court findings on p. 173 in that transcript: "Jerome Siegel, writer, and Joe Shuster, artists, collaborated in the creation of the comic strip character 'Superman' and created the same in 1933. The material appearing in the 'Superman' comic strip in the first issue of 'Action Comics' (June, 1938 issue, Plaintiffs Exhibit 12) was prepared by them in 1934."

7. *SC1*, 4–16. Throughout this book, references to *SCX* are shorthand for the Superman reprint volumes, Siegel, Shuster, et al., *Superman Chronicles* 1–9 (New York: DC Comics, 2006–2009). For a close reading of only this story, see Lund, "American Golem."

8. Cf. Cowan, "Seeing the Saviour." The term "Judeocentric" borrowed from Fingeroth, *Disguised as Clark Kent*, 25.

9. In Darowski, *Ages of Superman*, for example, only one mention of Superman's creators' Jewishness is ever made, and then in a context where Siegel and Shuster are not in focus; see O'Rourke and O'Rourke, "Morning Again," 122. This omission becomes all the more noticeable when one considers that the editor of that volume has said in an interview that "American identity" became a "through-line," or common theme, in that collection. See Yanes, "Darowski's Career."

10. Kaplan, *From Krakow to Krypton*, 13.

11. See, for example, Kaplan, *From Krakow to Krypton*; Sanderson, "Miller."

12. Fingeroth, *Disguised as Clark Kent*, chap. 4; Weinstein, *Up, Up, and Oy Vey!*, chap. 1; Kaplan, *From Krakow to Krypton*, chap. 3.

13. A dominant theme in Jones, *Men of Tomorrow*.

14. For example, Garrett, *Holy Superheroes!*; Brewer, *Who Needs a Superhero?*; Skelton, *Gospel*.

15. Reynolds, *Super Heroes*, 43; Loeb and Sale, *Superman for All Seasons*.
16. *SC2*, 34; cf. Ricca, *Super Boys*, 162–63.
17. Mietkiewicz, "Great Krypton!"
18. De Haven, *Our Hero*, 95–96 points out, "[a]lmost all of Superman's signature boilerplate [...] started on radio, as did many of the most durable elements of the mythology"; cf. Daniels, *Superman*, 54–57; Jones, *Men of Tomorrow*; Ricca, *Super Boys*.
19. Even with this cutoff, influences from others are unavoidable. Further, Shuster began delegating artwork early on, resulting in him playing a smaller role in the present study. Cf. Ricca, *Super Boys*, 162–163.
20. Kennedy, *Freedom from Fear*, 617–19.
21. De Haven, *Our Hero*, 72–73; Daniels, *Superman*, 63; Tye, *Superman*, 50–51; Ricca, *Super Boys*, 206; Welky, *Everything Was Better*, 142.
22. Cf. De Haven, *Our Hero*, 4–5.
23. Rimmon-Kenan, *Narrative Fiction*, 59–60.
24. On voices, see Rimmon-Kenan, *Narrative Fiction*, chap. 7.
25. *SC1*, 4; Rimmon-Kenan, *Narrative Fiction*, 62.
26. Rimmon-Kenan, *Narrative Fiction*, 61–62.
27. Rimmon-Kenan, *Narrative Fiction*, 65.
28. Byrne, Austin, and Williams, *Secret Revealed!*, 2:22.
29. Jarvis, *Male Body at War*, 44.
30. Wright, *Comic Book Nation*, 45–47; Murray, *Champions*, 214–29.
31. Goldstein, *Price of Whiteness* provides a survey of how Jewishness has been defined and redefined in the USA.
32. Charmé, "Varieties of Authenticity."
33. Charmé, "Varieties of Authenticity," 143.
34. Cf. Charmé et al., "Jewish Identities in Action," 139–40.
35. Crèvecoeur, *Letters*, 43–44. This definition remained a staple in discussions of American identity well into the twentieth century; cf. Schlesinger, "This New Man"; Mazlish, "Crevecoeur's New World."
36. Cf. Costello, *Secret Identity Crisis*, chap. 1.
37. Rubin, "Introduction," xvi.
38. Bellow, "Starting Out in Chicago," 5.
39. Whitfield, "Paradoxes," 248.
40. Whitfield, "Paradoxes," 249.

41. "Fudging and misjudging" Whitfield, "Paradoxes," 250.
42. Rubin, "Introduction," xvi–xvii.
43. Oirich and Randall, *The Amnesia Count-Down*; Schumer, *A Superhero for Our Time*; Kubert, *Yaakov & Isaac*; cf. Halter, *Shopping for Identity*; Jones, *Men of Tomorrow*.
44. Charmé et al., "Jewish Identities in Action."
45. Asad, *Anthropology of Islam*, 14.
46. Cf. Cohen, *Symbolic Construction*, 15; Anderson, *Imagined Communities*.
47. Brenner, *Prophets of the Past*; Roskies, *Usable Past*; Yerushalmi, *Zakhor*.
48. Wenger, *History Lessons*.
49. Cf. Brahm Levey, "Toward a Theory"; Walzer, "Liberalism and Jews."
50. Literature on the subject of Jewish American anti-prejudicial and rights activism includes Greenberg, *Troubling the Waters*; Galchinsky, *Jews and Human Rights*.
51. A case in point here can be found in writer-artist Will Eisner's most famous work, *A Contract with God*. In it, the character Frimme Hersch at one point abandons his Hasidic ways. *Contract*'s two versions of Frimme do not appear to be the same person, writes Yiddischist Jeremy Dauber: after abandoning his pious ways, shaving his beard, and getting into real estate, "one can see how complexly and problematically" Eisner has reproduced in Frimme the anti-Semitic image of the Jewish capitalist with thick lips and jowls to make his point. See Dauber, "Comic Books," 296–98.
52. Cf. Prell, *Fighting to Become Americans*.
53. Cf. Charmé et al., "Jewish Identities in Action," 124–25.

CHAPTER 2

Introducing the Jewish–Comics Connection

In anticipation of the then-upcoming Superman movie, *Man of Steel*, in a July 2013 *Huffington Post* article, religion scholar S. Brent Plate wrote: "Scratch the surface of almost all great comic books and we might find something startling similar: the roots of today's superheroes lie in a particular Jewish culture transplanted from Europe to the United States in the first half of the 20th-century."[1] This statement prompts numerous questions, and is problematic not least in its assumptions of a particular, transplantable European Jewish culture and its supposed retention in the USA. After all, Jewish communities in different European countries had their own cultures, and Jewish immigrants—particularly during the first half of the twentieth century, when many of Plate's superheroes were created—were encouraged to Americanize, something that many community leaders promoted and many first- and second-generation immigrants desired.[2] The claim is equally problematic in its assumption that those superheroes were conduits for this "particular" Jewish culture, not least since Plate himself, as one of his examples, later uses Wonder Woman. Far from being rooted in European Jewish culture, this character was the unmistakably Hellenic-inspired creation of William Moulton Marston, a WASPish Bostonian whose family traced its heritage back to the Battle of Hastings, who wanted to promote a particular vision of feminism with her.[3]

© The Editor(s) (if applicable) and The Author(s) 2016
M. Lund, *Re-Constructing the Man of Steel*,
DOI 10.1007/978-3-319-42960-1_2

Plate is far from alone in making grand claims about a supposed Jewish–comics connection. A vast literature on the subject has emerged since the mid-2000s, primarily in popular formats but also within academia. This literature is open to criticism on several levels: it lacks proper historicization and contextualization of its material; it applies essentialist perspectives to both characters and their creators; it bases much of its argument on erroneous assumptions, rooted in "common knowledge" and "accepted wisdom"; it makes grand statements from insufficient textual samples; and, in the case of academia, rather than directly examining primary sources, it uses questionable secondary sources with little or no source criticism.[4]

This chapter looks at how this literature portrays Superman, a central figure in the construction of the Jewish–comics connection, discussing recurrent tropes, "parallels," and intertexts, and touching upon how they have evolved over the years. It does so with the aim, in combination with the revised history of Superman presented in later chapters, of inspiring a revision of how sources and history are handled as the important study of Jews and comics continues to evolve.

INVENTING THE JEWISH–COMICS CONNECTION

In 1979, sociologist Herbert J. Gans wrote about the ethnic revival that a good deal of nostalgic writing celebrating immigrant culture and its *Gemeinschaft*—community—had started to appear, as more academics and writers from various ethnic groups entered the upper echelons of American society. He noted parenthetically that "an interesting study could be made of the extent to which writers from different ethnic groups, of both fiction and nonfiction, are pursuing nostalgic, contemporary, or future-oriented approaches to ethnicity."[5] Indeed, a nostalgic and celebratory literature on the topic of Jews and comics has emerged over the past decade, and while this book cannot constitute a full study of the type Gans envisioned, such a discussion can be useful in order to paint a fuller (but in no way complete) picture of the popular conception of the Jewish–comics connection.

Further, psychologist and rabbi Arthur Blecher has described how he decided to set aside his previous assumptions about Judaism and look at it critically. He found that

> a distinct pattern emerges from the printed pages of almost all Judaica published in America since the beginning of the twentieth century. Whether a

book is about God, or Scripture, or Jewish history or ritual observance, writers tend to reiterate a few specific concerns. One is continuity: The author takes pains to show that some particular manifestation of current Jewish practice is directly linked to ancient Judaism. Another topic is authenticity: The book makes assumptions about whether something is either intrinsically Jewish or the results of outside influence. Finally, the writers are preoccupied with worries about the survival of the Jewish way of life.[6]

This demonstrated for Blecher that "somehow a number of significant historical inaccuracies invaded the information American Jewish teachers have been presenting for over a century." These "false concepts," as Blecher labels them, are "myths in the sense of collective ideas that are untrue. [...] And as myths, they also contain valuable truths about the collective spirit of an enduring civilization."[7]

There is another meaning of myth that should also be applied here: for semiotician and literary theorist Roland Barthes, myth is a type of speech that, in being uttered, makes history "natural." That is to say, myth is a way of speaking about something that already exists, a symbol of any kind, and adding to it a meaning that promotes an idea or ideology that is not inherent in it, giving the historical and contingent the appearance of being eternal. In myth, "things lose the memory that they were once made."[8] Much of the extant literature on Jews and comics, it will be argued, treats Superman or the history of US comics this way, and in doing so distorts a more complex history of American Judaism and US comics, in order to celebrate Jewish identity in the twenty-first-century USA.

The myth of comics' and Superman's Jewishness has been a slowly emerging theme. Few early texts about Superman suggest any relation to Judaism. One of the first sources to claim a Jewish–comics connection was comics writer Jules Feiffer's 1965 essay, *The Great Comic Book Heroes*. Rather than claiming Superman as Jewish, however, Feiffer so identifies Will Eisner's 1940 creation, *The Spirit*.[9] Semiotician Umberto Eco, in his 1972 essay on Superman, focuses instead on *Superman*'s iterative scheme and its promotion of civic consciousness.[10] Leaning on Eco in a 1980 article, social theorist Thomas Andrae reads Superman as a transitional figure in the superman motif, changing it from a figure of menace into a "messiah" of sorts.[11]

Eight years later, in an exercise in creative etymology in conjunction with Superman's 50th anniversary, English scholar Gary Engle traces Superman's Kryptonian name, Kal-El, to a Hebrew name of God (El) and a Hebrew "root," *kal* (a word he derived from the root לקל), supposedly meaning "with lightness" or "swiftness" (actually, simply "light" or "swift"). By changing the latter word to *ḥal*, to which it ostensibly also "bears a connection," and claiming that it translates "roughly" as "everything" or "all" (actually the unrelated word כֹּל, pronounced *kol*), Engle suggested reading the name Kal-El as "all that God is." This then becomes the ground from which Engle suggests that "*Superman* raises the American immigrant experience to the level of religious myth."[12] Around this time, articles also started appearing in Jewish American-interest magazines and journals, which explicitly and emphatically highlighted the fact that many Golden Age comics creators were Jewish and, sometimes, made the case that so were their creations.[13]

Another important and oft-cited milestone in the Judaization of Superman was Feiffer's 1996 *New York Times* obituary for Jerry Siegel. In it, Feiffer writes that the character was the "ultimate assimilationist fantasy," wherein Siegel chronicled the "smart Jewish boy's American dream": "Acknowledge that, and you can better understand the symbolic meaning of the planet Krypton. It wasn't Krypton that Superman really came from; it was the planet Minsk or Lodz or Vilna or Warsaw."[14] Also in 1996, another article appeared that asked in its title: "Did You Know Superman is Jewish?" "Of course he is," answers masculinity scholar Harry Brod, calling the destruction of Superman's (in the referenced first 1938 appearance still unnamed) home planet a "holocaust," and coloring his piece with a haphazard mix of elements added by the character's Jewish creators long after his initial appearance and by other, often non-Jewish, writers and artists.[15]

It would take Brod 17 years to expand his article into a monograph, at which time the ground that he had once been one of the first to walk upon was well trod. By then, the type of superhero eisegesis that this book will address had grown exponentially. That Brod and Feiffer, along with some of the early writing in the Jewish American-interest press, were precursors to the efflorescence of publications that would begin around the mid-2000s is evidenced by the fact that they are cited in the first monograph on the subject of Jews and comics.[16] But none of these texts had the power to truly encourage an interpretive tradition; that inspiration would come from a masterpiece of fiction.

THE CHABON WATERSHED

The influence of novelist Michael Chabon's *The Amazing Adventures of Kavalier & Clay: A Novel* (2000) in the invention of the Jewish–comics connection cannot be overstated: it has become a staple, seemingly obligatory to cite when writing about Jews and comics.[17] The novel, which tells the story of Joe Kavalier and Sammy Clay, two young Jewish men in the

Golden Age comics business, lends significant narrative and thematic space to the Holocaust and prominently features the golem of Prague.[18] It is also a well-written book (as its Pulitzer Prize attests). Its allure for writers on Jews and comics, then, is entirely understandable, but it is difficult to prepare the uninitiated for the prominence it has gained in Jewish–comics connection literature.

Rabbi Simcha Weinstein, writer of the 2006 book *Up, Up, and Oy Vey! How Jewish History, Culture, and Values Shaped the Comic Book Superhero*, the first Jewish–comics connection monograph, credits Chabon with introducing millions of readers to what he labels "the Jewish–comic book connection."[19] The following year, in his book *Disguised as Clark Kent: Jews, Comics, and the Creation of the Superhero*, comic book writer and writing teacher Danny Fingeroth writes that he is attempting to recover a world described by Chabon in an article about Jewish comics legend Will Eisner, and that in his novel Chabon "explores [...] in depth" how golem myths fit into the superhero mix. Fingeroth seeks the comics creators' lost world in Eastern European Jewish tradition, as do most other Jewish–comics connection writers, without ever considering the fact that Chabon's novel only ventures into the Western European city of Prague, and that Eastern European Jews are described as foreign to the acculturated Prague-born Joe Kavalier.[20] Rounding off his 2008 book, *From Krakow to Krypton: Jews and Comic Books*, journalist and comedian Arie Kaplan writes that Chabon sees Superman as a "super-Jew." And, Kaplan continues, Chabon makes a "pretty good case for it in *Kavalier & Clay*," introducing a quote now near-ubiquitous in writing on Jews and comics, without regard to its fictionality: "They're all Jewish, superheroes. Superman, you don't think he's Jewish? Coming over from the old country, changing his name like that. Clark Kent, only a Jew would pick a name like that for himself."[21] Finally, in *Superman is Jewish? How Comic Book Superheroes Came to Serve Truth, Justice, and the Jewish-American Way* (2013), Harry Brod locates the superheroes' "secret origin" in a truncated version of the fictional Kavalier's interpretation of the meaning of the golem: "hope, in a time of desperation....[sic] a yearning that a few magic words and an artful hand might produce...escape."[22]

As will be argued in the next two sections, the books cited in the previous paragraph should be regarded not as journalistic criticism or scholarship, but as ethnically celebratory literature. Academic scholars have not been slow to follow the lead, however. In a 2006 volume on Jewish identity in postmodern America, literary critic Andrea Most writes that

Kavalier & Clay "*demonstrates* the usefulness" of reading American comics history as a story of negotiation of Jewish identities, before going on to claim that Chabon "*investigates*" these complex negotiations, "*shows*" how the historical (rather than Chabon's fictional) comics creators vented their desires, and "*tells Jewish history* as an integral part of American history," "*revealing*" how Jewish bodies were transformed.[23] That same year, Yiddishist Jeremy Dauber evoked Kavalier's experiences to support his claim that pre-WWII "Jewish matters of the moment lie strongly—but subtly—below the surface" in Eisner's *Spirit*.[24]

The editors of 2008's *The Jewish Graphic Novel: Critical Approaches* claim that Chabon "has made abundantly clear [that] there is a tightly woven and indelible relation between Jewish identity and the genesis of the superhero in the pantheon of American comics. Throughout, Chabon's novel makes strong connections between the identity of the Jewish artists and Kavalier and Clay's improbable creations."[25] Again, the "proof" is the Clark Kent quote cited above, now completely shorn of any humor it might originally have contained. In 2009, philosopher Jesse Kavadlo claimed that Superman is a kind of "super-immigrant" himself, on the basis of the same quote.[26] In his book about Superman and the Ku Klux Klan, journalist Rick Bowers includes *Kavalier & Clay* among his "Superman Sources."[27] When Italian scholar Marco Arnaudo makes a Superman–golem comparison in his 2013 *Myth of the Superhero*, his only reference is to Chabon.[28]

In this way, story and history have been conflated in recent years, providing a heroic narrative of evolution that brings the current, vibrant state of Jewish American comics production into continuity with the past, but also making an assumed part of it constitute the whole. This is not a novel observation; Jewish studies scholar Laurence Roth points out the same thing in his chapter in *Jewish Graphic Novel*, where he gives even more examples of how Chabon's novel has been elevated.[29] Similarly, Philip Roth scholar Derek Parker Royal, a frequent writer on Jews and comics whose work is discussed more below, wrote in a 2012 survey of the state of writing on Jews and comics that "it is curious how so many studies have referenced the novel as a way of almost legitimizing their projects."[30]

Chabon's novel is a work of fiction, not history. It tells us little about the past it presents and much about the time in which it was written; if it shows anything, it is that Chabon, a Jewish American born in 1963 and writing at the turn of the twentieth century, was comfortable enough in his Jewishness and in the USA to assert Jewish difference and to make claims about the past from a perspective that highlights and celebrates Jewishness. In that process, Chabon narrativized history to fit a specific, contemporary vision. Kavalier and Clay, although loosely based on several Jewish American pioneers of superheroes' Golden Age, are not real. By using Chabon's world and characters as legitimizers, by letting his imagined Jewish–comics connection serve as a cornerstone in arguing for an historical one, the cottage industry that has used his fiction as its foundation has chosen unstable ground upon which has been built a largely myth-based superstructure.

CONSIDERING THE JEWISH–COMICS CONNECTION

Popular Jewish–comics connection literature generally promotes anachronistic and implausible interpretations. Based in a type of benign essentialism, or "blood logic,"[31] writers often disregards factors other than Jewishness that might have influenced the creative process, seeking instead to promote a view of the comic book as a Jewish creation and seminal characters and series as Jewish characters and series. This is done by amplifying peripheral details, filling in gaps, or projecting present or recent developments backward into history. In these processes, elements from the 1940s Superman radio serial, the 1950s Superman TV series, and the 1978 Superman film are all treated as if they were part of the character as created by Siegel and Shuster, in effect having character development and publication history transcend the confines of historical progression. Indeed, throughout this literature, Superman is treated as if he somehow has a soul bestowed by Siegel and Shuster. As will be discussed more in Chap. 4, almost all writers make too much of Superman's adoptive parents, his childhood in rural Smallville, his move from the country to the city, and many other things that were not conceived for the original character or even by the original duo. Thus, for example, Weinstein links Superman to the rabbinical "Ethics of the Fathers," by citing the religious tractate's claim that "the world endures on three things: justice, truth, and peace" and Superman's standing for "truth, justice, and the American Way," even though that formulation first appeared in the 1950s TV series.[32] It is on the basis of anachronistic connections like this that Weinstein makes claims to a "persistent connection between Superman and Jewish culture."[33]

Each chapter of this book will discuss specific claims about Superman that are more clearly rooted in a theme or period, but before we can get into details, it is useful to look at two common overinterpretations of more general aspects of the character. The first is related to his Kryptonian name, Kal-El. As already noted, Gary Engle claimed that it could be read as "all that is God," but others have since changed the reading. Weinstein writes that the "prefix" Kal is the root of several Hebrew words meaning "lightness" or "swiftness" (the root *qll*, לֶלֶל, and the word *qal*, קַל, meaning "swift" or "light"), "vessel" (*kĕlî*, יְלִי), and "voice" (*qôl*, לוֹק), all of which he describes as apt "names" for the hero.[34] Kaplan echoes Engle's reading, without citing it.[35] Brod asks if it can really be "coincidental" that the name "spoken with a Hebrew pronunciation sounds like the Hebrew words for 'all is God' or 'all for God'?"[36]

None of these readings is right; or rather, all of them are potentially correct, since the Kryptonian name has only ever been rendered in English and thus can only be Hebraicized through speculation, and because the way the hypothetical Hebrew is "transcribed" gives no indication of which "k" sound the name supposedly begins with. By using the same loose rules and roots as the authors above, and with the right vocalization, the name Kal-El could theoretically also be "roughly" translated as having to do with the root לוכ (*kwl*, "seize"), אֶלֶכ (*kele*, "imprisonment"), the verb הֶלֶכ (*kâlâ*, "be complete," "be destroyed," "ruined," "waste away"), or some form of the verb לֶלֶכ (*qillel*) with the infinitive לֶלֶכ (*qallel*, "declare someone to be cursed"). Indeed, from the same basic ללל verbal root that Weinstein and Engle cite—with the root of *qal* also having the additional meaning of "insignificant, light"—the radically different "translation" "God is insignificant" (*Qal-ʾēl*) can also be constructed, giving Superman's name a "meaning" that fits far better with what is known about Siegel and Shuster's views about religion.[37]

Ultimately, however, all of these variations are equally meaningless. The notion that Superman was created with a Hebraic "original name" is itself faulty and the name Kal-El does not belong in a treatment of Siegel and Shuster's Superman in the first place. Jor-L, the name given to the alien baby Kal-L's father in the first week of the Superman comic strips in 1939, was lifted from a 1937 Siegel and Shuster strip, where that name, supposedly an "acronym" of Jerome Siegel, had been given to an alien policeman.[38] Julius Schwartz, Siegel and Shuster's friend and colleague, and a sometime ghostwriter on the comic strip, has noted the same thing, and added that "thus he [Siegel] is the father of Superman both as creator and amalgamation."[39] Further, while Engle's el-etymology has been appropriated, his identification of George Lowther, an announcer and producer on the Superman radio serial, as the Hebraic-sounding names'

originator has not been retained.[40] It was Lowther, in his 1942 novelization of Superman, who added an "e" to the names, making them Jor-el
and Kal-el. (Capitalization of the "e" came even later.) If this was an intentional Hebraism, it was more likely a Christianizing one, since Lowther
"larded" his book with Christian references.[41]

The second common general overinterpretation is the comparison
between Superman and the golem of Prague, made because both the
superhero and the now most well-known version of the latter are pro-
tectors. Some examples have already been discussed above, in connection with Michael Chabon's novel. In a second anachronistic twist, several
writers cite a 1998 comic book where Superman is explicitly called a
golem in homage to his Jewish creators. Although this comic book can
in no way tell us anything about Siegel and Shuster, it has been presented
as an "exploration of his [Superman's] Semitic origins" or as illustrating
that, "[c]learly, something about this Golem-like figure resonated" with
his creators.[42] Kaplan describes the golem as a "legendary creature magi-
cally conceived by Rabbi Judah Loew of medieval Prague to defend the
community from attacks by its anti-Semitic enemies" and quotes Jewish
comics creator Al Jaffe as saying that golems have served as a defense
mechanism: "They're [Jews are] always in an alien land, so that's why
they invented Golems!"[43] Calling the golem "Superman's supernatural
ancestor in Jewish lore," Brod gives an account of the figure where he
erroneously claims that "[i]n the various versions of golem stories the
golem is always brought to life by a scholar to protect the Jewish community against external threats."[44] After a meandering survey of pop cultural
golem appearances, he concludes, without citing a single example from
Siegel and Shuster's work: "Further, it seems clear that, consciously or not,
Siegel and Shuster were drawing on this tradition in bringing Superman to
the pages of the comics."[45]

But the golem-as-protector motif is not the ancient tradition these
writers claim. As German studies scholar Cathy S. Gelbin notes in her
book about golem traditions, "[t]oday, Jews and non-Jews alike relate the
golem with Jewish folk culture. It has become one of the most broadly
recognized signifiers of modern Jewish popular culture, no doubt in part
because the significant contribution of non-Jewish writers in the history
of this theme is not always recognized."[46] When a connection between
the golem and Rabbi Judah Loew of Prague are first made in the mid-
nineteenth century, the golem is a domestic servant, and when the first
written accounts of a golem protecting Jews against anti-Semitism appear

in the late 1800s, the golem regularly becomes a threat to the Jewish community as well, and has to be put down. It is only with Yudl Rosenberg's 1909 *Niflo'es Maharal* (*The Wondrous Deeds of the Maharal of Prague with the Golem*) that the golem becomes a benevolent protector. Rosenberg's story contained the first entirely benevolent and autonomous golem. As Curt Leviant, author, Yiddishist, and the first to translate the story into English notes, "[t]he myth of the golem who defends Jews during times of persecution, which many people nowadays mistakenly trace back to the sixteenth century, is actually a modern literary invention, a brilliant stroke created single-handedly by Yudl Rosenberg."[47] Leviant might be slightly overstating Rosenberg's innovativeness with regard to the protector motif, but Rosenberg's story about a protector that does not turn on its creator or charges has since, partly through dissemination in the name of a plagiarizer, become the most influential version. This version has attained widespread status as a standard narrative and has been projected back into history, while the belief that it is of older vintage has become a widely accepted myth.[48]

Furthermore, the development of the golem-as-protector did not take place in isolation; the nowadays well-known and globally disseminated version of the golem came about after significant back-and-forth between Jewish and German, often anti-Semitic, cultural producers.[49] As Gelbin and scholar of Jewish mysticism Moshe Idel have shown, it is difficult to claim a continuity of authentically Jewish golem traditions; the figure's use in any specific case is thus ambivalent without some statement of intent or evidence of underlying motivations that can connect it directly with Jewish versions.[50] Moreover, differences between the golem of Prague and Superman outweigh their one similarity; Superman, unlike golems in the literary and folkloric tradition, is born, not created; he is fully autonomous and a moral actor; he is capable of speech; and he is never put to rest, but is perpetually needed. Even if Siegel and Shuster knew about the benevolent protector version, for which there is no proof,[51] Superman's identity as a protector likely owed nothing to the golem and, as will be argued in Chap. 7, everything to the pop culture which it is established beyond doubt that they loved, which in those days was brimming with similar characters.[52]

As these examples should begin to illustrate, the small but growing Jewish–comics connection library suffers from a paucity of textual, biographical, or historical support for its interpretations, which is likely a reason for why this literature has relied so heavily on internal, mutual referencing. The resultant feedback loop may in turn account for the rapid emergence and sedimentation of a few common tropes, like the Hebraicist reading of Kal-El and the golem comparison. This feedback loop, I will argue, causes problems when its claims enter academic writing. Before turning to these issues, however, I want to make the case that the extant body of popular Jewish–comics connection literature is perhaps best regarded, in a non-pejorative sense, as myth-based heritage fabrication.[53]

FABRICATING JEWISH COMICS HERITAGE

Arthur Blecher's three key terms—continuity, authenticity, and survival—are useful in reading literature on Jews and comics. Indeed, Simcha Weinstein immediately anchors the superhero in a biblical tradition, citing "superpatriarchs and supermatriarchs" as their precursors. These stories, he claims, were retold by the children of Eastern European immigrants who "poured into New York's Lower East Side in the 1900s," refracted through the prism of daily life in the vein of Chabad-founder Schneur Zalman of Liadi's teachings about "living with the times."[54] While it is unlikely that Zalman's type of Orthodoxy was common among the immigrants Weinstein conjures,[55] its evocation allows him to establish in superheroes a religious authenticity, a sense that the heroes and the themes they represent are something intrinsically Jewish, and a continuity that links modern pop culture with scripture. From there, Weinstein can find connections everywhere, but only by constructing his subjects as scripturally learned far beyond what they are known to have been.

Weinstein describes his book as "a history, Torah (Bible) study session, and survey of pop culture all in one."[56] It fails as a history lesson, since it contains very little historical context and is often unselfconsciously a- or even antihistorical. Take for example his discussion of the Flash, a superfast character created in 1940 by non-Jewish writer Gardner Fox and Jewish artist Harry Lampert, and inspired in some measure by the Greek god Mercury. In the late 1950s, Flash was revamped and reintroduced by Jewish editor Julius Schwartz. On the basis of Schwarz's Jewishness, Weinstein uses the Flash to claim that "the concept of superspeed is rooted in biblical lore," and then presents a biblical story about the unnaturally speedy travels of Abraham's servant along with some medieval commentary that calls the servant's speed supernatural.[57] The book similarly fails as a pop culture survey, since it is highly limited in its choices and presentations of its material.

One could here engage in a nitpicking point-by-point empirical and rhetorical critique of Weinstein's presentation, but such a critique would miss the point of the book. Historical accuracy is not *Up, Up, and Oy Vey!*'s main concern, despite occasional claims to that effect; while the book should be read as an argument for a deep connection between Judaism and superheroes, it should not be taken at face value as arguing for a historically verifiable one. Where it truly shines is as a Torah lesson, presenting in its 127 pages an impressive array of scriptural, religious, and cultural Jewish traditions. Weinstein reads comics to answer the question of "[w]hat spiritual lessons can be gleaned from these super-heroes" and to "[tease] out the biblical archetypes embodied in famous comic book characters."[58] Few of these issues are dealt with in detail, but rather are introduced in a way that could inspire a reader's desire to know more.

Bookending Weinstein's lesson is his own life narrative of *teshuvah*, or return to Jewish religion. This lesson begins in a preface, where Weinstein writes about how he "lived a Clark Kent existence," wherein something was missing, until he embraced his "true, inner essence, [his] real iden-tity."[59] It ends on a note encouraging readerly *teshuvah*, situating it as a work of religious instruction.[60] Indeed, to claim that Weinstein uses com-ics for religio-cultural edification is uncontroversial; he has said so himself: "I have a bunch of apathetic art students who happen to be Jewish [...] But as a soon as I started using Superman as a tool to educate, they said, 'Oh, rabbi! Now we understand.' [...] With a title like Up, Up, and Oy Vey! it's clear I don't take myself too seriously with this."[61]

Similarly, Danny Fingeroth's book, for all its frequent overstatement, is self-admittedly speculative: "In this book," he writes, "I will be mak-ing speculations and tying facts together, attempting to indicate that there were and are – for the most part unconscious and subconscious – true Jewish content, meaning, and themes in various seminal superhero works."[62] Thus, like Weinstein, Fingeroth sets up a sense of continuity and authenticity, but one marked with a self-contradictory impulse to some-times conflate and sometimes separate Jews and immigrants in general, that recurs throughout the book: "When the facts of *Eastern European Jewish history and identity* were filtered through the talents of skilled and inspired *Jewish – and other – American-bred creators*, the result was the cultural phenomenon we know as the superhero. [...] The Jews and their history were the missing ingredients in creating this unique heroic archetype."[63]

While Fingeroth's analyses are always thought-provoking, *Disguised* is problematic. Fingeroth repeatedly essentializes and ascribes a collectively defined Jewishness to creators who were trying their best to create American popular culture.[64] Simultaneously, non-Jews are largely sidelined, as when non-Jewish editor Jim Shooter's refusal to let a character get away with genocide is chalked down to the lingering influence—"from beyond the grave"—of his deceased former mentor, Jewish editor Mort Weisinger.[65] Ultimately, the book becomes, toward its end, a near-explicit call to what Herbert Gans called "symbolic ethnicity," asserting a sense of difference that does not require institutional or prolonged engagement or, indeed, deep knowledge, as is evident for example in Fingeroth's erasure of one of the most important aspects of Judaism in order to call Superman a Moses-figure (discussed in Chap. 4). For Fingeroth, this symbolic identification centers on a sense of Jewish moral exceptionalism: "[t]he idea that Jews are like everybody else except, significantly, with a need to do the right thing, even if they themselves are far from perfect, might be a statement worth making over and over again."[66] In this narrative, the history of American comic books takes on the appearance of Jewish cultural production along an authentic continuum, simultaneously proposing and imposing a community of identity. Fingeroth provides little support for his interpretations and speculations, nor does he need to.

Arie Kaplan claims that "Jews almost single-handedly built the comic-book industry from the ground up" and writes that, "[l]ike many narratives about the Jewish people, this is the story of a tradition" handed down across generations.[67] Thus, like the other books, he frames his reading in terms of continuity and authenticity early on; Jews built the comic book business and Jews have since been its custodians. The better part of Kaplan's book, however, is devoted not to finding Jewish content in the comics themselves, but rather to showing what Jewish creators, fans, and others involved in the industry have contributed to contemporary pop culture. First, Kaplan stresses Jewish creations that range from superheroes to comics shops and conventions. Second, he stresses how those creators' work has been acknowledged as influences by such cultural luminaries as George Lucas, Steven Spielberg, comedian George Carlin, film- and television makers Kevin Smith and Joss Whedon, and how it has influenced such important contemporary cultural institutions as the *The National Lampoon*, *The Onion*, and *The Simpsons*.[68] In this light, *Krakow* reads less like an argument for the Jewishness of the comics industry and its products, and more like an example of "Jewhooing," the naming and claiming of Jews to emphasize Jewish contributions to civilization for purposes of ethnic pride and celebration. On the one hand, this practice shows that Jews can be assimilated; on the other hand, it shows anxieties about assimilation since the higher Jews climb on the social ladder and the more they blend in with majority society, the likelier it becomes that they will be named and claimed.[69]

Perhaps the most problematic popular book is the one written by Harry Brod. Stressing his academic credentials, Brod begins by making claims to scholarly rigor. He early establishes as one of his criteria that "one should be able to see some line of transmission by which the creators could plausibly have come into contact" with whatever "Jewish elements" one wants to claim are in the comics. This, he writes, "serves as a check against granting everyone a blanket license to just read whatever they wish into a work without offering any plausible account of how the meaning they're attributing to the work could possibly have gotten in there."[70] While this reads like a tacit acknowledgment that earlier Jewish–comics connection writing has lacked scholarly precision, Brod frequently falls into the same trap. For example, he invites readers to wonder if "the name of his home planet [Krypton is] really a secret invitation to decode Superman's encrypted secret identity as a crypto-Jew (Jews who, since the days of the Spanish Inquisition, have publicly given up their faith to escape persecution, but who remain Jews in the private lives and personal allegiance)?"[71]

Indeed, there are few examples where Brod adheres to his own rule: when discussing Jewish gender roles, his own academic specialty, he goes not to scholarly literature, but to *Fiddler on the Roof*; when discussing Jewish humor, his only source is a Lenny Bruce stand-up routine.[72] Rather, Brod's book is self-admittedly a future-oriented "exercise in reclamation," a continuity- and authenticity-centered attempt to "see to it that the stories of Superman and other comic book superheroes not be [...] lost as they are assimilated into mainstream culture [sic]." It is also, because of this claim, antihistorically oriented, since Superman and the other superheroes produced for the major American publishers were always intended for a broad mainstream audience.[73]

These writers, then, find their own meaning in the comics they read, and promote their interpretations within a vibrant and multifaceted, but also contentious, contemporary Jewish American order of discourse, aided by the increased visibility of Jewishness and ethnicity in contemporary consumer products and culture.[74] Broader acceptance of Jews in US culture after the ethnic revival and the advent of multiculturalism, outlined in the next chapter, has made assertions of ethnic particularity easier and less frightening. Conversely, increased social mobility and status has erected new obstacles; it can be difficult to assert ethnic pride and risk alienating non-Jewish friends, and the post-WWII Jewish American attainment of whiteness has brought with it a perception of Jews as part of the national, white, majority.

Since the late 1980s, tension between increasing US openness for Jewish assertiveness and fears of declining Jewish cohesiveness has inspired unease over the prospects of a Jewish American future.[75] Debaters like media theorist Douglas Rushkoff and legal scholar Alan M. Dershowitz have called for Jewish revival and reassessment of the community's contemporary paths and self-conceptions, looking to ensure American Judaism's survival by adapting to security, whiteness, and a modern (and, compared to earlier decades, more) open society.[76] Others, like the founders of the irreverent magazine *Heeb*, have adapted a more "tribalist" strategy of celebrating a distinct sense of Jewishness that reflects a sense of unease with having "become" the White Anglo-Saxon Protestants (WASPs) that once excluded Jewish Americans and mistreated others.[77]

It is in this context that books about Jews and comics appeared. They all argue for Jewish specificity and universalism, and they all claim that Jews created comics as Jews, but also that what they created held a broad appeal. This places the books among the American Judaica Blecher studied, suggesting that their writers are concerned with Jewish survival in a multicultural USA. At the same time, this Jewishness is a symbolic one, an exercise in popular culture genealogy that requires little commitment.[78] Thus, by Judaizing Superman, by naming the creators of a mainstay of American pop culture and claiming it as Jewish, they can assert difference, promote Jewish pride and interest in a younger generation, and, simultaneously, highlight Jewish contributions to US culture as a way of solidifying Jews' role in the creation of the modern USA; it provides a way of feeling both different and at home.

In doing this, the authors situate their discussed comics creators exclusively as Jews and read their work through an ethnic lens, in many cases projecting the current state of the comics industry backward. There is, of course, nothing wrong with this; Weinstein, Fingeroth, and Kaplan's books do not claim to be scholarship, and there is no reason why they should. As already noted, however, Brod does make claim to scholarly authority, despite purposely avoiding the entirety of comics scholarship, because academic writing is apparently "unfaithful" to the source material, ends up "falsifying the data," and sucks the fun out of something that is supposedly "inherently comic." As such, the book is problematic—there is, in a sense, "something wrong" with how it presents itself—and should be critiqued according to academic standards.[79]

Despite raising issues of contextualization and historicization, readings of the type presented by Weinstein, Fingeroth, and Kaplan actually represent an opportunity, by pointing to new and previously neglected areas of inquiry; at the very least, they provoke a response that takes them seriously and asks questions that have yet to be asked of the material.[80] In fact, the underlying idea of these books—that some comics creators' Jewishness has indeed impacted, consciously and unconsciously, on their creative work—also informs this book. There is however, a difference in approach; the coming chapters will attempt to situate Superman and his creators in their historical context in a way these authors have not. Conversely, as already hinted at, it is immensely problematic that the tendency of identifying Jews with the creation of the comic book, medium, and industry, and of viewing their work through a narrow lens of idealized Jewishness is not restricted to edifying or celebratory books. The tendency can also be found in academic writing, often with reference to the popular works discussed above. For that last reason, and for that reason alone, these popular works will continue to be unpacked in a critical dialogue that runs throughout this book.

COMICS JUDEOCENTRISM IN ACADEMIA

None of the above has been written as an attempt to delegitimize the books discussed. Setting out with that ambition would be a serious breach of the academic mission and a pointless exercise. Nonetheless, the identification of these works as belonging to a nonacademic order of discourse and to a nonacademic genre seems to be a sorely needed corrective within academic scholarship of Jews and comics. The consecration there of the celebratory speculation advanced in these books is widespread, often taking place through a generic conflation that breaks basic tenets of source criticism and that suffers from lacking historicization and contextualization. What follows is a small selection of texts of various kinds that use or promote these books in a way that helps turn ahistorical myth into accepted history, in the process muddling the historical record and making historically and contextually sensitive interpretation less accessible.

As in the popular literature, some scholars have recently attempted to claim superheroes, and Superman specifically, as golems. For example, aligning himself with the projects described above, Thomas Andrae claimed in 2010 to be able to finally confirm that Superman is "the latest in a long line of Jewish heroes with great strength," by citing an unpublished memoir by Jerry Siegel. In the manuscript, Superman's cocreator apparently recalls "being favorably impressed by a movie entitled *The Golem*," which Andrae identifies as the 1920 German Expressionist film *The Golem: How He Came into the World*, by non-Jewish directors Paul Wegener and Carl Boese.[81] Disregarding the film's non-Jewish origins and its anti-Semitic undertones, Andrae meanders about the golem's supposed dissemination into a wider culture in order to also get past the cited film's golem being an unruly monster, as most golems were before the protector motif became the standard. Andrae moves from Wegener and Boese's film to Mary Shelley's *Frankenstein*, and continues from there through horror films into science fiction "homo superior" figures, before landing in Superman, seemingly suggesting an undiluted transferal of the golem's properties throughout the entire journey.[82] In the end, Andrae adds nothing that has not already been claimed about the supposed Superman–golem connection.[83] (Further, in a different essay in the same volume, Andrae cites Fingeroth and Weinstein as having "recently acknowledged" that Superman was rooted in, until then, elided ideas of Jewish masculinity, although neither book says much on the topic.[84])

Andrae is not the first academic to use the above-discussed popular writers to make problematic claims. A 2007 issue of the academic journal *MELUS* contains a review of Weinstein's book that highlights the golem connection and Superman's "Hebrew" name, and in which the book is compared to four recent "Christian-oriented superhero studies." This comparison is inadvertently revealing: three of the cited books are works of normative Christian theology.[85] English scholar Cheryl Alexander Malcolm cites Weinstein in a cherry-picking essay on the X-Men and anti-Semitism.[86] *The Jewish Graphic Novel*'s "further reading" section includes Weinstein, Fingeroth, and Kaplan, uncommented and together with scholarly (and additional questionable) literature. Literary critic Stephen Tabachnick cites Weinstein, Fingeroth, and Kaplan in his 2014 book about Jewish belief and identity in graphic novels.[87] English scholar Chris Gavaler also includes all three in the bibliography of his unscholarly but university press-published 2015 *On the Origin of Superheroes: From the Big Bang to Action Comics No. 1*, although to what extent they are incorporated in the book's ill-defined and ill-presented argument is uncertain, since it contains no notes.[88]

As has already been discussed, Andrea Most cites Michael Chabon; along with the novelist, however, she also cites Brod and Kaplan to support her claim that it "takes only a small leap of the imagination" to read the "White, non-ethnic, all-American" superheroes as Jewish male assimilationist desires. "All the superheroes from Clark Kent/Superman to Peter Parker [Spider-Man] have double identities," she asserts before writing that "[t]hey spend their lives negotiating their different personae, an experience not unlike that of their Jewish creators, who needed to negotiate the Jewish/American divide with similar finesse in order to succeed in an antisemitic culture [sic]."[89] Most here assumes that a static, linear trajectory of the meaning of the secret identity trope can be established based solely on the fact that many creators were Jewish, which is a dubious claim for several reasons.

First, the period between Superman (1934) and Spider-Man (1962) saw the emergence of myriad superheroes with non-Jewish creators who had secret identities. Second, not all superheroes, whether created by Jews or non-Jews, have secret identities (the Fantastic Four, which appeared in 1961 and was created by the same Jewish American men who created Spider-Man, for example, did not). Third, Jewish strategies for maneuvering US majority society have changed significantly, as has the nature and extent of American anti-Semitism; similarly, American Jews' individual or collective anxieties about America or Americans' anxieties about American Jewry have neither been static nor uniform.[90] As a result of Most's claim, the histories of US superhero comics, Jewish American comics creators, and the realities of Jewish American male experiences are all made less accessible, not more.

Further, as a recurring voice of consecration, Derek Parker Royal consistently presents Weinstein, Fingeroth, and Kaplan's books as "scholarly studies," often bundling them together with other popular and academic works, and even with comics. Thus, for instance, in a 2013 book review in *MELUS*, Royal begins by noting that in recent years, "there has been a flurry of scholarly interest in comics and Jewish identity." He then reviews one scholarly volume (*The Jewish Graphic Novel*), two popular books (Brod's *Superman is Jewish?* and comics scholar and popular historian Fredrik Strömberg's *Jewish Images in the Comics: A Visual History*), and a comics anthology (*Yiddishkeit: Jewish Vernacular and the New Land*, edited by comics writer Harvey Pekar and historian Paul Buhle), as if they were all the same type of text. Also mentioning *Up, Up, and Oy Vey!*, *Disguised as Clark Kent, From Krakow to Krypton*, and *Siegel and Shuster's Funnyman: The First Jewish Superhero, From the Creators of Superman*, a reprint edition of a later Siegel and Shuster creation with a few introductory essays of questionable scholarly quality (including Andrae's two above-discussed works), Royal claims that they all—Weinstein, Fingeroth, and Kaplan as well as the editors of *The Jewish Graphic Novel*, the editors of *Yiddishkeit*, Strömberg, and Brod—have in common "a desire to define Jewish comics through a series of critical interrogations."[91]

In light of the discussion above, this characterization seems overstated. It becomes no less so when one considers that Strömberg's book, for example, is designed to show "how Jewish culture has been portrayed (positively and negatively) in comics in general, by Jewish as well as gentile creators"—that is, to be a broadly defined introduction to Jewish representations in comics writ large, rather than an attempt to define Jewish comics—and that *Yiddishkeit* is a collection of comics designed to tell stories from the history of a language, not to investigate the form in which those stories are presented.[92] Royal places the books in one single category, irrespective of their origins. Their writers, despite their own orientations or intentions, are attributed the same goal. In passing, Royal even seems to be defending Weinstein's book, which, he remarks, "some have argued, tends to posit a Jewish influence and signifiers without always making a persuasive case."[93] In an earlier review of *Funnyman*, in which Royal questions the essays' topical fittingness, but not, for example, Andrae's essentialistic golem speculation, he describes Fingeroth, who provides a foreword, as "himself an authority on the Jewish-inspired superhero."[94] Fingeroth is a popular speaker (in both senses of the word) on Jews and comics, but, as has already been noted, that does not make him an academic authority. In celebrating Fingeroth's work, and that of others who similarly neither abide by nor are beholden to the rules of academia, Royal is promoting a repetition of myth over critical research, to the detriment of both the study of Jews and comics and of the readers outside of the field who might one day benefit from fresh scholarship.

As a final example, in his book *Myth of the Superhero*, Marco Arnaudo cites Fingeroth and Weinstein, the latter so much that he gets his own entry in the index. Notably, while Arnaudo's book promises "close readings," his account of Superman's origin story does not cite the comics that contain it, but instead relies on Weinstein's account.[95] From there, Arnaudo jumps to the 1998 Superman story mentioned above, presenting it as an "extremely clear illustration" that both Superman in 1998 and—anachronistically—"as he was conceived in 1938," are "at least compatible with Jewish angels and golems and can also legitimately be understood as having derived from them."[96] In this discussion, as in the rest of his chapter on superheroes and religion, Arnaudo adds nothing new to the discussion of the Jewish–comics connection; he only rehashes popular interpretations and gives them the imprimatur of academic legitimacy.

The preceding discussion has only scratched the surface of contemporary scholarly writing about the Jewish–comics connection. Almost every academic text about Superman that considers his creators' Jewishness cites the same nonacademic literature, a literature that is slowly being consecrated as a canon for academic work on the topic of Jews and comics, broadly conceived. This must change; by relying on these works, the field keeps treading the same interpretive waters and getting nowhere. Indeed, it should be clear from this overview that correctives are sorely needed. Correction begins with contextualization and historicization, pursuits to which we now turn.

NOTES

1. Plate, "Superheroes Get Religion."
2. Cf. Satlow, *Creating Judaism*; Wenger, *History Lessons*; Sarna, *American Judaism*.
3. On Marston, see Lepore, *Wonder Woman*.
4. Cf. Lund, "The Mutant Problem."
5. Gans, "Symbolic Ethnicity," 199.
6. Blecher, *New American Judaism*, 1–2.
7. Blecher, *New American Judaism*, 5.
8. Barthes, *Mythologies*, 131–87.
9. Feiffer, "Minsk Theory," 39. Eisner in turn denied any Jewishness in *The Spirit* many times, sometimes vehemently, sometimes calling it an in-joke.
10. Eco, *Role of the Reader*, 107–24.
11. Andrae, "Menace to Messiah."
12. Engle, "What Makes Superman," 86.
13. For example, James, "ZAP! POW! BAM! OY!"; Weiss, "Secret Identities"; Schlam, "Contemporary Scribes"; Goodwin, "Cartoons and Jews."
14. Feiffer, "Minsk Theory," 698.

15. Brod, "Did You Know Superman Is Jewish?"
16. See the notes to chapter 1 in Weinstein, *Up, Up, and Oy Vey!*, 129.
17. Evocation of the novel is not limited to writing on Jews and comics. In place of scholarly works that provide this information, English scholar Charles Fanning begins his George McManus' work by citing Chabon's description of the popularity of comic strips. See Fanning, "McManus and Irish America," para. 1.
18. Chabon, *Kavalier & Clay*.
19. Weinstein, *Up, Up, and Oy Vey!*, 31.
20. Fingeroth, *Disguised as Clark Kent*, 20, 22, 33. Cf. Chabon, *Kavalier & Clay*, 24–25.
21. Kaplan, *From Krakow to Krypton*, 209. Weinstein uses this quote as epigraph for his chapter on Superman in *Up, Up, and Oy Vey!*, 21. Quote originally from Chabon, *Kavalier & Clay*, 585.
22. Brod, *Superman Is Jewish?*, 193. Ellipses in original. Quote originally from Chabon, *Kavalier & Clay*, 582.
23. Most, "Re-Imagining the Jew's Body," 19–20. Emphases added.
24. Dauber, "Comic Books," 287.
25. Baskind and Omer-Sherman, "Introduction," xxiii.
26. Kavadlo, "X-Istential X-Men," 41–42.
27. Bowers, *Superman vs. KKK*, 155.
28. Arnaudo, *Myth of the Superhero*, 29, 165n49. Not a single author in the field considers that Chabon's Jewish American characters are uncomfortable with the idea of bringing a golem to the comics page. See Chabon, *Kavalier & Clay*, 85–87.
29. Roth, "Contemporary American Jewish Comic Books," 4–7.
30. Royal, "Jewish Comics," 6.
31. Cf. Glenn, "In the Blood?"
32. Weinstein, *Up, Up, and Oy Vey!*, 28.
33. Weinstein, *Up, Up, and Oy Vey!*, 29.
34. Weinstein, *Up, Up, and Oy Vey!*, 27.
35. Kaplan, *From Krakow to Krypton*, 15.
36. Brod, *Superman Is Jewish?*, 5.
37. See, for example, Ricca, *Super Boys*. My sincere thanks to Ola Wikander for all his help with the Hebrew discussions in this book.
38. Strip reprinted in Daniels, *Superman*, 38–40. See also p. 25 for the origin of the name Jor-L. The name's first appearance is also discussed in Ricca, *Super Boys*, 109–10.
39. Schwartz, *Man of Two Worlds*, 143.

40. Engle, "What Makes Superman," 86.
41. On Lowther, see De Haven, *Our Hero*, 159, 194–95; Ricca, *Super Boys*, 204; Daniels, *Superman*, 71.
42. Weinstein, *Up, Up, and Oy Vey!*, 30–32; Kaplan, *From Krakow to Krypton*, 17–18; Brod, *Superman Is Jewish?*, 40.
43. Kaplan, *From Krakow to Krypton*, 16–17.
44. Brod, *Superman Is Jewish?*, 18, 35–41. Quotes from pp. 18 and 37.
45. Brod, *Superman Is Jewish?*, 41.
46. Gelbin, *The Golem Returns*, 13.
47. Leviant, "Introduction," xxv.
48. Rosenberg, *The Golem*; Gelbin, *The Golem Returns*, 90–92.
49. Cf. Gelbin, *The Golem Returns*; Rosenberg, *The Golem*. See also the treatment of ancient and medieval conceptions of golems in Idel, *Golem*.
50. Gelbin, *The Golem Returns*; Idel, *Golem*. For another problematic golem claim, centered on Captain America, that cites Weinstein as a "Jewish studies scholar," see DiPaolo, *War, Politics, Superheroes*, 152–54.
51. Cf. the discussion on p. 35 below.
52. On the duo's pop cultural habits, see for example Jones, *Men of Tomorrow*; Ricca, *Super Boys*.
53. On the fabrication of heritage, see Lowenthal, "Fabricating Heritage"; Wenger, *History Lessons*; cf. Hobsbawm, "Inventing Traditions."
54. Weinstein, *Up, Up, and Oy Vey!*, 16–17.
55. Cf. Sarna, *American Judaism*, 156–57.
56. Weinstein, *Up, Up, and Oy Vey!*, 18.
57. Weinstein, *Up, Up, and Oy Vey!*, 61–63.
58. Weinstein, *Up, Up, and Oy Vey!*, 17–18.
59. Weinstein, *Up, Up, and Oy Vey!*, 9–10.
60. Weinstein, *Up, Up, and Oy Vey!*, 119–27.
61. Elkin, "Super…Mensch?"
62. Fingeroth, *Disguised as Clark Kent*, 19.
63. Fingeroth, *Disguised as Clark Kent*, 20. Emphasis added.
64. For a particularly pronounced example, see Fingeroth, *Disguised as Clark Kent*, 53.
65. Fingeroth, *Disguised as Clark Kent*, 124–25.
66. Fingeroth, *Disguised as Clark Kent*, 134.

67. Kaplan, *From Krakow to Krypton*, xiv.
68. Kaplan, *From Krakow to Krypton*, 66–70, 72, 74, 79, 105.
69. Glenn, "In the Blood?"
70. Brod, *Superman Is Jewish?*, xxii.
71. Brod, *Superman Is Jewish?*, 5–6.
72. Brod, *Superman Is Jewish?*, 96, 106.
73. Brod, *Superman Is Jewish?*, xxvi; cf. Portnoy, "Superman Is a Glatt Goy" for a lengthier critique of the book.
74. Cf. Halter, *Shopping for Identity.*
75. Goldstein, *Price of Whiteness*, 223–39.
76. Dershowitz, *Vanishing American Jew*; Rushkoff, *Nothing Sacred.*
77. Goldstein, *Price of Whiteness*, 235–36; Novick, *Holocaust in American Life*, 191; Frye Jacobson, *Roots Too.*
78. Cf. Gans, "Symbolic Ethnicity."
79. Quotes from Brod, *Superman Is Jewish?*, xv–xvi. Again, See Portnoy, "Superman Is a Glatt Goy" for more about the problems with Brod's book.
80. Cf. Culler, "In Defense of Overinterpretation."
81. Andrae, "Jewish Superhero," 38–39; Boese and Wegener, *The Golem.*
82. Andrae, "Jewish Superhero," 38–39. On the occasionally argued Shelley–golem connection, see Gelbin, *The Golem Returns*, 35–37. For similarly essentialist treatment of golems in comics, see Weiner, "Marvel and the Golem."
83. Arie Kaplan, for example, makes a similar move with the Hulk. See Kaplan, *From Krakow to Krypton*, 209–10.
84. Andrae, "Funnyman, Jewish Masculinity," 51.
85. Weiner, "Review of Up, Up and Oy Vey!" The cited theologies are Skelton, *Gospel*; Brewer, *Who Needs a Superhero?*; Garrett, *Holy Superheroes!*
86. Malcolm, "Witness, Trauma, Remembrance," 156. For a critique of Malcolm's text and others like it, see Lund, "The Mutant Problem."
87. Tabachnick, *Quest for Jewish Belief*, 2, 64, for example, cites Kaplan and Tye as pointing out a golem connection. Tabachnick also references the 1998 Superman comic book in making his own golem-claim. Further suggestive of the "feedback loop" discussed above, he quotes Cheryl Malcolm's X-Men essay (on p. 73) in an error-ridden discussion of that series (one of his most striking errors is

the identification of Chris Claremont as the creator of Stan Lee and Jack Kirby's supervillain Magneto, who first appeared more than 15 years before Claremont wrote an X-Men comic).

88. Gavaler, *Origin of Superheroes*. One candidate for where they might have been used is pp. 41–42, where Gavaler includes a confused and abortive discussion of different uses of the word "golem."

89. Most, "Re-Imagining the Jew's Body," 19.

90. Brodkin, *How Jews Became White*; Prell, *Fighting to Become Americans*; Goldstein, *Price of Whiteness*; Dinnerstein, *Antisemitism in America*.

91. Royal, "Jewish Graphic Novel et al.," See also Royal, "Native Noir," para. 1n2.

92. Strömberg, *Jewish Images*, 8–9; Pekar, Buhle, and Hartman, *Yiddishkeit*.

93. Royal, "Jewish Graphic Novel et al.," 251.

94. Royal, "Siegel and Shuster's Funnyman Review," 364. See also Andrae, "Jewish Superhero," 38–41.

95. Arnaudo, *Myth of the Superhero*, 165n50.

96. Arnaudo, *Myth of the Superhero*, 29–30.

CHAPTER 3

The Jewish–Comics Connection Reconsidered

The appearance in the early twenty-first century of the Judeocentric comics criticism just discussed is unsurprising. Chabon's book is not alone in
suggesting a Jewish–comics connection; Jewish experiences and ideas have
been a steadily growing presence in alternative, underground, and biographical comics in recent years. Comics in general, and Jewish comics in
particular, have lately come in from the cultural cold, as it were. This owes
in large part to Jewish writer-artist Art Spiegelman and his Pulitzer Prize-
winning *Maus* (completed in 1991), a graphic retelling of his father's
experiences in the Holocaust and of their troubled relationship, which
today is perhaps the world's most famous long-form comic.[1] Also important in this process is the work of other initially peripheral Jewish writers
and artists like Harvey Pekar and Will Eisner, of non-Jewish underground
and alternative comics creators like R. Crumb, Denis Kitchen, Manuel
"Spain" Rodriguez, and Gilbert Shelton, and of non-Jewish mainstream
creators such as Frank Miller and Alan Moore.[2]

Today, works like Ben Katchor's *The Jew of New York* (1998, originally
serialized in the Jewish weekly *The Forward*), James Sturm's *The Golem's
Mighty Swing* (2001), and Joe Kubert's *Jew Gangster* (2004), for example,
tell Jewish American history to critical acclaim.[3] It must also be noted
that contemporary mainstream superhero comics now often contain overt
and self-consciously Jewish themes and explicitly Jewish characters. But
this has not always been regarded as a possibility or even as a desirable

© The Editor(s) (if applicable) and The Author(s) 2016
M. Lund, *Re-Constructing the Man of Steel*,
DOI 10.1007/978-3-319-42960-1_3

option. Before we can truly look at Siegel and Shuster and their work in context, we must look in some depth at the history of Jewish American identity formation and of US majority culture's relationship to its minorities. This history, with its many fissures and complexities, simultaneously bridges and divides the early Superman comics from both the contemporary Jewish American comics world and the Jewish–comics connection literature.

THE CHANGING FACE OF AMERICAN MAINSTREAM COMICS

Joe Simon, the Jewish cocreator with Jack Kirby of the blond, blue-eyed, hyper-patriotic, and flag-draped Captain America (first published in March 1941), recently told Danny Fingeroth that Jews and comics is a non-topic.[4] Indeed, Fingeroth notes that "to a man, none of the founders and creators of the superheroes that I interviewed in researching this book thought, when I first asked about it, that there was anything particularly Jewish about superheroes in general or any superhero in particular."[5] Similarly, toward the end of his life, Will Eisner volunteered the opinion that "none of the Jews I know, including myself, even attempted to introduce Jewish culture, which is something that a lot of people involved in the Jewish community think we did, but it's not true. All the characters created by Jewish cartoonists were WASPs."[6]

Such claims are all too easy to inflate. Just as it is overly simplistic to conclude that Jewish creators automatically created Jewish material, it would be naive to infer a blanket absence of intentional Jewish-themed signification from these and others' disavowals of reproduced Jewishness in early US superhero comic books. Furthermore, Jewish American comics creators like Siegel and Shuster's environments, socialization, and experiences would likely have impacted on them, despite their best efforts to create White Anglo-Saxon Protestant (WASP) characters. Indeed, as will be considered throughout this book, their use and nonuse of Jewish signification likely bear both the imprint of what anthropologist Karen Brodkin calls *ethnoracial assignment* and what sociologists Howard Winant and Michael Omi call *racial formation*, the larger social, political, and discursive contexts in which groups are assigned a place on either side of the perceived racial divide or along the ethnic spectrum.[7] These broad societal factors affect the ways in which identities can be constructed and represented. No matter how Americanized and assimilated Siegel, Shuster, and their Golden Age contemporaries might have considered themselves, Jews and non-Jews alike would have reminded them of their background.

But the cited claims nonetheless point to a fact that cannot be ignored. While many of the men (and it was mostly men) who ushered in the Golden Age of US superhero comics were Jewish in the halakhic sense—that is to say, their mothers were Jewish—and while many appear to have at least held on to some form of existential Jewish self-identification, there was little religious or traditional Judaism involved in their public and professional creative lives. Nor do they appear to have been strongly committed to secular cultural Judaism. The impact of and engagement with American majority culture in many early Jewish comics pioneers' lives and work is evident in, of all things, the recurrence of Christmas in comics history: since the early 1900s, it had been common for Americanized Jews, who wanted to show that they were no "greenhorns," to adapt American holidays and consumerism. Eisner, in the early stages of his career, published annual Christmas-themed stories in his weekly *Spirit* newspaper comic, in celebration of a holiday that he perceived as, "in effect, a national holiday celebrated as a secular event in every nation of western society."[8]

Max Gaines' son William, who took over the business after his father's death, perpetuated a similar practice when he hosted Christmas parties where he rewarded his predominantly Jewish staff with expensive gifts.[9] The Batman's cocreator Bob Kane, who in his autobiography seemingly tried to write any trace of Jewishness out of his life story, has been claimed as Jewish; the "mistake" that in Fingeroth's view "gives him away" as Jewish despite himself contrasts with one of the Kane autobiography's many references to Christmas: after describing what Fingeroth's regards as a very "Jewish meal," Kane adds that "[w]e all greeted my dad like he was Santa Claus."[10] While less eager to efface their backgrounds than Kane appears to have been, Jewish comics legends Stan Lee and Harvey Kurtzman do not in their autobiographies make any mention of Judaism in any definition as having played a significant role in their comics careers.[11]

(Incidentally, Harry Brod makes a claiming move similar to Fingeroth's with Stan Lee's biography. Pointing out [correctly] that Lee described his parents only as "Romanian immigrants" and [incorrectly] that Lee only mentions Jewishness "late in the game," in connection with his mixed marriage making adoption difficult, Brod writes: "It's perfectly legitimate for someone not to think their Jewishness had much of an impact on their work, but such a gap in his life story seems too much like avoidance *for me to fully accept.*"[12] What precisely Lee is avoiding or why Brod's acceptance should matter to him is difficult to answer, but these moments point to a sense of anxiety about the success of American Jewry's entry into US society. Confronting that anxiety by naming and claiming Jews, as discussed earlier, requires that the borders of Jewishness be patrolled. Such work rests on the construction of an imagined community through the establishment of common sentiment, built on perceived authentic and continuous tradition, to which Lee and Kane in their autobiographical self-representations do not conform.)

A primary reason for why so many talented Jews were involved in the early comic book business was that they wanted to work in illustration, but could not get jobs at upscale advertising and design firms because of restrictive hiring practices that kept them out, along with Italians, people of color, Asians, and Latinos.[13] Another reason was what comics historian Jean-Paul Gabilliet calls the "networking effect," a matter of ethno-religious social capital or previous contacts, through which friends, family, and associates helped each other out: Will Eisner and Bob Kane went to high school together and later tipped each other off about work; Stan Lee was hired by Martin Goodman, his cousin's husband; and a whole string of Jewish editors at DC was hired because of prior relationships with DC employees.[14] For most, however, working in comics was a job like any other, taken to pay the bills until they could begin walking the career path they wanted. Jerry Siegel did nothing to hide his career; he was doing what he wanted, but comics was not a vocation but for a select few.[15] Most were aware, in the beginning and for a long time afterward, that the industry was not held in high esteem.[16] Stan Lee, for instance, has claimed that he worked under a pseudonym because he was saving his real name (Stanley Martin Lieber) for the "Great American Novel" he was planning to one day write, rather than to hide his Jewish background.[17]

The swarm of superheroes that followed Superman was likely less a collective expression of Jewish secular messianic or utopian fervor, as Fingeroth would have it, than it was an expression of a venerated industry tradition. As one comics historian has put it, "[i]n the comic book industry, imitation was not only a high form of flattery, it was company policy."[18] Siegel and Shuster's tights-clad strongman was an almost overnight success; their publisher soon recruited Bob Kane in the hope of a repeat performance, and he was quickly joined on the bandwagon by a whole host of like-minded publishers, writers, and artists. Joining Jewish business partners Harry Donenfeld and Jack S. Liebowitz, who ran the publishing business that introduced Superman, and Stan Lee's relative Martin Goodman, were Protestant-run outfits like Leverett Gleason's Lev Gleason Publications and the Minnesotan Fawcett brothers' soon saunteringly moribund publishing house (DC eventually sued them over copyright infringement and won after a protracted legal battle).[19]

Over time, comics have become less denigrated, American society has become more open to celebrations of ethnic, cultural, and religious differences, and the comics industry has at least partly managed to reconcile the commercial impulses of the mainstream with the artistic and literary sensibilities that have long informed the underground and alternative scenes.[20] The re-ethnicization of American culture, which began in earnest in the late 1960s, has in part been one of a dialectical give-and-take between grass-roots movements, the government, and the business world, through culture, public policy, and commerce, which has both celebrated and commodified ethnicity and heritage.[21] Also beginning in the late 1960s, following trends in alternative and underground comics and concurrent with increasingly diverse but initially tokenistic ethnoracial representation in general, Jewish characters and issues began to appear more often in mainstream comics.

This too can be overstated: not all of these characters were created by Jews, nor were the connections usually deep. One prominent example is Roy Thomas, a lapsed Lutheran, who has been a tenacious advocate of golem stories, as well as the writer of several stories about the Holocaust, both of which are themes he has situated within a Jewish referential framework.[22] Another character that is often celebrated in Jewish–comics connection contexts is the X-Man Kitty Pryde, introduced in *Uncanny X-Men* #129 (January 1980), by writer Chris Claremont, whose mother is Jewish, and British-born Canadian artist John Byrne. Kitty's role in connection with Claremont is very easy to overstate, which happens in almost all of the books on the topic.[23] Kitty's Jewishness has little to do with Claremont, however; it was Byrne who suggested she be Jewish. But Byrne's readiness to suggest a Jewish X-Man in the first place, and Claremont's clear descriptions of Kitty as someone with whom he expected that readers could identify, is a telling indication of a more open conception of the role Jews and Jewishness could play in popular culture.

White ethnics had by the 1980s become unmarked. What would have been anathema a few decades earlier could now be accepted with a "why not."[24] To give a few further examples, Sabra, an Israeli superheroine clad in blue-and-white uniform most often displaying at least one *Magen David* (Star of David) in a prominent place, was created by non-Jewish creative duo Sal Buscema and Bill Mantlo in 1986.[25] The Golani, another Israeli superheroine, appeared in *Teenage Mutant Ninja Turtles Adventures*

#53–54 (February–March 1994), written by non-Jewish writer Stephen Murphy under the pseudonym Dean Clarrain. The 2002–2003 *Ultimate X-Men/Ultimates* crossover storyline, "Ultimate War," written by Scotsman Mark Millar, has a running gag in which a holographic computer repeatedly mixes martial arts and Judaica programs, resulting in, among other things, a group of Hasidic Jews wielding katana charging a group of superheroes, while simultaneously teaching Torah.[26] The list of similar characters and events could go on.

Simultaneously, existing characters have had their backgrounds rewritten through what is known in fandom as *retcon*, or retroactive continuity, a narrative convention common in serialized fictions. In its simplest definition, retcon is the alteration of previously established facts in a published continuity. Such alterations allow writers to motivate the resurrection of a dead character, to update a series to better fit the times, or to resolve conflicts in chronology. Retcon is also used to "fill in" gaps in character backgrounds and, sometimes, make them into almost entirely different characters. Through retcon, present needs and concerns of story (and business) redefine the very past upon which new stories are supposedly built.[27]

The character Magneto is an interesting example of such changes. When he first appeared in 1963, he was framed as a communist threat. As the civil rights movement grew stronger and more vocal, he gradually morphed into a white, fear-infused caricature of Black Power activism. After Chris Claremont took over writing duties, he eventually retconned Magneto into a Holocaust survivor of undefined ethnicity; in Claremont's days, the Holocaust was used mainly in Cold War terms, as a heavy-handed warning about the cost of moral compromise.[28] In the years since, however, Magneto's Jewishness has been assumed by readers. His identity, however, remained fuzzy for years, and the character's Jewishness did not make it into continuity until the 2008–2009 miniseries *X-Men: Magneto Testament*, wherein Korean American writer Greg Pak and Italian artist Carmine di Giandomenico made the character unambiguously Jewish.[29]

The trajectory of the character Ragman, who first appeared in 1976, can similarly serve as an instructive example of a change in Jewish and non-Jewish attitudes toward Jewish representation that has informed recent readings of superhero comics. Although Ragman was regarded as Jewish by some fans, Jewish comics creators Joe Kubert and Robert Kanigher's "Tatterdemalion of Justice" was explicitly identified as Irish. As Kanigher relayed to a reader who commented on the character's "obvious Jewishness" (Rory's father looked "either Jewish or Italian, and junk-dealing [the family trade] was a fairly common occupation for both groups at the time"), that "if Rory [Regan, the Ragman] was meant to be Jewish, he'd have a Jewish name–as Bette [Berg, a supporting character] does! She's Jewish–Rory is of Irish descent."[30] Eventually, however, in the early 1990s, readers' long-standing assumptions about the Ragman being Jewish were retconned into official continuity. Protagonist Rory Regan became Rory Reganiewicz. Rather than donning a simple costume made of old rags, the character was now said to wear a patchwork "suit of souls" created in sixteenth-century Prague, by a rabbinical council using the same magic that had allowed rabbi Judah Loew to create his legendary golem.[31]

By 2010, the Ragman's Jewish background was so well established in continuity that an entire story could be devoted to him conversing with a rabbi about his father, who had worn the suit in his youth. In the story, titled *Suit of Souls* and written by Greek American Christos N. Gage, Gerry (born Jerzy) Reganiewicz, fought the Nazis and protected the Warsaw ghetto until fleeing the day before its fall. Rory wonders why his father fled, and why he kept his Jewish roots a secret for the rest of his life. The rabbi reveals that it was the souls inhabiting the costume that forced Gerry to flee the conflagration engulfing the ghetto, since the suit was especially vulnerable to fire. Through this, Gerry is redeemed, giving the story cathartic closure: he had neither been a coward nor ashamed to call himself a Jew but, rather, had felt unworthy to do so because of what he had erroneously thought of as his own cowardice.[32] Responding to readers' assumptions and reflecting changing cultural attitudes, then, the course of the Ragman's publication history has seen the character go from being an Irishman created by Jews to being an overtly Jewish superhero, whose most intimate Jewish family history is written by a non-Jewish writer.

Suit of Souls, of course, is an example of the use of ethnic history almost on the level of cultural myth. The golem and the Holocaust, which have both been inscribed as cultural symbols in the American imaginary, serve here to give an air of mystery and pathos to character development by virtue of their broad recognition. But they do so without depth. As such, the comic displays the optionality and malleability of identity in twenty-first-century America and the ways in which the market has responded to many contemporary Americans' desires for ethnic difference and representation.[33] But, as Jewish community activist and educator David

Wolkin points out in a flippant but insightful review, *Suit of Souls* trades on a few common mass culture representational tropes. "The first red flag was the rabbi," he writes, and reproduces an image of a bespectacled, balding, short, and slightly awkward man, the stock *nebbishy* rabbi. The major themes of the story are "[g]uilt and shame, my friends, with a little twist of self-loathing. What could be more Jewish than that?" (Note on page 166 below, that Larry Tye makes a strikingly similar argument, perhaps jokingly but without Wolkin's sarcasm, in relation to Superman's dual identities.) Further, the backstory connects with anti-Semitism through reference to the Blood Libel and Ku Klux Klan, and through the Holocaust.

Worst of all, Wolkin goes on, the revelation that Gerry had not himself chosen to flee comes from a Nazi soul trapped in the suit, a soul that is then released from bondage because of its actions: "I—I'm moving on," the Nazi says before pointing out how easy his own release was, "Unglaublich—to find redemption in such a small thing."[34] By having this ending, the story represents the Nazi genocide of Jews in the peculiarly redemptive and affirmative manner that is a hallmark of the Americanization of the Holocaust as described by, among others, historian Alvin H. Rosenfeld. Rosenfeld writes that the cruelties and deprivations of the Nazi genocide of Jews are so alien to the American mindset, pragmatic in its approach to history and accustomed to an ethos of goodness, innocence, optimism, liberty, diversity, and equality, that they are virtually incomprehensible: "The Holocaust has had to enter American consciousness, therefore, in ways that Americans could readily understand on their own terms. These are terms that promote a tendency to individualize, heroize, moralize, idealize, and universalize."[35] Thus, as happens in *Suit of Souls*, the Holocaust in the USA often takes the form of a redemptive and affirmative story peopled more with survivors and rescuers—even "good Nazis"—than victims.

As characters appear and reappear in the large and ever-expanding fictional universes of DC and Marvel, the major superhero publishers, characterization becomes more nuanced. As this happens, it sometimes just "makes sense" to make a character Jewish for narrative or personal reasons, as happened in the Judaizing trajectory of the character Moon Knight, created in 1975 by writer Doug Moench and artist Don Perlin. Moench, who is not Jewish, felt that since the character's secret identity was that of Mark Spector, an often Jewish name (Moench had a Jewish friend of that name), the character should be Jewish. A later Jewish writer then provided the character with "an elderly, bearded Orthodox rabbi" for a father.[36] Other times Judaization helps to push the action forward, and on occasion it honors a creator, as was the case with the Thing and Jack Kirby in 2002.

The Thing, a gruff superhero created by Kirby and Stan Lee in 1961, is a member of *The Fantastic Four*'s eponymous quartet of protagonists. While his backstory had been explored many times in the intervening decades, through flashbacks to his youth spent in a gang on "Yancy Street," his service in the Air Force, and so on, he had never been provided an ethno-religious background. Lee denies having thought of the Thing as Jewish, stating that when he created his characters, he wanted them to be "enjoyed by people all around the world of varying faiths and so forth, and [...] tried to keep everything kind of neutral."[37] It had long been assumed that there was much of Kirby in the Thing. Indeed, Kirby himself has said that he saw the character as in part himself: "If you'll notice the way the Thing talks and acts, you'll find that the Thing is really Jack Kirby [...] He has my manners, he has my manner of speech, and he thinks the way I do. He's excitable, and you'll find that he's very, very active among people, and he can muscle his way through a crowd. I find I'm that sort of person."[38] Since the artist was known to have made a drawing of the character in a yarmulke and *tallit* (prayer shawl), holding a *siddur* (prayer book), which originated privately as a Chanukah card in 1975, it was deemed appropriate that the fictional curmudgeon officially be made Jewish in a retcon, which was orchestrated by non-Jewish editor Tom Brevoort and writer Karl Kesel.[39] In an interesting reversal, Brevoort appears to think that Kirby intended for the character to be Jewish, while neither Fingeroth nor Kaplan gives Kirby's greeting card image much stock in that regard.[40]

The discussion has now come full circle, but the picture has changed somewhat. There has always been a number of talented Jews on the forefront of the US comics industry: the question is what that means. It is not constructive to simply assume and assert that there is something we can call Jewish content in mainstream US comic books simply because they were created by Jews, especially in light of the fact that Jewish signification in those comics is not the exclusive domain of Jewish creators. Kirby's homemade Chanukah card is not of a kind with the mass-produced *Fantastic Four* #1; one is contracted work meant to be sold on the mass market, the other a private joke between a Jewish artist and a coreligionist fan. It might be concluded from this survey that the issue of Jews in comics should be considered to be clear-cut that there is nothing Jewish at all about superhero comics. That would be an error. Quite to the contrary, the Jewish–comics connection envelops a far more complex history than the work done to date would suggest, one that connects with historical issues and perceptions of race and ethnicity, class, and gender.

THE SYNTHESIS OF JUDAISM AND AMERICA

Many of the early innovators and pioneers in US comic book history were Jewish.[41] Jerry Siegel and Joe Shuster were Jewish, as was Max Gaines, the man most often held to be the inventor of the American comic book and one of the people credited as having discovered Superman. So was his son William who, among other things, cocreated the pop culture staple *MAD Magazine* (1952) with Jewish artists and writers Harvey Kurtzman, Al Feldstein, and Will Elder. Stan Lee is Jewish, and so was fellow comics legend Jack Kirby, with whom Lee (along with non-Jewish Steve Ditko and a handful of others) created the Marvel Universe as we know it today, and who contributed several other aspects to the form and business of comics that are still in widespread use. Chris Claremont, the British-born writer who went on to popularize those mutants far beyond what their originators could ever dream, in the son of a Jewish mother.[42] Will Eisner, one of US comics' celebrated grand old men, was also Jewish. The list could go on for pages. What their Jewishness meant for these men, however, was not necessarily the same as it means for their Jewish interpreters today.

As much recent scholarship has convincingly argued, American Judaism is not simply an expression of a timeless Jewish tradition transplanted to the USA. More and more, the literature on Jewish American history (and of Jews and other ethnicities in general) has come to understand ethnic identity as "invented" and recreated over time, often in dialogue with hegemonic majority cultural formations.[43] While many of its manifestations have roots in European developments following the Enlightenment and Jewish emancipation, American Judaism is in large measure a US creation. Indeed, for many Jewish immigrants, coming to the USA entailed a literal and symbolic abandonment of the Old World; either in transit or upon arrival, artifacts like photographs were thrown into the water and some considered prayer shawls and *tefillin*, the small leather boxes used for ritual Jewish prayer, to be excess baggage.[44] Historian of Judaism Jonathan D. Sarna notes in the introduction to his seminal *American Judaism: A New History*, that "in America [...] Judaism has had to adapt to a religious environment shaped by the denominational character of American Protestantism, the canons of free market competition, the ideals of freedom, and the reality of diversity." American Judaism must therefore be studied within a larger historical framework:

> For American Judaism, this means paying attention to American history, Jewish history, and the history of American religion. Second, the term 'religion' needs to be constructed broadly, so as to include not only 'secular' movements but also those opposed to religion altogether. [...] Third, diversity must be accepted as a fact and analyzed. Finally [...] [s]ocial, economic, political, cultural, and psychological factors affecting religious life must constantly be borne in mind.[45]

From early on, the USA's Jewish communities responded to developments in US democracy: when the Constitution was signed ("in a time when constitution writing was all the rage") each of the country's synagogues rewrote their own constitutions, incorporating "large dollops of republican rhetoric," according to Sarna; even before the Bill of Rights had been ratified, at least one congregation included a formal "bill of rights" in its own constitution.[46] The major branches of religious American Judaism— Reform, Conservative, and Orthodox—are in large measure founded and developed on a pattern established by Protestant denominationalism or otherwise a reaction to such emulation, and they initially emphasized respectability and decorum so as to not appear strange in the majority's eyes.[47] All three have been greatly influenced by the USA's competitive religious marketplace. The appearance of a whole host of smaller alternatives for Jewish religious practice and a large number of nonreligious Jewish movements and subcultures further displays the diversity inspired by an ever-expanding marketplace of ideas.

Demographic influx in waves of immigration from different parts of Europe continued to episodically trigger reshaping of American Judaism until the country's borders were more or less closed by restrictive immigration laws in 1924, but by then the community was embroiled in a power struggle of sorts between established American Jews and Eastern European newcomers. Postwar suburbanization prompted additional transformations, and the late-1960s rise of ethnic consciousness, growing remembrance of the Holocaust, and the Israeli Six-Day War in 1967 inspired a new type of Jewish self-identification that realized, to use Judaism scholar Jacob Neusner's pointed phrasing, "in a poignant way the conflicting demands of Jewish Americans to be intensely Jewish, but only once in a while, and not exacting much of a cost in meaningful difference from others."[48]

Similarly, as Beth Wenger has noted, the very history of American Judaism has been fashioned "virtually from whole cloth."[49] As opposed to Jewish communities in other countries, American Jews had immigrated to a new country and, with a few early exceptions, immediately found themselves enfranchised to a greater degree than ever before. There was no officially sanctioned segregation or oppression in the USA and no binding way for a Jewish American establishment to enforce cohesion, as had often been the case in Europe. Many believed that "America was different" and, in the narratives they created, American Jews consequently situated themselves as "insiders in the national culture, participants in its creation, and equal members of American democracy from its inception."[50]

Conversely, the USA has not simply imposed a ready-made culture on its Jewish population.[51] Despite the historically recurrent arguments of nativists, white supremacists, and other homegrown xenophobes throughout the last century, American culture has always been a "mongrel" culture. The word mongrel is not here used in a pejorative sense, but in the dictionary sense, meaning that it is both the result of the interbreeding of diverse breeds or strains and, at least in some measure, of unknown origin. One of the most thorough chroniclers of Jewish contributions to this mix is Stephen Whitfield, whose *In Search of Jewish American Culture* is an attempt to address the questions of how US culture has differed because of the presence of Jews and how American Jews invented a distinctive culture without the feeling of living in exile.[52]

Jewish American history, then, is in many ways a history of the encounter with the USA, a history of both voluntary Americanization inspired by the country's pull and promise and a story of Americanization forced upon American Jewry by the push of anti-Semitism and nativist sentiment. It is also a history of opposition to and anxieties about Americanization. Further, by virtue of being addressed to mainstream audiences, Jewish American mass cultural production was no different from non-Jewish mass cultural production; because it was guided by commercial concerns and aiming for a broad appeal to satisfy popular tastes, trying to not assail reigning norms was a key concern.[53] Thus, US history should be taken into account in any discussion of Jewish American creativity.

WHITENESS AND ETHNICITY: GROUNDING RACE, GENDER, AND CLASS

For Jews, as for the USA's other ethnic, racial, cultural, and religious minorities, participation and mobility in US society has historically been conditional. The USA, founded as it was on ideals of justice, liberty, and equality of opportunity, was also built on a foundation of those largely unspoken cultural assumptions that were most comfortable to the white men of means at the top of the socioeconomic pyramid.[54] Throughout the twentieth century, US culture underwent a slow shift in regard to the perceived place of non-WASPs, in a process that was racialized, classed, and gendered. These changes in the relationships between Jews and US society and to Americanization were reflected in how the majority perceived and represented American Jewry, and in how American Jews perceived and represented the majority and each other. This history is central to understanding Siegel and Shuster's Superman and his later interpreters.

A ground for American identity was established gradually after the Revolution in the form of whiteness, which conferred fitness for inclusion, citizenship, and participation. As one memorable formulation puts it: "White privilege is like an invisible weightless knapsack of special provisions, assurances, tools, maps, guides, codebooks, passports, visas, clothes, compass, emergency gear, and blank checks."[55] Whiteness does not refer exclusively to phenotypical characteristics, but to a sociocultural complex of values, ideas, and behaviors, often unreflexively perceived as the norm. As such, it is a concept that has also always been related to classed and gendered behaviors and conventions. For immigrants, escaping dominance and oppression, and gaining access to equality of opportunity has often required adherence to the same conventions and structures that once kept one down. Importantly, as film scholar Richard Dyer has noted, whiteness is "a matter of ascription – white people are who white people say are white. This has a profoundly controlling effect."[56]

With slavery, blackness became stigmatized as servile and whiteness became a privileged condition by contrast and constant distinction; supposed black inferiority reinforced supposed white supremacy.[57] Indeed, as historian David R. Roediger has convincingly argued, whiteness and blackness developed together in the USA, the former being defined over and against the latter over the first 65 years of the nineteenth century. Whiteness as a powerful social fact grew out of wage laborers' proximity to and distancing from chattel slavery, the lingering power of forceful

Revolutionary Era rhetoric about "political slavery," and anxieties about the rise and discipline of industrial capitalism. This ideology was not only a trickle down from the ruling classes but also an active discourse within working class environments.[58] Economic competition following the emancipation of US slaves in the Civil War exacerbated these feelings.[59] For workers, according to Roediger, whiteness functioned as a "psychological wage": "That is, status and privileges conferred by race could be used to make up for alienating and exploitative class relationships. [...] Workers could, and did, define and accept their class positions by fashioning identities as 'not slaves' or as 'not Blacks'."[60]

By the mid-nineteenth century, the USA had developed its own form of unmarked romantic nationalism in which "real" Americans were grounded as white, free, and independent. "Americans tended to racialize others and consider themselves simply human," writes historian of racism George M. Frederickson, noting that white Americans constructed themselves as "citizens of the 'Universal Yankee Nation' and beneficiaries of what was promised to 'all men' by the Declaration of Independence."[61] Whiteness also evolved into a gendered phenomenon, with men working out their anxieties about citizenship and wage labor by stressing occupational independence, production, and the masculine ability to provide for their dependents.[62] Simultaneously, affluent Jewish and other immigrant women began modeling themselves on the "womanly" virtues of the Protestant elite and embraced domesticity, hoping to hide or efface their culture's divergence from the norm, while working-class immigrant women were stigmatized for their nonconformity.[63] Thus, by the time the great late nineteenth- and early twentieth-century waves of "new immigrants" of Eastern and Southern European origin brought many first-generation superhero comics creators' families to the USA, a discourse of whiteness had become a prominent feature in the nation's identity climate.

What Roediger calls the "long early 20th century," the period from 1890 to 1945, began with increasing pressure on Jews and other immigrants to assimilate, to Americanize, and to "whiten." The concept of race early on gained a plural meaning. Late nineteenth-century estimates could claim that there were between 2 and 63 races, depending on whether the concept was conceived in terms of "color races" (white, black, Native American, Asian) or "nation races" (e.g. Jews, Polacks, Italians, Slavs), as well as an "American" race and, perhaps most confusingly, an "English-speaking" race. In this climate, "new immigrants" were made "conditionally white," or racially situated "in between" hard racism and full inclusion, neither fully white nor nonwhite.[64] By the turn of the twentieth century, immigrants and others were being classified according to these ill-defined schemas of "race" and were granted social mobility and the rights of full citizenship accordingly. Similarly, hiring patterns and wage discrimination were often influenced by ethnoracial assignations.[65]

Nonetheless, the establishment in the South of the Jim Crow system of institutionalized segregation of blacks and somewhat lesser northern segregation of that group ensured that no group was ever as far outside society as African Americans.[66] Part of the "new immigrants'" meeting with the USA entailed learning, through the encounter with white supremacy, to see and disparage race in order to fit in and to escape the worst forms of oppression.[67] Immigrants and their children quickly learned that "the worst thing one could be in this Promised Land was 'colored'."[68]

"New immigrant" women had their own particular set of fears of racialization, and risked being regarded as "oriental" and therefore ugly or open to sexual exploitation if their complexion was too dark, or their hair the wrong color or too curly. Homemakers took great care to make a clean and white home, but were still deemed inbetween, because keeping their families thriving (or simply alive) often required "unwomanly" physical labor.[69] Jewish women were particularly subjected to the anxieties of those who feared the influx of "new immigrant" "races"; the so-called Ghetto Girl, garishly dressed, desirous of material comforts and pleasures, overly autonomous, and lacking in decorum, became a negative image that was the opposite of the normative white bourgeois woman. This figure expressed both non-Jewish stereotypes about Jews and Jewish American worries about the dangers posed by the less Americanized to their own inclusion, powerfully symbolizing what needed to be contained and disciplined away for Jewish well-being and acceptance in the USA.[70]

In 1908, Jewish playwright Israel Zangwill wrote "The Melting Pot," a play about the daughter of a Russian nobleman who had played a part in the 1903 Kishinev pogrom and a Jew, the lone survivor in his family of that same explosion of anti-Semitism. The youths find love with each other and reject the Old World for the USA, into which they expect to assimilate. The play rested in part on the idea that immigrants would Americanize through marriage. With its praise of intermarriage, the play seemed to suggest that "racial amalgamation was a prerequisite to becoming true Americans." This idea, which would continue to be prevalent in US pop culture in the first decades of the twentieth century, helped popularize the concept of the Melting Pot. The Melting Pot idea emphasized

"America as the place where old prejudices would be submerged and the peoples of Europe would be unified into a new, more potent race."[71]

In 1915, around the time when the first generation of Jewish comics pioneers was coming into the world, President Woodrow Wilson spoke the following words to 4000 newly naturalized citizens:

> You cannot dedicate yourself to America unless you become in every respect and with every purpose of your will thorough Americans. You cannot become thorough Americans if you think of yourselves in groups. America does not consist of groups. A man who thinks of himself as belonging to a particular national group in America has not yet become an American, and the man who goes among you to trade upon your nationality is no worthy son to live under the Stars and Stripes.[72]

Such harsh pro-Americanizing rhetoric remained common following WWI; by 1924, in part from pressure exerted by a then-powerful Ku Klux Klan and other racist, nativist, and "100 % Americanist" groups and individuals, the USA's borders had been more or less closed through strict immigration legislation that marked "new immigrants" as racially undesirable, if still less so than people of color.

Some regarded this legislation as a sort of "lid" on the Melting Pot: those immigrants who had already come were now widely expected to melt into the USA through assimilation, Americanization, and whitening. Also following restriction, as immigrants Americanized, rural African Americans, Asians, Mexicans, and white "hillbillies" increasingly entered the less desirable areas of work, in turn becoming the most "foreign" of city dwellers and somewhat alleviating anti-immigrant sentiment.[73] Housing covenants designed to keep people of color out of white neighborhoods, racist and racialist representations in pop culture, along with segregation in movie houses and nightclubs, and "aggressive Americanization" in public schooling, further instilled immigrants and their children with awareness of the color line and their own inbetween status.[74] Still, by the time Siegel and Shuster created Superman, US anti-Semitism was reaching unprecedented levels.[75] It is within this restrictive context and identity climate, with a strong pull toward Americanization and a strong push in anti-Semitism that Siegel and Shuster did their work. As will be seen throughout the rest of the book, but most clearly in Chaps. 8 and 9, this affected how their Superman took shape. The books that treat those stories today, however, emerged out of a very different situation, which owes much to postwar developments.

ETHNIC WHITENESS AND ETHNIC CELEBRATION

After WWII, "new immigrants" were increasingly regarded as "white ethnics," in ways that both opened up a path into whiteness and coerced them to walk it. Americans styled themselves as more inclusive and anti-racist in rhetoric, but the racial projects of the war years were largely kept to one side of the color line; white and whitening America organized for inclusion and exclusion at the same time.[76] In the postwar years, with the emergence of a liberal Cold War consensus culture, white ethnics became part of an American mainstream that stressed the universal sameness of humankind. Ethnicity became a sign of assimilable "minor" difference, as opposed to supposedly inherent racial difference.[77]

With much discrimination and many obstacles to white ethnic social mobility gone, and following the rise of black militancy in the mid-to-late 1960s, white ethnic consciousness started to emerge, in part because white privilege had become more visible and sometimes uncomfortable. Members of many groups that had been whitened began uncovering forgotten histories and celebrating heritages. This phenomenon, labeled an ethnic revival, is often explained in terms of "Hansen's Law"; named after its originator, historian Marcus Lee Hansen, the Law rested on the idea that "what the second generation wanted to forget, the third wanted to remember." While there had never been a complete "death or slumber of ethnicity" in America, there certainly was a surge of popular ethnic interest beginning in the 1960s. Historian Mathew Frye Jacobson writes:

> What is missing from the standard Hansen's Law reckoning are the surrounding cultural, institutional, and political forces: trade presses and television networks, which produced mass paperbacks and TV shows like *Roots*; news agencies, like *Time Magazine*, which turned the roots phenomenon into a roots craze by providing instructions in genealogical research; publishers, scholars, and universities, which produced studies like *World of Our Fathers* and offered college credits for *Roots*–inflected family histories; and politicians like Gerald Ford and Jimmy Carter, who sanctioned a vision of "ethnic heritage" that had vast implications not only for individuals and families but for the nation itself and for reigning notions of "Americanness."[78]

Through the efforts of academia, the culture industries, the mass marketplace, and the state, the USA emerged as not a homogenizing Melting Pot, but a multicultural Mosaic. These developments "mark the emergence of a wholly new syntax of nationality and belonging – a change in personal feeling for some, perhaps, but a change in public language for all."[79] This shift did not supplant whiteness, but changed its ground from WASPishness to ethnic "Ellis Island whiteness." The USA was celebrated as a "nation of immigrants," retaining the attending exclusions inherent in such a concept and creating a new type of white supremacism. Since the 1960s, ethnic hyphenation has become "a natural idiom of national belonging in this nation of immigrants," writes Frye Jacobson.[80] "Ethnicization has itself become normative," echoes historian Marilyn Halter, "a part of the Americanization process."[81] Ethnicity has become the prototype of Americanness. Immigrant heritage is the new whiteness, an identity "denoting relatively recent arrival, underdog credentials, and innocence in white supremacy's history of conquest and enslavement."[82]

These developments reverberated in questions of class and gender, both of which were connected with consumption. Mass culture consumption has long served as a means of assimilation, which has helped break down traditional boundaries between groups. Halter notes that visible ethnicity has historically been associated with the lifestyles of the lower classes. Accents, ethnic foods, and other markers of difference were effaced among the upwardly mobile in the name of Americanization, and regarded as signs of failed assimilation. Halter writes that

[a]s the economy boomed after World War II, participation in mass consumer society had a homogenizing effect. The drive of the second generation to assimilate as rapidly as possible coincided with the availability and affordability of goods and an accompanying mass marketing approach. This was an era when socioeconomic advancement often meant denial of one's immigrant past and ethnic heritage, a betrayal that could readily translate into self-hate and anomie. The sustenance of face-to-face, co-ethnic communities was replaced by the palliative of mass-produced material goods that rapidly filled suburban households but often left the inhabitants inside with a profound sense of spiritual dislocation.[83]

The dominant Jewish American gender stereotype of the 1970s and 1980s was the Jewish American Princess. She was an unpassionate figure of passive consumption and consumerism, a product of integration into the middle class and the frustrated expectations of those who had achieved the dream and found it lacking. As such, she epitomized demanding and withholding middle-class life. Significantly, the Princess was not a figure of difference, but of sameness: "one absolutely does not have to be Jewish to achieve even an advanced state of JAPitude," quipped one comedian, listing such Princesses as Jackie Onassis, Cher, and Nancy Reagan, among others.[84]

Still, since the 1960s, American culture and consumption has aimed increasingly at demassification, serving for consumers as a way to assert an identity different from their neighbors.[85] "American popular culture reenacted the debate between integration and diversity in the 1970s," writes historian Bruce Schulman: "The nation's moviehouses, record stores, and dance clubs witnessed an extended, if not always conscious or articulate, dispute between the fading integrationist ideal and the emerging [cultural] nationalist sensibility."[86] The 1990 US census indicated that a reversal in the relationship to ethnic identification had occurred: the more educated and successful were more likely to identify with ethnic designations. The signs of difference that were once eschewed, notably foods, were increasingly consumed as a means to assert identity.[87] The relationship between marked and unmarked, then, had changed to the point of reversal.

In this process, forgotten literatures were retrieved, beginning for Jewish Americans with the 1960 reissue of Abraham Cahan's 1917 novel *The Rise of David Levinski*. School children and college students were sent on "heritage hunts." America's 1976 bicentennial celebration adopted ethnic diversity as a central motif. By the Statue of Liberty's centenary ten years later, the conceit of the USA as a "nation of immigrants" had become an article of civil-religious faith. Americans undertook genealogical archaeologies at a precipitous pace after the 1977 airing of the TV miniseries *Roots*. Ethnic history, "heritage tourism," cook books of "authentic" recipes (including the *Holocaust Survivor Cookbook*, "[t]he most important cookbook you'll ever own"), the romantization of the European *shtetl* and the immigrant Lower East Side, and a host of other heritage projects have made American Jews and other ethnic and racial groups more educated about their pasts, and more attached to them.[88] Jewish Americans, like many other groups, "rediscovered their families, their ethnicity, their spirituality. They looked back–but almost exclusively at themselves."[89]

The phenomenon of ethnic celebration, and of symbolic ethnicity which frequently accompanies it, is often shrouded in sentiment and nostalgia, as is evident, for example, in the discussion about Jewish–comics literature above. On this note, we have returned to Herbert Gans' observations about ethnic revival writing. It is in the light of the discussed developments that Chabon's novel and the popular literature are best understood. Since contemporary US formations of national and ethnic identity are the results of long, and often painful processes, and because opportunities to publically celebrate ethnicity are of relatively recent vintage, the historian must be careful, lest interpretation be similarly inflected with myth and uncritical celebration.

As will be discussed in the pages to come, the absence of overtly Jewish characters or other Jewish significations in something like Siegel and Shuster's Superman does not mean that Jewish concerns and experiences are absent from the work. Nor does the inverse, the presence of Jewish characters and Jewish significations in these comics, mean that Jewish concerns and experiences are dominant. Rather, the rest of this book will attempt to contextualize Superman comics that have previously been read narrowly through a lens of sentimental and nostalgic Jewishness, and situate them within the tumultuous pre-WWII meeting of Judaism and Americanism and of Jewishness and Americanness. This is done to investigate how the two ideals converged and intersected in Superman. In the remaining chapters, I will present alternative interpretations of Superman that illustrate not only how different a critical reading of the stories in which this history is kept in mind of necessity becomes but also what unintended, and sometimes troubling, consequences that Judeocentric readings can have, if their logics are fully unpacked.

NOTES

1. Spiegelman, *Maus*; cf. Geis, *Considering Maus*.
2. For a history of the underground and alternative comics scenes, Sabin, *Comics, Comix & Graphic Novels*. Note also the lack of women in this list. As Oksman, *Keep Their Noses?* points out, female cartoonists in general, and Jewish cartoonists in particular, have been given little attention in either fan culture or comics scholarship.
3. Katchor, *Jew of NY*; Sturm, *Golem's Mighty Swing*; Kubert, *Jew Gangster*.
4. Quoted in Fingeroth, *Disguised as Clark Kent*, 24.
5. Fingeroth, *Disguised as Clark Kent*, 25.
6. Kronenberg, "Auteur Theory," 229.
7. Brodkin, *How Jews Became White*, 1–3, 21–22; Omi and Winant, *Racial Formation*.
8. Eisner, *Christmas Spirit*, 5; cf. Takaki, *Different Mirror*, 282; Heinze, *Adapting to Abundance*.
9. Hajdu, *Ten-Cent Plague*, 188.

10. Fingeroth, *Disguised as Clark Kent*, 52–54.
11. Lee and Mair, *Excelsior!*; Kane, *Batman*; Kurtzman, *My Life*.
12. Brod, *Superman Is Jewish?*, 90.
13. Jones, *Men of Tomorrow*, 134–35; Hajdu, *Ten-Cent Plague*, 25–26.
14. Gabilliet, *Of Comics and Men*, 160–63; Lee and Mair, *Excelsior!*, 22–25; Schumacher, *Dreamer's Life*, 21–24; Andelman, *A Spirited Life*, 36, 41.
15. Tye, *Superman*, 48–49.
16. Jones, *Men of Tomorrow*, 168–70, 237–42; Wright, *Comic Book Nation*, 7, 33–35; Gabilliet, *Of Comics and Men*, pt. 3; Beaty, *Comics Versus Art*; Hajdu, *Ten-Cent Plague*; Schumacher, *Dreamer's Life*, 33–34; Nyberg, *Seal of Approval*; cf. Lee and Mair, *Excelsior!*, 56–57; Eisner and Miller, *Eisner/Miller*, chap. 15.
17. Brevoort and Lee, The Jewish Thing; Lee and Mair, *Excelsior!*, 26–27.
18. Wright, *Comic Book Nation*, 15–22; cf. Gabilliet, *Of Comics and Men*, 18–19; Jones, *Men of Tomorrow*, 147–56, 165–66; Lee and Mair, *Excelsior!*, 62–64; Fingeroth, *Disguised as Clark Kent*, 28–29.
19. Cf. Jones, *Men of Tomorrow*, 165–66, 187–88, 262, 13–22; Murray, *Champions*, 17–30.
20. Both Marvel and DC have established "adult" imprints that publish mature comics, meaning both more violent and more philosophically inclined (and sometimes both). But, as Jewish comics writer, artist, and teacher Joe Kubert's *Yossel* and *Jew Gangster* indicate, they are willing to gamble and move outside their traditional comfort zones.
21. Halter, *Shopping for Identity*.
22. On Thomas' background, see Cooke, Thomas Interview. Thomas notes that "I went to a parochial Lutheran school, but I'm not religious." Thomas' use of golems is enumerated but not contextualized in Weiner, "Marvel and the Golem."
23. For example, over two decades of Kitty continuity and characterization are reduced to a few examples of explicit Jewish signification in Weinstein, *Up, Up, and Oy Vey!*, 113–14; Kaplan, *From Krakow to Krypton*, 120–23; Malcolm, "Witness, Trauma, Remembrance," 154–55, 159.
24. Sanderson, "Claremont Pt. 2," 51; James, "ZAP! POW! BAM! OY!," 50.

25. Sabra first appeared in Mantlo and Buscema, *Power in the Promised Land*.
26. Millar et al., *Ultimate X-Men Vol. 5: Ultimate War*.
27. For a short time in the early 1950s, Captain America appeared in comic books as a "commie smasher." The attempted revival of the character was unsuccessful, but not so his March 1964 revival in *The Avengers* #4. Since this version of the character was said to have been frozen in a block of ice for 20 years, the "commie smasher" Captain was rewritten to fit continuity; returning in the early 1970s, the 1950s version of the character was now "revealed" to have been a fan of the real Captain America who went insane after taking a serum that gave him enhanced strength. The conflict between the two Captains was then used to deliver commentary on Cold War policies. See the discussion in Costello, *Secret Identity Crisis*, 105–7.
28. For a longer discussion about this history, see Lund, "The Mutant Problem."
29. Pak and Di Giandomenico, *Magneto Testament*.
30. See the letters page in Kanigher, *75–25 or Die!*
31. Fleming, Giffen, and Broderick, *The Folktale*.
32. Gage, *Suit of Souls*.
33. Cf. Halter, *Shopping for Identity*; Frye Jacobson, *Roots Too*.
34. Wolkin, "Ragman."
35. Rosenfeld, *End of Holocaust*, 59–61; cf. Novick, *Holocaust in American Life*; Flanzbaum, *Americanization of Holocaust*.
36. This trajectory is described in Fingeroth, *Disguised as Clark Kent*, 136–37.
37. Brevoort and Lee, The Jewish Thing.
38. Quoted in Evanier, *Kirby*, 124.
39. See Weiss, "Comic Superhero Revealed"; Brevoort and Lee, The Jewish Thing; Kirby's card in Evanier, *Kirby*, 212.
40. Fingeroth, *Disguised as Clark Kent*, 137–38; Kaplan, *From Krakow to Krypton*, 100; Breevort in Gross, "It's a Jewish Thing."
41. Comic strips, on the other hand, was largely a WASPish preserve. There were exceptions to this rule, such as Rube Goldberg and Harry Hershfield, but Jews were largely kept out of the business. Cf. Goodwin, "Cartoons and Jews"; Moss, "Racial Anxiety."
42. Fingeroth, *Disguised as Clark Kent*, 121, describes Claremont as "half-Jewish"; Claremont notes in Kaplan, *From Krakow to*

Krypton, 122, that "from a cultural point of view, certainly through my family, I know what it's like to be Jewish!"

43. For some examples, see Conzen and Gerber, "Invention of Ethnicity"; Roskies, *Usable Past*; Wenger, *History Lessons*; "Inventing American Jewry"; Satlow, *Creating Judaism*; Prell, *Fighting to Become Americans*, 14–17.

44. Sarna, *American Judaism*, 156–57; Halter, *Shopping for Identity*, 78–80.

45. Sarna, *American Judaism*, xvi–xvii.

46. Sarna, *American Judaism*, 42–44.

47. See Sarna, *American Judaism*; Kaplan, *Companion to American Judaism*; Blecher, *New American Judaism*. Satlow, *Creating Judaism*, chap. 1, offers a similar perspective along with a helpful comparative view of contemporary Israeli Judaism.

48. On the role of different generations of immigration, see Kaplan, *Companion to American Judaism*, pt. 1; Sarna, *American Judaism*; on the influence of the postwar suburban Jewish experience, see Kaplan, *Contemporary American Judaism*; Neusner, *Judaism in Modern Times*, chap. 8, argues for the emergence of an "American Judaism of Holocaust and Redemption" following the attempted destruction of European Jewry in the Holocaust and the perceived redemption achieved through the establishment of the state of Israel and its performance in the 1967 Six-Day War (220).

49. Wenger, *History Lessons*, 15.

50. Wenger, *History Lessons*, 15–29.

51. Nor, for that matter, on any other group; cf. Takaki, *Different Mirror*.

52. Whitfield, *American Jewish Culture*.

53. Sarna, *American Judaism*, 330–31; this, as Patterson, *Grand Expectations*, 347 points out, is common to commercial cultural production in general.

54. Cf. Mazur, *Americanization of Religious Minorities*; Michael, *Identity and the Failure of America*.

55. McIntosh, "White Privilege and Male Privilege," 1–2.

56. Quote from Dyer, *White*, 48; see also Brodkin, *How Jews Became White*; Goldstein, *Price of Whiteness*; Ignatiev, *How the Irish Became White*. White skin, however, seems to have been a prerequisite for entering the Melting Pot. In fact, Nathan Glazer has argued that an important reason for the failure of the Melting Pot, leading to

Americans having to concede that they "are all multiculturalists now," is that the theory did not account for the country's African American population. See his somewhat defeatist *Multiculturalists*.
57. Brodkin, *How Jews Became White*, chap. 2 (esp. p. 70).
58. Cf. Roediger, *Wages of Whiteness*; pp. 27–31 provide examples of the type of Revolutionary rhetoric that helped make white self-definition in opposition to slavery so tempting.
59. Fredrickson, *Racism*, 76–92; Roediger, *Wages of Whiteness*.
60. Roediger, *Wages of Whiteness*, 13.
61. Fredrickson, *Racism*, 73.
62. Roediger, *Wages of Whiteness*.
63. Prell, *Fighting to Become Americans*, 7–8; Brodkin, *How Jews Became White*, chap. 3.
64. Roediger, *Working toward Whiteness*, 10–13 ; Brodkin, *How Jews Became White*, 25–35. Brodkin, on pp. 1–2 also notes that Jews in the US have experienced a "kind of double vision that comes from racial middleness: of an experience of marginality vis-à-vis whiteness, and an experience of whiteness vis-à-vis blackness."
65. Roediger, *Working toward Whiteness*.
66. Fredrickson, *Racism*, chap. 3; Roediger, *Working toward Whiteness*.
67. Roediger, *Working toward Whiteness*, chaps. 3–4.
68. Conzen and Gerber, "Invention of Ethnicity."
69. Roediger, *Working toward Whiteness*, 186–91.
70. Prell, *Fighting to Become Americans*, chap. 1.
71. Goldstein, *Price of Whiteness*, 99; Prell, *Fighting to Become Americans*, 69.
72. Wilson, "Naturalized Citizens."
73. Roediger, *Working toward Whiteness*, 18–21, chap. 5.
74. Roediger, *Working toward Whiteness*, 157–84, 193–95; cf. Dollinger, *Quest for Inclusion*, 148–49.
75. Dinnerstein, *Antisemitism in America*, chap. 6; Lipstadt, *Beyond Belief*, 127; Shogan, *Prelude to Catastrophe*, 108–9.
76. Roediger, *Working toward Whiteness*, 235–44; cf. Takaki, *Double Victory*.
77. Frye Jacobson, *Roots Too*, 31–34; Schulman, *Seventies*, 58.
78. Frye Jacobson, *Roots Too*, 4.
79. Frye Jacobson, *Roots Too*, 4–6.
80. Frye Jacobson, *Roots Too*, 6–10, 177–80; cf. pp. 59–69 and chap. 7.

81. Halter, *Shopping for Identity*, 78; Frye Jacobson, *Roots Too*, 75, 128.
82. Frye Jacobson, *Roots Too*, 317.
83. Halter, *Shopping for Identity*, 42; cf. Heinze, *Adapting to Abundance*; Smith, *Hard-Boiled*.
84. Prell, *Fighting to Become Americans*, chap. 6; quote from p. 190.
85. Halter, *Shopping for Identity*.
86. Schulman, *Seventies*, 72.
87. Halter, *Shopping for Identity*, chap. 1.
88. Cf. Frye Jacobson, *Roots Too*; Roskies, *Usable Past*; Diner, Shandler, and Wenger, *Remembering the LES*.
89. Schulman, *Seventies*, 77.

CHAPTER 4

And So Begins a Startling Adventure

"Doomed planet. Desperate scientists. Last hope. Kindly couple." These words, paired with simple visuals—close-ups of Krypton, Superman's Kryptonian parents, baby Kal-El's shuttle, and the Kents—are the only origin story writer Grant Morrison and artists Frank Quitely provide for Superman in their 2005–2008 miniseries *All-Star Superman*.[1] It is a simple, yet incredibly effective, way of activating readers' knowledge; after all, everybody knows Superman's story, right? The problem with that assumption is that, while the story is indeed well known, it has been retold numerous times, and always with some measure of difference. This fact might not be important for the average reader, but it is crucial for critical analysis. This chapter will therefore linger on Superman's origin story and the way it has been used in Jewish–comics connection literature, to claim that superman should be read as an immigrant, a refugee created in response to Nazism, and a Moses figure.

In a long list of different—but supposedly compatible—ostensible Jewish inspirations for Superman, which can serve here as an introduction to the Jewish themes most often discussed in the Jewish–comics connection literature, Harry Brod summarizes his view:

Superman is "the hero from Ellis Island, personified as an (undocumented) alien who had been naturalized by the ultimate American couple, Eben and Sarah Kent." Immigrant refugee baby Kal-El had been sent to Earth by his

© The Editor(s) (if applicable) and The Author(s) 2016
M. Lund, *Re-Constructing the Man of Steel*,
DOI 10.1007/978-3-319-42960-1_4

parents when they, along with his entire culture, were annihilated in the great holocaust of the destruction of his home planet, populated by what were said to be "highly evolved inhabitants." In the context of the time, his story echoes that of the "Kindertransports" of Europe, via which Jewish children were evacuated to safe countries to escape the Nazis, leaving their parents behind.

Set adrift in a very advanced basket of bulrushes, Kal-El undertook a journey recalling that of Moses, adrift on the Nile. The change from his native Kryptonian name Kal-El to the adoptive and adaptive Clark Kent (like the change of Siegel's family name, and those of millions of Jews, at Ellis Island[2]), and his later movement from the small town of Smallville to the big city of Metropolis, mirrored Jewish immigration patterns. American Jews and American superheroes share an urban environment. [...] [T]he natural habitat of the superheroes created by Jews is the streets of the cities.[3]

As will be shown below, this characterization takes significant liberties with Jewish history and projects several later traits and aspects of the Superman metatext back onto Siegel and Shuster's work.

SUPER-IMMIGRANT?

Along with Brod above, Larry Tye calls Superman "the ultimate foreigner, escaping to America from his intergalactic shtetl and shedding his Jewish name [sic] for Clark Kent" (even though he has earlier explicitly noted that the early Superman has no knowledge of his alien origins).[4] Danny Fingeroth regards Superman as the "embodiment of all those lone immigrants" who came to the USA, seeking safety and success, from an Old World, to which they could not return.[5] With reference to unnamed and unsourced pop culture scholars, Arie Kaplan calls Superman "the ultimate metaphor for the Jewish experience."[6] The writers are all on shaky ground when they make these connections.

The first telling of Superman's origin, which was apparently conceived in the rush to meet a deadline,[7] was a hastily added one-page introduction to the character. Appearing only in a single panel, "a distant planet" (it was first named Krypton in a ghostwritten sequence of the daily comic strip published on January 16, 1939[8]) was "destroyed by old age," providing an easy "scientific explanation of Clark Kent's amazing strength."[9] In a comparison likely adapted from novelist Philip Wylie's 1930 science fiction novel *Gladiator*, one of Superman's most commonly suggested inspirations, the hero is said to have come from a planet whose inhabitant's "physical structure was millions of years advanced of our own." This, readers are assured, is not as incredible as it sounds: "For even today on our world exist creatures with *super-strength!* The lowly ant can support weights hundreds of times its own[.] The grasshopper leaps what to a man would be the space of several city blocks."[10] (Compare Wylie: "Did you ever watch an ant carry many times its weight? Or see a grasshopper jump fifty times its length? The insects have better muscles and nerves than we have. And I improved your body till it was relatively that strong."[11])

At Max Gaines' urging, *Superman* #1 (Summer 1939) contained a slightly expanded origin story. Krypton, now called a "doomed planet," was still only allotted one panel before Superman's childhood and discovery of his powers again took center stage.[12] After this, Krypton would not reappear for years. It next showed up in a single Sunday comic strip, published on November 25, 1945, as an introduction to another retelling of Superman's origin. After that, the planet was not seen until *Superman* #52 (May/June 1948), when it was somewhat fleshed out in a story that was not scripted by Siegel, whose contract with the publisher had ended. What little was known about the planet under Siegel and Shuster did not mark it as a *shtetl*, as Tye would have it, since it is never suggested that the parts of Krypton that we get to see are enclaves. Nor was Krypton, as Brod claims below, a source of formative "heritage" for the superhero. The planet, as far as this Superman is concerned, is completely unknown. Narratively, it is inconsequential.

Given Krypton's low profile in these years, it is surprising how much anachronism has seeped into readings of the planet and of Superman's early days more generally. Brod has already been quoted about the alien baby, using the names Eben and Sarah for his adoptive parents. Simcha Weinstein writes that Superman is found "in a midwestern [sic] cornfield by Jonathan and Martha Kent."[13] Clearly, the two writers choose different sources for naming the Kents, but neither references Siegel and Shuster's work: Eben and Sarah were so named by George Lowther in the same 1942 Superman novelization that introduced the name Kal-El, and the names Martha and Jonathan first appeared in the early 1950s. In *Superman* #1, only the adoptive mother has a name: Mary.[14] Furthermore, the first version of the origin story mentions only a singular "passing motorist" finding the alien baby and turning him over to an orphanage.[15]

Brod also claims that in recent decades, a "de-Jewification" of Superman has occurred, and that "[h]is heroic persona and values appeared to be rooted not so much in his Kryptonian heritage as in the values imparted to him by his adoptive parents and their family farm home in Smallville."[16] The move from Smallville to Metropolis never happened for Siegel and Shuster's Superman. Smallville had not been conceived in any form prior to WWII, and Metropolis was still Cleveland when these origin stories were told. Moreover, in none of the early origin stories does Superman have either a small-town or farm upbringing. The images of his childhood in *Superman* #1 suggest he was a city dweller from the beginning, reflecting both the general urbanization of US pop culture that appeared in step with the urbanization of the country as a whole and, more important, which will be discussed more in Chap. 8, the urban understanding of his creators.[17] The Kent farm was another of Lowther's additions.[18] Kansas would not be named as Superman's home until 1978's *Superman: The Movie*, a fact that Tye acknowledges in a long endnote to a passage that nonetheless anachronistically identifies Siegel and Shuster's Kents as "Kansas farmers."[19]

Superman's alien origin has come to play an important role in defining who he is in recent comics stories. In some versions, he knows the dead language of Krypton, his birth-planet; he studies Krypton's culture; he even occasionally expresses himself in Kryptonian religious terms ("By Rao!"). The use of Krypton as Superman's longed-for lost home and heritage has become increasingly common since 1960, when Siegel, returning to DC after a 12-year exile due to a financial falling-out with the owners of Superman's copyright, wrote a story that explored the planet more deeply than ever before.[20] Guided by editor Mort Weisinger, Siegel delved into personal issues with Superman and Clark Kent, the character and series in the process perhaps becoming more "ethnic" in some respects. When the character first appeared, however, those ideas were still far off; the first published incarnation of Superman "was above caring that he had been sundered from his homeworld [sic] and his parents. His charm was his laughing invulnerability."[21] Indeed, one Superman editor would a few years later positively remark directly on Superman's inability to reconnect with his home planet.[22] Nowhere in those early years are there hints of any of what Tye calls Superman's "lingering heartsickness."[23]

Further, Tye writes that "Superman was a refugee who had escaped to America from a world about to explode, just as the Shusters and Siegels did in fleeing Europe before the Holocaust."[24] But that is a supra-historical interpretation that erases the respective historical specificities of both the Siegels' and Shusters' personal migratory experiences and of the Holocaust: Siegel's parents immigrated in 1900, to escape after conscription and attempts at conversion; Shuster's mother left Russian insecurity and anti-Semitism for Canada in 1912, and his father, whom she met in Rotterdam en route, followed soon after, out of love.[25] Rather, as Chap. 7 will show, when situated biographically, and historically within Jewish American discourses, the original Superman instead appears as an Americanization fantasy in tune with its time. If Superman was an immigrant in any way but by default, he was one fully at home in his new country, neither undocumented nor there illegally, having in both of Siegel and Shuster's comic book versions explicitly been turned over to an orphanage and consequently properly entered into the system.

Still, it may well be true that the distant planet's destruction could have been a reference to the "old country," but in that case it is not a nostalgic one. Like the Lithuania from which Siegel's parents had come, a "shadowy world far beyond his understanding or care" as one of his biographers puts it, Krypton as it first appears is inconsequential and even denigrated, dismissed as a world dying of "old age" and "doomed."[26] As Beth Wenger has shown, a comparative "gaze toward Europe" was a constant thread in the construction of Jewish American heritage in the late nineteenth through the mid-twentieth centuries. Although they often betrayed ambiguities or longings, references to the world left behind commonly stressed the "sharp break" with the past that occurred in the USA.[27] When filtered through the popular culture Siegel and Shuster loved and bonded around, the destruction of Krypton and Superman's reinvention as a champion of the people makes eminent sense: only on Earth, or in the New World, was the alien truly empowered; Superman came from outside and shed all traces of outsiderhood and connections to the "old country" except those he could use to serve his new home. And he did so with great conviction, as we will see in Chap. 5.

Rather, claiming Superman as an immigrant allows for a passing statement of difference and ethnic pride. This is the case, for example, in Brod's comments above, where he points out how Kryptonians in one origin story were called "highly evolved inhabitants." Brod implies that this description should be read as a celebratory reference to European Jews (as Kaplan does elsewhere, when he characterizes them as "a race of brilliant scientists"[28]); of course, reading it that way requires omitting the rest of the sentence in which the phrasing appears, which points to the same type of biological, sci-fi-tinged evolution mentioned in *Action* #1: Kryptonians, the narrative goes on, "were capable of incredible feats of strength…leaping great heights and distances…lifting and smashing heavy weights…possessing impenetrable skins."[29] But this kind of omission is a common means of myth-making.

SUPER-MOSES?

Simcha Weinstein claims that, rather than pop cultural sources that have often elsewhere been suggested and frequently attested by the creators themselves, Siegel and Shuster's Jewish heritage "was perhaps their greatest inspiration." In order to support this claim, Weinstein looks to the origin story as presented in *Superman* #1, and not to the first version, from *Action* #1.[30] The latter origin story, he writes, "draws heavily on Jewish geographical, historical, and biblical sources." According to Weinstein, Superman's journey from Krypton to Earth "closely reflects" the story of Moses: both figures are raised in foreign cultures; both have "inspirational talks" with father figures; and both have speech impediments.[31]

Besides being rife with ahistorical projections of later additions to Superman continuity, this "parallel" drawing is often counterintuitive. As already noted, Superman's childhood is not infused with any sense of foreignness. What Weinstein calls "inspirational talks" are between Superman and his "adoptive father," and between Moses and God through the burning bush, respectively. These comparisons between speakers are forced, at best. They are also inaccurate, since the "inspirational talk" Superman receives comes from both his adoptive parents, not just the father. Moreover, the comic book's talk is universalistic. While Superman's adoptive father tells him to hide "this great strength of [his]" from people, because others will fear him if they know about it, his mother ends the talk by urging him to use his power "to assist humanity" when the "proper time comes." The Biblical talk, conversely, is particularistic: God tells Moses that "I shall dispatch you to Pharaoh and you shall take my people the children of Israel out of Egypt."[32] Again, a more likely intertext is Wylie's novel, wherein the protagonist is told by his father that people will fear and hate him for his strength: "Some day you'll find a use for it – a big, noble, use – and then you can make it work and be proud of it. Until that day, you have to be humble like all the rest of us."[33] Finally, Weinstein's comparison between Moses and Clark's respective speech impediments is unconvincing, since Moses' impediment seems to have been permanent (Ex. 4:10), while Clark's stuttering is an occasional, and clearly affected behavior, rooted in Superman's masquerading as a weakling, about which more is said in Chap. 9.

Still, it is unsurprising that Arie Kaplan and Harry Brod also draw the Moses "parallel" in passing.[34] Apparently drawing on Kaplan, Weinstein, and Fingeroth, Tye writes that the name Kal-El "suggests that the alien superbaby was not just a Jew but a very special one. Like Moses." He goes on to note that both were "rescued by non-Jews and raised in foreign cultures – Moses by Pharaoh's daughter, Kal-El by Kansas [sic] farmers named Kent – and the adoptive parents quickly learned how exceptional their foundlings were." As a final touch that contorts the Bible, he claims that "[t]he narratives of Krypton's birth and death borrowed the language of Genesis [wherein the world is born, but does not die]. Kal-El's escape to Earth was the story of Exodus [albeit without any Exodus ever taking place]."[35] Marco Arnaudo also repeats the parallel. With reference to Weinstein, Arnaudo claims that the destruction of Krypton through natural disaster and baby Superman's flight "echo the Moses story *so precisely*" that it is "highly likely" that Siegel and Shuster's Jewish background had at least some measure of influence. The "precise" echo that Arnaudo cites, however, is with Moses being put in a basket and, stretching the comparison incredibly thin, with the human-ordered mass murder that followed pharaoh's order to drown every male child in Exodus.[36] Historian David Welky, without citing any source, states in a similarly flat way that "Superman's origin story is similar to the tale of Moses, whose parents saved from [sic] certain death by setting him adrift in an ark of bulrushes – a low-tech predecessor of Kal-El's spaceship – from which he emerged as the deliverer of a people."[37]

All of these comparisons are unconvincing in their anachronism or their generality, but even if one accepts Moses as an inspiration—which he might well have been—it is difficult to see what the significance of his use would be: the story of an infant sent from its home to another place resides on the level of a general structure. Kal-El's journey indeed resembled that of Moses' trip down the Nile, but in the same vague way that one can draw "parallels" to Sargon of Akkad's childhood basket-ride, from which the Moses story itself borrows heavily, or to Jesus' being sent from heaven.[38] Nonetheless, the Judeocentric interpretation is being defended forcefully. As Tye puts it, the "evidence that he was a Jew did not stop other faiths from claiming Superman as their own," while Brod laments what he calls a "steady and persistent […] de-Jewification" of Superman's "original Jewish sensibilities."[39] Similarly, Arnaudo asserts "the profound Jewish roots of the superhero comic," which he claims are being "recodified" when Superman is framed with Christological elements.[40]

These defensive claims are problematic, not least because there is, in fact, much textual evidence to support a Christologization of Superman long before Brod's asserted 2006 date, the release of the undeniably Christologizing *Superman Returns*, directed by Jewish American Bryan Singer. Christological framing has been prominent in works by comic book creators, film- and TV-makers, and Christian theologians for a long time.[41] As noted, Christologization of Superman is suggested as early as Lowther's 1942 novelization. Notably, in the 1978 Superman blockbuster, script doctor Tom Mankiewicz, himself of Jewish descent, intentionally cast Superman's origins in Christological terms: "I tried to have Brando symbolize God in that long speech when he sends Clark down to Earth. 'I have sent them you, my only son.' If that's not God sending Christ to Earth, it's as close as you can get without offending the church-going public."[42]

To date, however, Danny Fingeroth is the only popular writer to even consider a potential Jesus "parallel" as anything but latter-day Christian "appropriation" or worse. Fingeroth writes that the "main metaphor systems at war for credit for the inspiration for Superman are Moses and Jesus."[43] Ultimately, and unsurprisingly, he writes that the fact that Moses is "by chance plucked from the water by Pharaoh's daughter and adopted into her family–albeit Egyptian royalty, as opposed to the struggling farm-family Kents of the [as noted, post-WWII, non-Siegel and Shuster-created] Superman mythos—makes Moses more akin to Superman than Jesus," and adds in self-reflexive candor that "here we may be in the realm of partisan argument." He continues, in a way suggestive of the mythic quality of the "parallel," that

> both Moses' and Superman's future greatness is a combination of innate good qualities and good foster parenting. Interestingly, Moses ends up returning to and becoming the leader of the people who sent him away, whereas Superman, unable to so return, changes and inspires the society that took him in. It would be as if Moses became Pharaoh and "changed the system from within."[44]

That "as if" shows how tenuous the connection is. In Fingeroth's version, turning Superman into Moses requires the erasure of Judaism: Moses' renunciation of Egyptian royalty and his return to his people lie at the very center of Jewish historiography, theology, culture, and peoplehood. If Moses had had no people, and if he had stayed behind, there would be no Exodus. Without that people, that narrative, and the mnemonic techniques established at the end of 40 years' wandering (in Deut.), there would be no Judaism in any form resembling what we recognize by that word, historically and in the present.[45]

Nonetheless, the Moses-parallel provides a good illustration of interpretive sedimentation in Jewish–comics connection literature. In his otherwise excellent biography of Siegel and Shuster, literary critic Brad Ricca enters into a discussion about possible religious influences on Superman's creation. Although Siegel and Shuster had been raised in Jewish homes, writes Ricca, they tended to distrust the religion of their "old world parents." But, he continues, there are "several parallels" between Superman and Moses. Presenting a confused composite of Kaplan, Weinstein, and Fingeroth, Ricca outlines these "parallels": each is adopted as an infant, and, as grown men, each "embraces his true background to save his adopted people," something that neither Moses nor Siegel and Shuster's Superman does.[46] Moses embraces his true background and leaves his adopted people, whereas, as already discussed, Superman's Kryptonian origins were a nonissue in Sigel and Shuster's run. Ricca's connection with Jesus is equally tenuous, but he concludes that Superman's religious inspiration was a compromise between Judaism's realistic focus on human experience and history, Christianity's "ultra-human" focus on metaphysics and theology, and science.[47] Neither of Ricca's sources provide any hint as to why Siegel and Shuster would have used either figure or do much to help resolve the tension between the "metaphor systems" currently at war over Superman.

Siegel and Shuster's Superman, then, is not who and what the popular Jewish–comics connection books try to make him, because the past in which he is placed is rarely the history from which he emerged. More concretely, in references to another "metaphor system" that has been largely ignored in the Jewish–comics connection literature, popular comics historian Les Daniels acknowledges that Superman's story recalls both Moses and Jesus, and that there are parallel stories in many cultures, but concludes that the character was a secular American messiah. He continues: "Nothing of the kind was consciously on his [Siegel's] mind, apparently: his explanation for dropping Superman down from the sky was that it 'just happened that way.' And Shuster echoed him: 'We just thought it was a good idea.'"[48] In another interview, Shuster said that the idea came about when "Jerry reversed the usual formula of the superhero who goes to another planet. He put the superhero in ordinary, familiar surroundings

instead of the other way around, as was done in most science fiction."[49]
The type of connection suggested here, to pop culture, is discussed more
in Chap. 7.

COSMIC REFUGEE?

Weinstein writes about the 1939 *Superman* #1—rather than the early
1938 *Action* #1—that "[j]ust as the baby Superman was sent away from
Krypton to avoid the mass destruction of his people, many Jewish children were sent on the Kindertransports to seek safety with families in
England."[50] Many popular writers have made the same claim; Kaplan, for
instance, writes that, "[i]f read a certain way," the story "also reflects the
saga of the *Kindertransports*."[51] Brod, citing Kaplan, writes that, "in the
context of the time," Superman's story "echoes" the *Kindertransports*.[52]
And Tye claims that "the destruction of Kal-El's planet and people also
calls to mind the Nazi Holocaust that was brewing when Jerry and Joe
were publishing their first comic, and it summons up as well the effort
to save Jewish children through *Kindertransports*. Superman's lingering
heartsickness was survivor's guilt."[53]

The problem with this reading is that, first, as already noted, Krypton
and Kryptonians played a negligible role in the comic book origin stories. Second, and more important, the *Kindertransports* could not have
been "echoed" or "reflected" in the *Action* #1 story, which is the only
one that could possibly matter in a historically sensitive reading. The first
ships did not leave a European port until December 1938, eight months
after this comic book was published. It is true that, when Siegel wrote his
famous, self-aggrandizing 1975 press-release rant against the then-recently
announced *Superman* movie about which he had not been approached by
the studio, he did claim that among the things that inspired him to create Superman was hearing about the oppression of Jews in Nazi Germany
(quoted at length below). But it is difficult to determine how much of
this is an a posteriori construction. Siegel told many conflicting versions
of how Superman was born over the years, so he is not overly reliable on
this point, but, as Chap. 6 shows, he never told a story that can be said to
suggest special concern for the oppressed in Germany.

In 1934, when Superman was created, reports from Germany rarely
mentioned ill-treatment of Jews as anything special, and the Nazi regime
had yet to engage in its genocidal program.[54] It is true that by the time
Superman #1 came out, Jewish children were being sent to relative safety

in England, but the program was conceived as a temporary measure, and the refugees were expected to return to their homes and families when the "crisis was over."[55] As historian Peter Novick puts it: "Before 1941, and surely before the outbreak of the European War in September 1939, it appeared to be a matter of Jews escaping from likely persecution, not certain death. The Holocaust, now long in the established past, was then in the unimagined future." The *Kinderstransports*, he adds somewhat pointedly, were not considered "a matter of saving children from the gas chambers."[56] Thus, the fact that so many writers have used the suffering of European Jews in those uncertain days to Judaize Superman says very little about the character. But it does say something about the time in which they wrote, a time when a general interest in the Holocaust remains pervasive in Jewish American culture, and in US culture at large, but also a time when concrete historical knowledge about what the Holocaust was is limited and waning.[57]

If Superman is not Moses, a refugee, or an immigrant longing for the Old World, what is he? Although it is important to not take everything in it at face value, Siegel's antagonistic 1975 press release contains a passage in which he describes what led him to conceive Superman in the early thirties. That passage introduces many of the themes discussed in the rest of this book:

> Listening to President Roosevelt's "fireside chats"...being unemployed during the depression and knowing helplessness and fear. Hearing and reading of the oppression and slaughter of helpless, oppressed jews [sic] in Nazi Germany...seeing movies depicting the horrors and privation suffered by the downtrodden...reading of gallant, crusading heroes in the pulps, and seeing equally crusading heroes on the screen in feature films and movie serials (often pitted against malevolent, grasping, ruthless madmen) I had the urge to help...help the despairing masses, somehow.[58]

Following a model that roughly parallels these claims, the rest of the book will discuss how Superman fits into and discusses Roosevelt's New Deal and the Jewish American turn toward the Democratic Party; the war in Europe, the rise of Nazism in Germany, and US anti-Semitism; and the pop culture of the day and its impact on Jewish Americanization. It will then turn to two themes that were important in the days before WWII, but which are absent from Siegel's writing above, as well as in much of the Jewish–comics connection literature: race and gender as they were imagined in the Great Depression.

NOTES

1. Morrison and Quitely, *All-Star Superman*.
2. Here, Brod is engaging in further myth-reproduction. Almost all Ellis Island name-change stories are false. Inspectors at Ellis Island never actually wrote down immigrants' names, but rather double-checked them against passenger manifestoes provided by the steam ship companies. Most likely, any name changes were instigated by the immigrants themselves or were caused by ticket clerks' errors. For more information, see Cannato, *American Passage*; Sutton, "Name Not Changed."
3. Brod, *Superman Is Jewish?*, 9–10 5.
4. Tye, *Superman*, 40–41, 50, 66.
5. Fingeroth, *Disguised as Clark Kent*, 44–45.
6. Kaplan, *From Krakow to Krypton*, 14.
7. Interestingly, an unpublished version of Superman, Siegel produced with Russell Keaton, had a more developed origin story in which Superman traveled back in time rather than from outer space. See Trexler, "Hidden History."
8. Jones, *Men of Tomorrow*, 145; strip reprinted in Daniels, *Superman*, 28–40.
9. *SC1*, 4; cf. Jones, *Men of Tomorrow*, 122–24; Tye, *Superman*, 30–31.
10. On Wylie, see Jones, *Men of Tomorrow*, 35–36; Tye, *Superman*, 32–33; Ricca, *Super Boys*, 130–33. Ricca also suggests that the idea might have been "swiped" from science fiction promoter and writer Hugo Gernsback, who had run an article in one of his magazines in 1931 (p. 154).
11. Wylie, *Gladiator*, 51.
12. *SC1*, 195–196; Daniels, *Superman*, 44. In the Sunday strip, Krypton is called an "amazing planet," but then clearly in connection with its sci-fi framed inhabitants. See Siegel and Shuster, *Sunday Classics*, 3.
13. Weinstein, *Up, Up, and Oy Vey!*, 26.
14. Mary named in *SC1*, 195; De Haven, *Our Hero*, 156–62.
15. *SC1*, 4.
16. Brod, *Superman Is Jewish?*, 14.
17. *SC1*, 196; cf. Chambliss and Svitavsky, "Pulp to Superhero."
18. De Haven, *Our Hero*, 159.
19. Tye, *Superman*, 318.

20. Siegel, Boring, and Kaye, "Superman's Return to Krypton."
21. Jones, *Men of Tomorrow*, 286–89; cf. De Haven, *Our Hero*, 115–17.
22. Lepore, *Wonder Woman*, 238.
23. Tye, *Superman*, 66.
24. Tye, *Superman*, 78.
25. Ricca, *Super Boys*, 10–12, 298–99.
26. *SC1*, 4, 196; quote from Ricca, *Super Boys*, 18.
27. Wenger, *History Lessons*, 44–50.
28. Kaplan, *From Krakow to Krypton*, 14.
29. Strip reprinted in Andrae, Blum, and Coddington, "Supermen and Kids," 18. See also Siegel and Shuster, *Sunday Classics*, 3, 11.
30. See, for instance, the many references made by Siegel and Shuster in Andrae, Blum, and Coddington, "Supermen and Kids."
31. Weinstein, *Up, Up, and Oy Vey!*, 26.
32. Weinstein, *Up, Up, and Oy Vey!*, 26.
33. Wylie, *Gladiator*, 51.
34. Kaplan, *From Krakow to Krypton*, 14; Brod, *Superman Is Jewish?*, 5, 9.
35. Tye, *Superman*, 65–66.
36. Arnaudo, *Myth of the Superhero*, 29–30. Emphasis added.
37. Welky, *Everything Was Better*, 133.
38. See, for instance, Nigosian, *From Ancient Writings to Sacred Texts*, 54 ff.
39. Tye, *Superman*, 65–67; Brod, *Superman Is Jewish?*, 14–18.
40. Arnaudo, *Myth of the Superhero*, 47.
41. Examples include Donner, *Superman: The Movie*; Singer, *Superman Returns*; Nutter, "Pilot"; Skelton, *Gospel*.
42. Quoted in Rossen, *Superman Vs. Hollywood*, 72.
43. Fingeroth, *Disguised as Clark Kent*, 44.
44. Fingeroth, *Disguised as Clark Kent*, 45.
45. Cf. Assmann, *Religion and Cultural Memory*, 16–21.
46. Ricca, *Super Boys*, 131, 355n37.
47. Ricca, *Super Boys*, 131–33.
48. Daniels, *Superman*, 19.
49. Andrae, Blum, and Coddington, "Supermen and Kids," 15.
50. Weinstein, *Up, Up, and Oy Vey!*, 24.
51. Kaplan, *From Krakow to Krypton*, 14.
52. Brod, *Superman Is Jewish?*, 9.

53. Tye, *Superman*, 66.
54. Lipstadt, *Beyond Belief*; Bauer, *History of the Holocaust*.
55. Oppenheimer et al., "Kindertransport"; "Rising to the Moment"; United States Holocaust Memorial Museum, "Kindertransport, 1938–1940."
56. Novick, *Holocaust in American Life*, 49–50.
57. Cf. Novick, *Holocaust in American Life*; Rosenfeld, *End of Holocaust*.
58. Siegel, "Victimization of Superman's Originators," 8. Ellipses in original.

CHAPTER 5

Superman, Champion of the Oppressed

When Superman first appeared, he did not battle supervillains and alien beings, or save the world from cosmic calamity time and again. Rather, what was most important for Siegel and Shuster's early Superman is evident from his earliest adventures, in which, for example, he forced a war-profiteering munitions manufacturer to enlist in a South American army to experience the consequences of his callousness, expressed in simple terms with the phrase "[m]en are cheap – munitions, expensive!" He also subjected a mine owner and his blasé party guests, the idle and careless rich, to a cave in to demonstrate the consequences of disregard for employee safety and well-being for those most affected.[1] Other early examples included a boxer whose manager had destroyed his career for personal gain, a football player endangered by bookies, underprivileged children in slums or orphanages, beaten wives, and the wrongfully accused. This Superman was "[d]edicated to assisting the helpless and oppressed,"[2] a defender of individuals who, through no fault of their own, had fallen on hard times. Set against these poor souls were the criminals, businessmen, and politicians whose unbridled self-interest almost invariably and immediately threatened dire and undeserved consequences for the innocent, and only a few of these villains ever repented.[3]

Superman's unflagging desire to do good, "his unceasing battle against evil and injustice,"[4] is a trait frequently confirmed by indirect presentation. His own desires, if he has any, never get in the way, and his righteous

© The Editor(s) (if applicable) and The Author(s) 2016   83
M. Lund, *Re-Constructing the Man of Steel*,
DOI 10.1007/978-3-319-42960-1_5

fury is pragmatically sublimated into constructive action; when a man he knows is killed in a "hit-skip" accident, for instance, Superman "declares war on reckless drivers."[5] There are also many examples of direct definition of this dedication, for example, when it is shown that Superman does not wait for people to need him before springing into action, but takes an active role in searching for "someone in need of assistance."[6] Even as elements of science fiction became more common in the comic books, he remained grounded. The "Ultra-Humanite," the first supervillain he faced (*Action* #13, June 1939), coveted world domination; interestingly, "Ultra" pursued ascendancy as "[t]he head of a vast ring of evil enterprises" and was first revealed when Superman clamped down on a violent taxi cartel.[7] Similarly, when Luthor, who in time would become Superman's greatest foe, first appeared in *Action* #23 (April 1940), he displayed a criminal imagination that contrasted Superman perfectly: Luthor was the ultimate war-profiteer, seeking personal power by engineering a world war, exploiting entire nations and threatening to send untold millions to their deaths.[8] With enemies like these, the scale of villainy no doubt increased, but Superman's concerns remained the same; he would not abandon the downtrodden.

Arie Kaplan writes that "[i]t's not too far a stretch to surmise that Siegel's and Shuster's obsession with social justice came from their Jewish background," adding that "Jewish ethics largely revolve around the concept of *tikkun olam*, or healing the world."[9] Similarly, Simcha Weinstein sees in Krypton's destruction the Lurianic school of Kabbalah's idea of the *shevirat ha-kelim* (the breaking of vessels meant to hold divine light, which was then dispersed and has to be returned in order to restore creation), and suggests that Superman personifies *tikkun*, which he describes as a "universal message."[10] Although he does not here cite Weinstein (but he does elsewhere), it would appear that Larry Tye bases himself on the Rabbi when he writes, in a truncated form, that the "explosion of Krypton conjures up images from the mystical Kabbalah, where the divine vessel was shattered and Jews were called on to perform *tikkun ha-olam* by repairing the vessel and the world."[11]

It is an exciting reading, but the Lurianic conception of *tikkun* (with less focus on the *olam*, or world[12]) was neither primarily ethical nor universalistic; it was a call to religious orthodoxy and the performance of intricate contemplative and theurgic rites.[13] Scholar of Jewish mysticism Joseph Dan, noting that *tikkun* is a "nationalistic ideology," describes its achievement as "the ultimate redemption, bringing perfection first and foremost to God himself, and as a result – to the universe, to humanity, and to the people of Israel." This *tikkun* is carried out with "the Torah, the halakhah, and the totality of Jewish tradition. Thus, [...] the practical message of this mythology is an ultraorthodox one. A believer in the *tikkun* does not deviate from Jewish traditional orthodoxy."[14]

However, neither Weinstein nor Tye connects further with Lurianic *tikkun*; rather, like Kaplan, they tie into a present-day formulation of *tikkun olam* that places social activism at the center of Judaism. This conception is a post-Holocaust phenomenon: *tikkun olam* was considered in these terms only in the 1950s and has gained widespread popularity only since the 1970s, becoming a "catch-all" term and presented as an age-old and venerable Jewish tradition, rather than the latest form of a historically protean concept.[15] The designation of Superman as a performer of *tikkun olam*, then, is myth-making that divorces the character from his historical context and projects a recently elevated and naturalized concept backward into history. By engaging in this type of myth-making, this writing obscures the actual textual framing of Superman's activism, which is often highly suggestive of the New Deal.

SUPER NEW-DEALER

Kaplan also writes that the Jewish "obsession" with *tikkun olam* led some Jews to embrace the ideals of the Communist Party and that Siegel and Shuster's fascination with social problems came from their "own youth during the Depression," but that despite Superman's being "a man of the people" early in his career, his "endearing 'Socialist cheerleader' phase" ended abruptly.[16] It is true that Superman displayed some socialist tendencies in his earliest adventures, but if Siegel and Shuster ever embraced socialism, it would appear that by the end of the 1930s they had come to the same conclusion that many other native-born Jewish Americans had reached: "[L]eftism belonged to the immigrant experience, and if they were to integrate into the American mainstream, their politics would have to move to the center."[17]

Superman's birth at the height of the Great Depression came sometime between a 1933 legislative flurry called the Hundred Days, when President Franklin Delano Roosevelt and a bipartisan coalition introduced several programs that instilled much-needed hope and optimism in the economically ailing USA, and the 1935 so-called Second New Deal, when rapid social and legislative reform swept the nation.[18] As President-elect,

Roosevelt was vocal about the need for action, and immediately after his inauguration moved to make good on his words, "with spectacular vigor."[19] His inaugural address contained a searing indictment of those perceived to have caused the country's hardships:

> [O]ur distress comes from no failure of substance. We are stricken by no plague of locusts. [...] Nature still offers her bounty and human efforts have multiplied it. Plenty is at our doorstep, but a generous use of it languishes in the very sight of the supply. Primarily this is because the rulers of the exchange of mankind's goods have failed, through their own incompetence, have admitted their failure, and abdicated. Practices of the unscrupulous money changers stand indicted in the court of public opinion, rejected by the hearts and minds of men.

It was also in this speech that Roosevelt famously said that "the only thing we have to fear is fear itself. [...] In every dark hour of our national life a leadership of frankness and vigor has met with that understanding and support of the people themselves which is essential to victory. I am convinced that you will again give that support to leadership in these critical days."[20]

A few days later, in the first of his popular fireside radio chats, Roosevelt again asked for Americans' confidence and help: "Let us unite in banishing fear. We have provided the machinery to restore our financial system; it is up to you to support and make it work. It is your problem no less than mine. Together we cannot fail."[21] Although representatives from the business world were involved directly in administration policy making, business interests and bankers, portrayed as greedy speculators and self-serving employers, took several hard hits in presidential addresses that fed popular anti-business sentiment. Dissatisfied employees, union organizers, and others who felt encouraged by Roosevelt's legislative outline and rhetoric projected their own, more far-reaching, agendas onto them.[22] More important, the president's claim to be championing the cause of the "forgotten man at the bottom of the economic pyramid" was kept vivid in the minds of New Dealers.[23]

Superman and his creators, it would seem, were among those who took the president's words to heart. Roosevelt himself never appeared in Superman comics from this period (although he did in one of Siegel and Shuster's earlier spy comics[24]), which might have been because the White House kept close tabs on how the President's image was used.[25] His presence can be strongly felt, however, and one Superman story was clearly intended as a (voluntary) public service announcement; in Action #26 (July 1940), Superman fights phony doctors selling sugar pills that they claim are a powerful remedy for "infantile paralysis [polio] and other forms of bone and joint malformations."[26] The story ends with Superman being credited for another victory in the penultimate panel of the last page, leaving room at page's end for the following message to readers: "Help fight infantile paralysis! Contribute to President Roosevelt's fund!"[27]

All the books about Jews and comics mention the Depression in passing, but few connections between it and Superman's activism and struggles are ever made.[28] Conversely, in situating Superman as a political metaphor, comic historian Christopher Murray has suggested that Superman comics "could be read as a parable of America's recovery from the Depression, with the destruction of Krypton representing the economic catastrophe." In this reading, Superman's flight from Krypton becomes a flight from the Dust Bowl and, with geographical anachronism, "his childhood in Kansas [sic] represents his identification with the agricultural workers in the Midwest."[29]

Reading Krypton's destruction as a recasting of the stock market crash might be going too far, but any reading of the early Superman should consider a political metaphor perspective. For Superman, "evil"—whether that word is understood as connoting extraterritoriality (as it often does in contemporary superhero comics) or metaphysics (as in religious notions about good and evil as transcendent concepts)—is not a cosmic concept, but something ordinary.[30] The oppressed for whom Superman fought these evils were the poor, the tired, the huddled masses yearning to breathe free, and the battle was fought for their security and for a change in their conditions. The freedom to seek these integral parts of the American experience was in Superman's world curtailed by a seemingly endless stream of self-serving curs who could not, and would not, see the plight of their fellow men.

While Superman was created in the early days of the New Deal, he was not published until it had all but petered out. The end of reform did not mean the end of pursuing the New Deal's goals, however. Achieving security, the "leitmotif" of the government's actions and programs during the New Deal, remained an important goal.[31] Superman, showing his support for this way of thinking from his earliest adventures, took on crooked politicians, war profiteers, and callous capitalists, exemplified, in an above-cited story, by a mine owner who rationalized his disregard for employee

safety or well-being by saying that "I'm a business man, not a humanitar-
ian!"[32] Superman's actions continued to tie him to the hegemonic, normative, and largely myth-based New Deal ethos throughout the prewar
period: in *Action* #11 (April 1939), for example, he turns the tables on
stock brokers who knowingly sell useless stock, leaving them ruined while
reimbursing their swindled customers.[33] In *Action* #13 (June 1939), he
takes up trust-busting, then still a part of the Roosevelt White House's
struggle, and identified himself with such concerns directly: "*Cab protec-
tive league*, eh? Sounds like just the sort of set-up I like to break down!"[34]

Among the clearest convergences of the New Deal's struggle for
recovery and Superman can be found in *Superman* #4 (Spring 1940).
The story begins with the murder of Paul Dorgan, a sociologist who is
about to reveal that "sinister persons or forces plan to deliberately stave
off the return of national prosperity." Clark wonders what all the excitement is about; "Haven't you heard," he is asked in response, "[t]he nation
is being paralyzed by a wave of major strikes in all major industries."
"There's disorder everywhere." Surprised, Clark confesses to have "had
no inkling!" Immediately, he wonders "if after all there isn't perhaps some
basis in Dorgan's contention that sinister forces seek to retard the nation's
return to prosperity?"[35] Superman's investigation reveals that businessman
J.E. Curtis plots to stymie recovery through industrial sabotage. Clearly
anchoring reading in the economic and political situation and discourse of
the day, Curtis, who has been promised important concessions by a foreign
nation if he is able to "wreck America's economic structure," attempts to
"launch a financial upheaval that will panic the stock-exchange and plunge
the country into its worst depression!"[36] Superman swiftly stops the plot,
killing his and, by extension the nation's, foe. After publishing an exposé
as Clark Kent, he is asked how he got the material. He replies: "That
does'nt [sic] matter. What *is* important is that the nation is once again
returning to its march toward prosperity."[37]

Another clear example of the severity with which Superman comics
treated the Depression and where the blame was placed can be found in
Superman #5 (Summer 1940). Like the story above, it is anchored in the
New Deal, the Depression, and the conspiratorial thinking that has always
accompanied them: "An unexpected wave of unemployment hits the
country as millions suffer from hunger, business staggers, and the United
States is faced with the worst depression in its history!"[38] Clark asks the
wrong questions when interviewing some businessmen, which leads to
a bomber plane being sent to blow up the *Daily Planet*, an attempt to

frame him for murder, and finally to him being thrown down an elevator shaft, all to cover up a sinister conspiracy. One businessman involved in the scheme, thinking that no one is listening, indulges in some helpful exposition suggestive of the Depression's anti-business climate, which a hidden Superman overhears: "Pretty slick the way we continue to pile up profits while the rest of the country goes bankrupt, eh?" Superman discovers that Luthor is behind this fictional depression and, in a fit of Depression-era hyperbole, is said to be "plotting the *downfall of present day civilization!*"[39] As always, Superman foils the plot. Like the previous example, the story personalizes the financial situation and frames Superman's work with a happy ending: "Most important of all is that the menace is removed – and that the nation is returning to its former prosperity."[40]

By showing recovery achieved, this short, self-contained comic book story offered some small measure of catharsis to its readership. With its indictment of "the rulers of the exchange of mankind's goods" and its prosperity cheerleading, the story comes close to New Deal propaganda and ties into official American political culture. Indeed, this representation closely mirrors the president' public treatment of the Depression: "Roosevelt's oratory formed an expository style that presented problems in an individualized way, without reducing them to impersonal or generic situations, echoes of the practice common to Hollywood cinema of personalizing conflicts and problems by reducing them to individual stories or personal cases." Roosevelt's speech writers were instructed to "close each chat on a high note," making the speeches "close to reality, documentary, participant" like much 1930s culture, but importantly with a "Hollywood-like happy ending, meant to give the nation confidence."[41]

For Roosevelt, "change was [the] keynote" and "[s]ecurity was the touchstone."[42] Similarly, in his battle for justice, Superman did not merely pursue security from the predations of the self-serving, but actively worked for change. Many of the people he fought seem to have been irredeemably evil, especially those who paid for their crimes with their lives ("A well-deserved fate!"[43]). Others were given the benefit of the doubt. In *Action* #8 (January 1939), Superman listens to the mother of a gang member facing assault and battery charges: "Of course he talks tough – what's more he *is* tough, your honor – but he's only like all the other boys in our neighborhood....Hard, resentful, underprivileged. He's my only son, sir[.] He might have been a good boy except for his environment. He still might be – if you'll be merciful!"[44] Convinced by the argument, but certain that the court will not listen, Superman sets out to save the other members of the defendant's gang who, having become a liability, are soon set up by their fence.[45]

After stopping the youngsters' break-in attempts and scaring them straight, Superman expresses his belief that they are not alone to blame for turning to crime, echoing the concept of "environmentalism," "the sense that crime and poverty is a social problem, a product of poverty and slums" that historian Morris Dickstein calls a "major theme of the thirties."[46] "It's not entirely your fault you're delinquent," says Superman, "it's these slums – your poor living conditions – if there was only some way I could remedy it!" A solution immediately presents itself; grabbing a newspaper, Superman reads that the government has stepped in to "erect modern housing projects" after a natural disaster. By deciding to demolish the slum and thereby force the government to step in, and presumably effect change for the better in the boys' lives, Superman is tapping into the same "utopian optimism inherent in all social engineering: we can deal with this problem, we can fix it."[47] With his actions, the hero puts social welfare and the combatting of the causes of crime in the government's hands, suggesting not a celebration of unilateral individualism but a liberal collectivist ideological bent.

Even after editorial policy put Superman's social justice focus on the back-burner, and fewer stories explicitly dealt with social themes, reformist idealism did not disappear entirely. Again suggesting collectivist New Dealerism, a Superman story in *World's Finest Comics* #4 (Winter 1941) begins on a dramatic note: "Confronted by an obsolete and dangerous street railway situation, the crusading *Man of Tomorrow* launches a campaign to modernize public transportation in *Metropolis* before lives are lost." Metropolis' aging streetcars suffer a series of accidents, but the Metropolis Railway Company's president refuses to replace them. Once Superman shows him the victims of this neglect, however, the president's position immediately changes: "Horrible! I – I never before realized lives and limbs are worth more than dollars and cents!" With newfound compassion, the executive offers to "begin replacing street cars [sic] with modern buses and continue to do so as circumstances permit." Unfortunately, Dan Bransom, a "prominent civic reformer," demands that the company "[t]oss out all the street cars and replace all of them with buses at once. All or nothing!" Suspicious, Superman notes that "Bransom deliberately gummed up the proceedings when reform was definitely in sight – I'm going to trail him and try to learn what that means." Bransom, it turns out, presented the dispute as a zero-sum game because he has arranged for a commission for himself on bus sales, so he can "clean up" in the expected changeover. When confronted, he shows his true colors, tossing Lois Lane off a cliff as he tries to make good his escape.[48]

The story ties into two aspects of Depression life. First, New Dealers had repeatedly learned from, for example, Catholic radio-preacher Father Charles Coughlin's slide away from the Roosevelt camp toward fascism and anti-Semitism, populist physician Francis Everett Townsend's abortive plan to dispose of one category of surplus workers (the elderly) by introducing an unrealistic monthly stipend, and populist Democratic politician Huey Long's New Deal-endangering "Share Our Wealth Society," that not everyone claiming to have the people's "best interests" in mind was on the same track.[49] Bransom's actions thus played to memories that reformers can turn out to be "reformers" (scare quotes in original[50]). Textually, this serves to abridge the existence in the real world of differing visions of reform and to make them fit with the dualistic mold that marked Superman comics. Second, and perhaps more important, the lack of any suggestion that public transportation become state-run or of any challenge to private ownership, along with the sympathetic portrayal of the railway company's president, shows that Superman shared the New Deal's aim, which was not to abolish capitalism, but to devolatilize it and to distribute its benefits more evenly.[51]

A stronger indictment of heartless capitalism had been published a few months earlier in *World's Finest* #3 (Fall 1941), beginning with a denunciation of "deliberate mass murder" as the "most foul of all crimes." The story's "mass murder" is a series of train accidents orchestrated by Thornton Bigsby, "one of the most powerful industrialists in the nation!" His purpose is not ideological: the accidents serve only as part of a scheme to drive down a railway company's stock, so that Bigsby can buy a controlling interest "for a song." Superman had faced many greedy men in his years as superhero, but Bigsby, encountered toward the end of the Depression, was the pinnacle of "evil" as something ordinary, a "cold-blooded mass-murderer" willing to kill indiscriminately in his quest for profit.[52] The New Deal had sought to install a system of checks and balances to reduce or at least manage risk, to referee the market in a way that would prevent the rampant self-interest said to have driven America into the Depression. When that pursuit was individualized in Superman comics, this self-interest took the shape of unchecked capitalism manifested as cold-blooded greed and ambition, untrammeled even by concern for human life.

SUPERMAN'S POLITICS

Despite his oftentimes juvenile presentation, then, the early Superman was highly political. Tirelessly fighting for the downtrodden, he was the first "super New Dealer" and remained the foremost as others followed in his footsteps.[53] In taking action and reaching out to the "forgotten man," Superman seemingly took to heart what the president had said upon taking office:

> The measure of the restoration lies in the extent to which we apply social values more noble than mere monetary profit. Happiness lies not in the mere possession of money; it lies in the joy of achievement, in the thrill of creative effort. The joy and moral stimulation of work no longer must be forgotten in the mad chase of evanescent profits. *These dark days will be worth all they cost us if they teach us that our true destiny is not to be ministered unto but to minister to ourselves and to our fellow men.*[54]

By turning against the vested interests of the business world, Roosevelt knew that he was not making many friends among "the old enemies of peace – business and financial monopoly, speculation, reckless banking, class antagonism, sectionalism, war profiteering." He acknowledged as much in a 1936 campaign speech: "Never before in all our history have these forces been so united against one candidate as they stand today. They are unanimous in their hate for me – and I welcome their hatred." Adding insult to injury, he went on to say that "I should like to have it said of my first Administration that in it the forces of selfishness and of lust for power met their match. I should like to have it said of my second Administration that in it these forces met their master."[55]

No doubt Roosevelt's charm and optimism played an important role in winning support among the people, in the halls of power, in the press corps, and with public opinion-makers whose audiences numbered in the millions, like gossipmonger Walter Winchell and Father Coughlin, before the latter became disaffected with the president, abandoned the New Deal, and moved toward virulent and outspoken anti-Semitism.[56] Through the making and implementation of policy and his speeches, but even more so in his many press conferences, staged photos, newsreels, and intimate fireside chats, Roosevelt and his staff carefully cultivated the image of a president of and for the people that earned him a "fame that resembled that of movie stardom." Many even had of him on their walls.[57] Throughout the Depression, Roosevelt promised and, to a lesser extent, delivered jobs to the unemployed, listened to others than the moneyed elites, and championed social justice, extending his hand not only to the old-guard whites of the country but to all, or at least most, of its citizens (historian David M. Kennedy notes the "New Deal's consistently inclusionary ethos"[58]).

Indeed, Roosevelt actively cultivated the patriotism and political loyalties of minorities.[59] Inspired by the president's inclusive rhetoric, his appointment of Jews to several important government positions, his labor politics, and, especially for those who saw that this would make Sabbath observance easier, his support of a five-day workweek, many, if not most, American Jews regarded the president as a friend. As a vital part of the ethnic constituency core of the New Deal coalition, an overwhelming majority showed their support in a palpable way, giving him their vote in the elections that won him an unprecedented four terms in the Oval Office: an estimated 82 percent of American Jews voted for Roosevelt in 1932; 85 percent in 1936; and even, in 1940 and 1944, when the president began losing support among other minorities, 90 percent of American Jews still voted for him.[60] Republican Jonah Goldstein summed up the situation when he quipped, in a lamenting tone, that "[t]he Jews now have three *velten* [worlds]. *Die velt* [this world], *yenneh velt* [the world to come], and Roosevelt."[61]

About the Jewish American identification with Democratic liberalism that began during the Roosevelt years, historian Marc Dollinger writes that "[t]hey [American Jews] have worked their way to the top of American political, economic, and cultural life and established their community as the best-known defenders of the nation's downtrodden and oppressed."[62] This was not an entirely new phenomenon, since Jews and liberalism have historically converged as a product of emancipation in exile, but part of the allure of liberal politics during the Depression was their usefulness for American Jews who hoped to make the move from the social margins into the mainstream.[63] Jews have often supported liberal governments because two of the ideology's central tenets have converged with Jewish interests and values: individual freedom and social justice. Emancipation gave Jews access to majority society and freed them from the constraints of ghetto authority structures, but only in a meritocratic and tolerant society could they remain truly free. Thus, Jews have supported liberal regimes in part out of self-interest. In political philosopher Michael Walzer's words: "Liberal emancipation, liberal universalism: this is the particularism of the Jews, at least of the Jews in exile."[64]

The speculation that led Arie Kaplan into discussing *tikkun olam* above, that Siegel and Shuster's "obsession" with social justice came from their Jewish background, should not be dismissed, however. The Jewish prophetic tradition and the importance of *tzedakah* (charity) and *gemilut hasidim* (acts of loving kindness) are often cited as underlying reasons for why liberalism has been so inviting for Jews: like traditional Judaism, liberalism privileges social justice.[65] Siegel might not have been observant, as most of his recent biographers note, but since he "liberally steals names from biblical history and other pulp stories" in his pre-Superman work, it is clear that he was not a complete stranger to the Torah, a body of literature that often stresses identification with the poor and oppressed and fosters, in Walzer's words, "a suspicion not so much of wealth or power as of the moral complacency and arrogance that commonly accompany them."[66] (This, of course, is also a sentiment evident in Roosevelt's denunciation of "the forces of selfishness and of lust for power" quoted above).

Welfare has never been an abstract religious principle in Jewish history; it has historically been a concrete presence in Jewish communal life, taking the form of charity, mutual aid societies, and communal organizations. Cleveland around the Depression was no different in this respect.[67] That Siegel would have been aware of Jewish charity practices is likely, since his mother was an influential presence in Cleveland's Jewish community and charity organizations like the Orthodox Jewish Orphans Home, and her name shows up "in the minutes of nearly every Jewish association in Cleveland as a board member, host, secretary, or organizer."[68]

Notably, the fervor with which Superman undertook his fight went beyond that of most New Dealers' and the range of his distrust of those with power over others extended beyond the realms of finance and politics: the hero found foes of the common man in orphanages, prisons, law enforcement, the judiciary, and among those who abused the trust of others implicit in certain social roles. Superman's dedication, then, does not appear to have been (only) an expression of the zeal of the converted brought about by the appearance of a charming leader in Roosevelt, nor is it a trait particular to the height of the Depression and the heyday of the New Deal. Rather, Superman's activism was a prolonged effort that continued well after the New Deal lost steam and popular support for Roosevelt was on the decline. By contrast, the less grounded Captain Marvel, created by non-Jewish creators C.C. Beck and Bill Parker and published by Minnesotan Protestant publisher W.H. Fawcett, for example, began his career in *Whiz Comics* #2 (February 1940) by fighting sabotage and invasion, and did not highlight social issues to anywhere near the same extent as Superman; perhaps an indication that the liberal moment was beginning to lose momentum, Captain Marvel outsold Superman shortly after his introduction.[69]

Thus, Superman appears to be a particularly convinced advocate of social justice for individuals victimized by social factors beyond their control, as was the case with much Depression-era Jewish American liberal commitment.[70] This is not to suggest, as Danny Fingeroth does, that Superman was conceived as a *tzaddik*,[71] a righteous man, but only that Siegel's Jewish Glenville socialization and environment, which would likely have incorporated the then-common and strong tendency of linking Judaism and American values as fundamentally compatible, had imparted in him a strong sense of justice and communitarian obligation. That background, combined with the writer's enthusiastic consumption of American popular culture, perhaps fostered an ideological predisposition to accept Roosevelt and New Deal collectivism as enthusiastically as he did when the president asked for the people's help.[72] Indeed, given the nature and the studied near-ubiquity of the "Roosevelt magic," the president's public image and the charm with which it was infused, and Roosevelt's courting of Jewish Americans, it is not at all Surprising that Superman, the self-abnegating social crusader, would be cast as a liberal reformer in the New Deal vein when addressing a mainstream audience, and that he would remain so as late as 1941.

NOTES

1. *SC1*, 17–44.
2. *SC1*, 70.
3. A few contrite foes can be found in *SC1*, 29, 44; *SC7*, 149.
4. E.g. *SC1*, 140; *SC2*, 4, 18, 105, 119; *SC7*, 58.
5. *SC1*, 153–166.
6. *SC2*, 32, 46.
7. *SC1*, 190.
8. *SC3*, 17–44.
9. Kaplan, *From Krakow to Krypton*, 19.
10. Weinstein, *Up, Up, and Oy Vey!*, 28.
11. Tye, *Superman*, 66.
12. Cooper, "*Tikkun Olam* Catch-All," 47.
13. Fine, "Art of Metoscopy," 330–32.

14. Dan, *Kabbalah*, 78.
15. Cf. Rosenthal, "Tikkun Ha-Olam"; Cooper, "*Tikkun Olam* Catch-All"; Jacobs, "History of 'Tikkun'." *Tikkun olam*'s recent emergence into the spotlight, and the speed with which it gained recognition is clearly visible in the platform-documents of Reform Judaism: the 1976 "Centenary Perspective" makes no mention of *tikkun*, whereas 1997's "Reform Judaism & Zionism" speaks about the Reform Judaism's "historic commitment to tikkun olam." Worth noting here is that Kaplan's book originated in three articles first published in *Reform Judaism Magazine*, starting fall 2003.
16. Kaplan, *From Krakow to Krypton*, 19–20.
17. Dollinger, *Quest for Inclusion*, 7.
18. On the Hundred Days and the New Deal, see Kennedy, *Freedom from Fear*.
19. Kennedy, *Freedom from Fear*, 134–35.
20. Roosevelt, "First Inaugural."
21. Roosevelt, "Banking Crisis"; cf. Kennedy, *Freedom from Fear*, 136–137: "[T]ens of millions of Americans tuned in" to listen to Roosevelt as, "[i]n a voice at once commanding and avuncular, masterful yet intimate, he soothed the nervous nation."
22. E.g. Kennedy, *Freedom from Fear*, 187, 291–292, 328.
23. Terms first used in Roosevelt, "Forgotten Man."
24. Ricca, *Super Boys*, 111.
25. Cf. Muscio, *Hollywood's New Deal*.
26. *SC4*, 5.
27. *SC4*, 17.
28. Cf. Fingeroth, *Disguised as Clark Kent*, 46–47; Kaplan, *From Krakow to Krypton*, 13, 20; Weinstein, *Up, Up, and Oy Vey!*, 22; Brod, *Superman Is Jewish?*, 13, notes that "Superman's values have been recognized at the time of his debut as very much those of a New Dealer," but makes nothing more of it.
29. Murray, *Champions*, 13.
30. Cf. the configuration of "evil" in Roosevelt, "Works Relief": "There are chiselers in every walk of life; there are those in every industry who are guilty of unfair practices, every profession has its black sheep, but long experience in government has taught me that the exceptional instances of wrongdoing in government are probably less numerous than in almost every other line of endeavor. The most effective means of preventing such evils in this work

relief program will be the eternal vigilance of the American people themselves."

31. Kennedy, *Freedom from Fear*, 363–65; cf. esp. Roosevelt, "Four Freedoms."
32. *SC1*, 32–44; cf. Kennedy, *Freedom from Fear*, 291–96.
33. *SC1*, 140–52.
34. *SC1*, 181.
35. *SC3*, 72–73.
36. *SC3*, 83.
37. *SC3*, 84.
38. *SC3*, 153.
39. *SC3*, 165. Emphasis added. According to Ashley, *Time Machines*, 113–114, many believed in the latter days of the Depression that civilization could be on its last legs. Cf. Thurber, *Thurber Carnival*, 31.

    See also Siegel and Shuster, *Sunday Classics*. In one Sunday strip arc, Superman foils a plot by sinister men who, through hypnosis, cause a crime spree with the ultimate aim of raising enough capital from pillaging the country to one day seize control of the government (12–16). In another Sunday strip arc, Superman similarly foils the plots of the "Lamite," a man who for years has "worked to soak up this nation's wealth" and has blackmailed people to do his sinister, selfish bidding (33–40).
40. *SC3*, 165.
41. Muscio, *Hollywood's New Deal*, 33.
42. Kennedy, *Freedom from Fear*, 245–46; cf. the explicit references to reform in *SC3*, 131; *SC7*, 149.
43. *SC4*, 65.
44. *SC1*, 98.
45. *SC1*, 100–101; Superman's skepticism might be a critique of the federal "war on crime's" harsh attitudes, discussed in Appier, "Path to Crime."
46. Dickstein, *Dancing in the Dark*, 242.
47. *SC1*, 97–100; cf. Dickstein, *Dancing in the Dark*, 242; Appier, "Path to Crime."
48. *SC7*, 140–52.
49. Cf. Kennedy, *Freedom from Fear*, 218–242, 283–284.
50. *SC7*, 152.
51. Kennedy, *Freedom from Fear*, 372, 364; cf. Muscio, *Hollywood's New Deal*, 7–8.

52. *SC6*, 177–89.
53. Cf. Wright, *Comic Book Nation*, 24.
54. Roosevelt, "First Inaugural." Emphasis added.
55. Roosevelt, "Madison Square."
56. Roosevelt's hold on the people is evident from, for example, the 14,000 unsolicited songs sent to him during his presidency, as seen in Maney, "They Sang"; cf. Gabler, *Winchell*; Brinkley, *Voices of Protest*; Kennedy, *Freedom from Fear*, 227–34.
57. Cf. Muscio, *Hollywood's New Deal*, 23, pp. 20–35, 77–81.
58. Kennedy, *Freedom from Fear*, 379; cf. Roediger, *Working toward Whiteness*, chap. 7; Takaki, *Different Mirror*, 332–35 for a different perspective.
59. Cf. Kennedy, "On This Day: May 8, 1875," 750.
60. Cf. Hertzberg, *Jews in America*, 282–300; Kennedy, *Freedom from Fear*, 216; Sarna, *American Judaism*, 257–58; Dollinger, *Quest for Inclusion*, chap. 1; according to Arad, *Rise of Nazism*, 130, "more than 15 percent of Roosevelt's top-level appointees [...] were Jews"; voting statistics from Shogan, *Prelude to Catastrophe*, 8, 186, 225.
61. Quoted in Shogan, *Prelude to Catastrophe*, 6.
62. Dollinger, *Quest for Inclusion*, 3.
63. Walzer, "Liberalism and Jews."
64. Walzer, "Liberalism and Jews," 6.
65. Walzer, "Liberalism and Jews," 6–9; Brahm Levey, "Toward a Theory," 67–68.
66. Walzer, "Liberalism and Jews," 6; for some remarks on Siegel's religiosity, see Ricca, *Super Boys*, 92, 131; Tye, *Superman*, 67; Jones, *Men of Tomorrow*, 84–85.
67. See Gartner, *Jews of Cleveland*, 290–294, for a picture of mutual aid and charity activities in Cleveland's Jewish community.
68. Ricca, *Super Boys*, 92, 199–200; Tye, *Superman*, 77.
69. Cf. Parker and Beck, "[Untitled Captain Marvel Story #1]"; "[Untitled Captain Marvel Story #2]"; "[Untitled Captain Marvel Story #3]"; Jones, *Men of Tomorrow*, 165–66.
70. Dollinger, *Quest for Inclusion*, 20–21.
71. Fingeroth, *Disguised as Clark Kent*, 47.
72. Cf. Kaplan and Mittelman, "Judaism and Democracy"; Wenger, *History Lessons*; Sarna, "Cult of Synthesis"; Dollinger, *Quest for Inclusion*.

CHAPTER 6

Patriot Number One

Simcha Weinstein's Superman chapter begins by conjuring up images of the November 1938 *Kristallnacht*: "The planet needed a hero – fast," he continues, disregarding the facts—which he later cites—that the hero he is about to discuss had been created years before and was already known to the world.[1] Weinstein also identifies *Action* #1–2's fictional South American nation "San Monte," which will be discussed later, as a "thinly disguised Nazi Germany," and describes Adolphus Runyan, a scientist who in *Superman* #2 (Fall 1939) has invented a gas powerful enough to penetrate gas masks, as "a thinly disguised caricature of Adolf Hitler, who really used poison gas."[2] While it is true that Hitler had sanctioned the use of poison gas in a September 1939 decree, which "granted" mentally ill and hereditarily sick people the "grace" of death,[3] it is unlikely that Siegel and Shuster would have known this, much less had time to incorporate it into the referenced issue, which was most likely already on newsstands by that date. And despite the similarity in first names, the Adolphus Runyan that appears in the comic book is no Hitler, nor even a villain. When Clark Kent asks him what he intends to do with his invention during an interview, Runyan replies: "I'll turn it over to our war department—but only in the case of a defensive war!"[4] Indeed, Runyan is unequivocally presented as a principled, patriotic inventor who ultimately gives his life to prevent his formula from falling into war profiteers' hands. Weinstein, then, is

© The Editor(s) (if applicable) and The Author(s) 2016
M. Lund, *Re-Constructing the Man of Steel*,
DOI 10.1007/978-3-319-42960-1_6

here creating myth with Superman, subsuming the character's historical relationship with war in the 1930s and early 1940s under post-Holocaust knowledge and concerns.

This is not a process restricted to Jewish–comics connection literature. It is often common in general academic comics history to see claims that comic books were ahead of the rest of the USA in advocating the nation's entry into WWII, and, in many cases, that this was connected with the Jewish American presence in the comics industry. According to comics historian Bradford Wright, "[c]omic books actually had launched their own propaganda effort long before the federal government. Many of the young artists creating comic books were Jewish and liberal. Morally repelled by the Nazis, they expressed their politics in their work."[5] Summarizing his argument in an essay about Jewish Americans and WWII-era comic books, comics scholar Nicholas Yanes writes:

> Jewish American comic book creators were philosophically united under FDR's presidency because of his desire to bring the country into World War II. Consequently, comic books in the late 30s and early 40s motivated America's entry into the war effort. Comic book creators supported the war because they had heard rumors of the Holocaust, and because they believed that the war would come to U.S. soil if America did not interfere soon.[6]

However, the early appearances of stand-ins for Nazis and other belligerents can all too easily be overstated as signifying an interventionist, pro-war stance or as marking a response to the Jewish situation in Nazi-occupied Europe. This chapter will discuss how Superman handled war and intervention, but since this topic ties into a larger discourse in comics history more explicitly than any of the earlier ones, a small detour into more general comics history is necessary before it can be addressed.

JEWISH AMERICAN COMICS CREATORS AND SUPERHEROIC INTERVENTIONISM

In his essay about superheroes before and during WWII, Yanes writes: "Comic books uniquely pushed for the U.S. to enter the war because the Jewish Americans who created the American comic book industry had personal stakes in a U.S. victory, and they understood that patriotism was synonymous with sacrifice." Comic books in the late 1930s and early 1940s, he continues, did not only reflect American anxieties about the looming war, but "contained propaganda in clear support for America's entry into combat. The reason was that Jewish Americans were the first to see the danger Hitler represented."[7] The master's thesis from which Yanes excerpted and developed this essay presents the proposed Jewish–comics connection in more all-encompassing terms: discussing an advertisement for war bonds and stamps written and signed by Jewish American Treasury Secretary Henry Morgenthau, Jr. and published in a June 1942 comic book, undated in the thesis but published after US entry into the war, Yanes writes that this "plea to support the war appearing in comic books is significant because Morgenthau was a Jew using a Jewish medium to motivate the country to support a war that would help save the lives of European Jews."[8] These broad claims are historically problematic for several reasons.

Morgenthau hated Hitler and was at the time of the advertisement poised to become one of the most active Jewish members of the Roosevelt administration when it came to this issue,[9] but concluding that propaganda bearing his name somehow integrated with assumed broad-based Jewish-motivated anti-Nazi initiatives in the comic book industry is overly reductive. Similar ads appeared everywhere on WWII's American home front, during what was an unprecedented propaganda and fund-raising flurry.[10] At no stage of this process, nor at any point in the war, did the US government publically focus on the plight of European Jews with anything but symbolic gestures.[11] Yanes' "Jewish medium" statement in effect reduces an official request for Americans to sacrifice for the greater good to an unhistorically cohesive, activist, and informed Jewish American response to Nazi anti-Semitism.[12]

It is impossible today, with the tragic benefit of hindsight, to imagine just how people reacted to news about Nazi atrocities. But it cannot be assumed that all Jewish American comics creators were equally informed, that they all believed what they heard, or that they acted upon their knowledge in similar ways. Indeed, evidence suggests that events were underreported in part out of caution, so as to not fall victim to the type of exaggerated "atrocity stories" that had been reported during WWI, and in part because the centrality of anti-Semitism to the Nazi ideology was for a long time severely underestimated.[13] Many were unwilling to acknowledge what was happening or unable to understand. The scale and depth of Nazi atrocities had no precedent. Furthermore, up until early 1941, according to Holocaust historian Yehuda Bauer, it is possible that even "the Nazis – with the possible exception of Hitler himself – were not conscious of the full implications of the murderous ingredient of their own ideology."[14]

Jewish comics pioneer Joe Kubert writes in the foreword to his counterfactual 2005 Holocaust memoir, *Yossel: April 19, 1943*, that he regarded the stories about events in Poland that he heard in his home to be "[h]orrible fairy tales" not to be believed. Only after the war did he see them confirmed.[15] Even Supreme Court Justice Felix Frankfurter, one of Roosevelt's Jewish associates, was unable to believe an eyewitness account related to him in person in summer 1943.[16] The anti-Nazi activities of Jewish Americans were less unified and far more complex than Yanes' vertical integration perspective suggests. One does well to heed the words of historian Gulie Ne'eman Arad: "While no historian can disown Auschwitz when writing about any facet of this period, to situate the analysis within a closed referential framework of its catastrophic ending, when the real became unreal by the reality of the unthinkable, is likely to engender a *supra*-historical interpretation."[17] Arad also notes that Jewish Americans were experiencing the "height of their Americanization process" in the 1930s and 1940s: "[I]t was this enigmatically framed experience – their wish to gain acceptance at the height of rejection – which had a most significant bearing on shaping their defensive response to the Jewish catastrophe. Their Americanization experience played a more powerful role in determining American Jewry's response to the atrocities in Europe than the events themselves, and it is to their American context that American Jews resonated and responded most readily."[18]

Perhaps the most problematic issue of Yanes' argument, however, is the attempt to propose a special relationship between comic books and the White House and, presumably, more specifically a Jewish connection between the two, by naming Morgenthau and claiming the "Jewish medium." Yanes points to the use of the phrase "Keep 'Em Flying!," which he identifies as "Wonder Woman's battle cry," as an "important aspect" of the advertisement.[19] This phrase did not originate with Wonder Woman, nor was it in any way unique to comic books; it was the US Army Air Corps' then-recently adopted and highly visible slogan, the use of which was actively promoted by the War Department.[20] Even if that were not the case, the reference to Wonder Woman undermines the claim to a Jewish connection and the claiming of the "Jewish medium," for reasons already discussed.

Beyond Wonder Woman, not every superhero fighting the war was created by Jews, and not every superhero created by Jews fought in the war;

again, although understandable and most likely part of the explanation for why comic books were so active in propaganda, Yanes and others' references to Jewish concerns gloss over a much more complex history. The comic book in which the cited advertisement was published had stories scripted by Jewish writer-artist Carl Burgos, born Max Finkelstein, as well as by non-Jewish writers like Mickey Spillane and Bill Everett, a descendant of the English poet and painter William Blake.[21] Another famous example, *Daredevil Fights Hitler* (July 1941), was published by lapsed Protestant and leftist Leverett Gleason. The comic book was a hastily assembled comic book that featured a group of superheroes attacking a large picture of the Nazi dictator on its cover. The exact genesis of the content remains uncertain: Wright credits Gleason with its interventionist position, while journalist and popular comics historian Gerard Jones names a group of Jewish and non-Jewish artists and writers.[22] Regardless of the comic book's origin, however, Gleason was the final arbiter of whether *Daredevil* would see print, a decision which "revealed Lev's politics: liberal, secular, progressive, and resolutely anti-fascist."[23] In early 1942, Will Eisner even received a letter in which one of his business partners asked Eisner to "caution" his openly anti-Semitic employee Bob Powell "about working too much anti-Nazi stuff" into a feature he was working on.[24] Meanwhile, neither Superman nor the Batman, who both had Jewish creators, took an active part in the fighting; instead, they stayed stateside and focused on civilian life, linking American consumer culture with democracy in preparation for the postwar years.[25]

Thus, the notion that Jewish American comics creators were uniquely or particularly vehement in their resistance to Nazism because of a joint opposition to Nazi anti-Semitism is problematic because it assumes a degree of cohesion and a level of knowledge that cannot be verified, and because it employs a narrow ethnic lens to read a much more diverse material. Reading these comics in their own time, rather than simply assuming that the appearance of Nazis represents a Jewishly-informed pro-war stance, produces very different results.

SUPERMAN AND WAR

Isolationism, the idea that Americans "could choose whether and when to participate in the world," along with the exceptionalist idea that America was "not simply distant from the Old World but different from it as well," defined the very essence of American national identity for many, influenced foreign policy, and helped shape popular opinion.[26] After WWI, a war about which Americans remained unenthused and that many tellingly called the "European War," the USA took on a less internationalist attitude: isolationism may have been most pronounced in the Midwest, writes David M. Kennedy, but people of all sexes, ages, religions, and political persuasions, from across the ethnic spectrum and from all regions of the nation, "shared in the postwar years a feeling of apathy toward Europe, not to mention the rest of the wretchedly quarrelsome world, that bordered on disgust."[27] Isolationism was never a unified ideology or movement, but a widely and strongly felt sentiment, made all the more fervent by the Depression.[28]

Isolationist rhetoric in these days was often harsh: "Ninety-nine Americans out of a hundred [...] would today regard as an imbecile anyone who suggests that, in the event of another European war, the United States should again participate in it," one commentator wrote in 1935.[29] That year, American isolationism "hardened from mere indifference to the outside world into studied, active repudiation of anything that smacked of international political or military engagement."[30] As Europe's hope of avoiding war diminished, Americans legislated neutrality, marched for peace, and waxed pacifistic; a 1937 poll indicated that 95 percent of Americans felt that the country should stay out of any future war and, while majority opinion was decidedly anti-Hitler by late 1939, there was then still little desire for active involvement abroad.[31] A July 1941 Gallup poll asked: "If you were asked to vote today on the question of the United States entering the war now against Germany and Italy, how would you vote – to get into the war now or to stay out of the war?" Despite the question's awkward phrasing, the response was clear: 79 percent answered that they would vote for America to "stay out."[32]

One of the "European War's" most enduring legacies in the USA was the indictment of profiteers, the "merchants of death [who made] obscene profits from the war"; authors and poets like John Dos Passos, E.E. Cummings, and Ernest Hemingway fed public disillusion, while many public intellectuals argued that the war had been fought to make the world safe, not for democracy, but for Wall Street bankers and arms manufacturers. The sentiment was further reinforced after spring 1934 by the Nye Committee's "isolationist preachments" and "indignant condemnation of the crimes of big business, which had somehow, the committee insisted (though never proved), covertly forced the Wilson administration into war." The argument was overdrawn but it fell on receptive ears, especially in the Depression's antibusiness climate.[33]

This isolationist memory seems to have influenced those early Superman comic books that dealt with war, which was repeatedly shown as resulting from greed and profiteering rather than from any political or ideological differences between belligerents. Such simple reasoning appeared in *Action Comics* #1–2, which at least in part was created when the Nye Committee was still in the public eye. In those stories, Superman tracks a bill that will "embroil" the USA with Europe to Emil Norvell, a wealthy munitions magnate who has already sunk his talons into the warring South American republic "San Monte." When confronted, the opposing commanders can give no reason for why they are fighting: "We're not angry at each other!" Superman sets the record straight: "Gentlemen, it is clear that you've been fighting only to promote the sale of munitions! – Why not shake hands and make up?" They do so, and their war ends. The indictment is clear: war profiteers, willing to ruthlessly throw even the isolationist USA to the wolves if it increases their profit margins, are the cause of wars.[34] As noted above, Weinstein calls "San Monte" a "thinly disguised Nazi Germany," but if there is any real-world corollary to the conflict, Brad Ricca makes a more convincing case for the 1932–1938 Chaco War between Paraguay and Bolivia, which he notes was covered "almost every day" by the *Cleveland Plain Dealer,* a paper that Siegel read.[35]

Next, in *Action* #22–23 (March–April 1940), published during the period of relative and strange calm in Europe between September 1939 and May 1940, known as the "Phony War,"[36] Luthor tries to engineer a global conflict so he can benefit from the ensuing chaos. The story begins when the fictional European nation Toran invades Galonia, fictionalizing the then-recent joint German-Soviet invasion of Poland. Lita Laverne, an actress and Toran spy, asks Clark to tell her "about the great nations. Do you think they are in sympathy with the *Toran's* invasion of *Galonia*?" Suspicious of her intentions, but without missing a beat, Clark replies that "[t]he democracies are definitely opposed to aggressor nations."[37] Significantly, the expected type, timing, and tenor of that opposition is not suggested. England and France had responded with declarations of war but did not engage in direct warfare, while the USA had responded in conscience but not in action.[38]

Knowledge of US unwillingness to get involved in another European war and painful memories of the last time they did are evident in the "Toran-Galonian" war story; Lita hatches a plan to sink a neutral ocean liner to bring other countries into the war, recalling the 1915 sinking of the British *Lusitania* that killed 128 American passengers and "stunned the United States out of its complacency and brought the Great War home to its people for the first time," and the story's battlefield scenes visually bring the then-recent and unpopular conflict's harrowing trench warfare to mind.[39] On his way to cover the war, cuing the reading of these images, Clark sums up American attitudes: "So once again the world is being flung into a terrible conflagration! How senseless!"[40]

To return to where this chapter began, the story in which Adolphus Runyan appeared, titled "Superman Champions Universal Peace!," was familiar in structure and message. After Clark's interview is cut short by "three evil-looking men," Runyan is found dead. Superman follows the men's trail to "Boravia, a small country exhausting its life blood in a senseless civil war" and to the powerful munitions magnate Lubane, who is "promoting this war and profiting off the death and misery of others!"[41] During the confrontation, Lubane drops a vial of Runyan's gas from fear of the menacing Superman and chokes to death. Satisfied that there is "one less vulture" in the world, Superman barges in on a deadlocked peace negotiation between the Boravian belligerents and threatens to collapse the whole room on top of its occupants if they do not make peace.[42] The tactic works and soon a disguised Superman walks "thru the rejoicing city": "And to think that just a few minutes ago these happy people were under the dread shadow of war!"[43] Again, the "merchants of death" were the true culprits in war and, again, the conflict is easily ended when their corrupting influence is gone. Such was Superman's way, "undeniably pacifistic" in the words of one *New Yorker* writer in 1940, "though not in the ordinary, do-nothing sense of the word. If Superman disapproves of a war, he simply stops it."[44]

SUPERMAN ENDS THE WAR

The "Toran–Galonian" war appeared shortly after another piece relating to the declared but still unfought war in Europe. The two-page story, "How Superman Would End the War," published in *Look Magazine* on February 27, 1940, expressed the duality of US reactions to the invasion of Poland and its aftermath.[45] As David Kennedy summarizes, "[p]ublic opinion and official policy alike hung quivering between hope and fear – hope that with American help the Allies could defeat Hitler, and fear that events might yet suck the United States into the conflict."[46] In the comic, Superman, true to form, smashes the German Siegfried line and invites the French soldiers on the Maginot line to "[c]ome and get 'em [the

Nazi soldiers]!" Proceeding to "Hitler's retreat," Superman grabs the German dictator and tells him that "I'd like to land a strictly non-Aryan sock on your jaw, but there's no time for that! You're coming with me while I visit a certain pal of yours."[47] After snatching up Stalin, Hitler's "pal," Superman soon has "the scoundrels responsible for Europe's present ills" standing trial in front of the League of Nations, where they are found guilty "of modern history's greatest crime – unprovoked aggression against defenseless countries."[48]

With reference to Weinstein, film and literary critic Marc DiPaolo sees this story as a "good reason" to regard Superman as a golem. In his view, it "is a simple, evocative wish-fulfillment narrative that suggests that Siegel and Shuster wished that some powerful force would intervene in Europe and stop the advance of both Communism and Fascism, be that force God, the United States, or Superman." DiPaolo then simply summarizes the plot as if it were self-explanatory and moves on to stories, published decades later, that explained why DC's superheroes did not "take it upon themselves to defeat Hitler, either on Earth-2 [the then-current designation for the Golden Age 'reality' among DC's many parallel universes] or in our own reality [sic]."[49]

However, it bears mention that the *Look* story was commissioned, and thus perhaps less wish fulfillment than it was contract fulfillment. Superman intervened because *Look* wondered what would happen if he did, but his intervention was not framed as a call for the USA to do the same. Despite having largely been the brainchild of President Woodrow Wilson, the USA never joined the League of Nations. In fact, the League had become "strictly taboo" in US political discourse by the 1924 presidential elections, "openly spurned" by Roosevelt in 1932, and the manifest weakness of its members during the 1935–1936 Italo–Ethiopian War "confirmed American distrust and fed isolationist sentiment."[50] Superman, as an American, would naturally be horrified by the Molotov–Ribbentroppacters' bellicosity and by the dictators' lacking sense of democratic fair play,[51] but he leaves the fighting to the French and does not presume to pass judgment himself. In handing Hitler and Stalin over, Superman makes it clear that this is in the League's hands and thus a European matter. In "ending the war," Superman was framed as the American aid that would help the European democracies win the war and keep the USA out of the fray.

Perhaps most notable is Superman's passing comment about wanting to give Hitler "a strictly non-Aryan sock." While possibly a way of forestalling

emerging criticism that Superman was himself promoting fascist or totalitarian ideas to impressionable children,[52] the verbal jab was undoubtedly
a way of sniping at Nazi anti-Semitism and perhaps even intended as a
"strictly Semitic sock." But, while the story's meaning is indeed seemingly self-evident, it should be situated beyond the fact that Siegel and
Shuster were Jewish. By this time, a majority of the American population
was negatively disposed toward Hitler and Stalin, and ridicule of both dictators was fairly common.[53] When the comic was published, full-scale war
was threatening to erupt in Europe, putting a fine point on discourses on
national unity in the USA. More and more, American identity was recon-
ceived as resting in ideology and in the sharing of certain universalistic
values, rather than in ethnicity.[54]

Nazi anti-Semitism was criticized in the US press, and American anthro-
pologists and eugenicists alike distanced themselves from such thinking. The
once-common term "race" was becoming all but inapplicable in the subdi-
vision of whites and in academic circles the terms "Aryan" and "Semitic"
were relegated to the realm of linguistics.[55] Even Edgar Rice Burroughs,
Tarzan's eugenicist and white supremacist creator (about whom more is
said in Chap. 7), had by 1938 satirized the Nazis ("Zanis") in his serialized novel, *Carson of Venus*.[56] Race, writes sociologist Nathan Glazer, "now
meant – in large measure because of Hitler and his racism – what we today
understand as race, physical difference. [...] Mobilization in World War
II meant accentuating our tolerance, our diversity, against the racism and
intolerance of Hitler."[57] Roosevelt, Hollywood, and government anti-fifth
column propaganda even identified incitement of race hatreds as a chief
tactic of the hidden enemy.[58] (So would Superman, in front of Congress, in
a 1942 comic strip; in it, he says he can best serve the country on the home
front, battling our "most insidious foes ... the hidden maggots – the trai-
tors, the Fifth Columnists, the potential Quislings who will do all in their
power to halt our production of war materials. I will be on the alert for the
old totalitarian trick of creating disunity by spreading race hatreds."[59])

Despite still having more than a few issues with overt and structural
racism of its own, the USA would not let the overtly politicized racism
of the Nazi regime stand unopposed, and the nation discursively defined
itself over and against the Nazis' mistreatment of Jews with greater, albeit
still white, inclusiveness. Thus, Superman did not cross any line of consensus when he too denounced Nazi racial theory with its emphasis on
"Aryan" superiority. Read as part of the whole comic, the "non-Aryan
sock" comment serves mainly to cast Hitler as despicable from a general-

ized, unmarked, "American" point of view, not too different from, for example, Nazi-mocking articles in magazines like *Time*, several of which printed the term "Aryan" in scare quotes.[60] If the "non-Aryan" comment was meant to express sympathy for Jewish suffering under Nazi oppression, Siegel approached it in an indirect, but in those days common, way. Superman's reference likely simultaneously juxtaposes "Aryan" with both "Jewish" and "American," a sort of "New Man" that immigrants were told to become, and many wanted to be.[61] The racial reference would then signify a refusal to be categorized according to the Nazis' alien thinking, and the hero comes off as asserting the compatibility of Jewish and American identity in the face of Nazi and US anti-Semitism and contributing to a then-emerging "wartime discourse that condemned all forms of racism and bigotry as 'un-American'."[62]

There were many Jewish-organized boycotts and protests, but there was also much internal debate about how to frame the discourse. At the time, explicit concerns about European Jews were largely underreported, and protest, rescue, and relief efforts were often sublimated or co-opted into consensus politics and expressed as a "universal" issue. Stephen Wise, a Reform rabbi, Zionist, and activist, for example, was loath to embarrass Roosevelt with demands or manifestations. As late as August 1943, he would tell his supporters that "[w]e are Americans first, last, and at all times. Nothing else that we are [...] qualifies our Americanism. [...] Our first and sternest task, in common with all other citizens of our beloved country is to win the anti-Fascist war. Unless that war be lost, all else is lost." Wise's view was echoed by most Jewish American organizations and their publications.[63] Those involved in the mostly behind-the-scenes debate about how the USA as a nation could address or intervene in the Jewish situation in Europe frequently found that little either could or would be done within the White House or without, in terms of large-scale action.[64] Hitler and his goose-stepping goons were doubtlessly perceived as a menace in US majority opinion by the time Superman "ended" the war, but one to be opposed only insofar as it constituted a threat to national security, a task to which the superhero would soon turn, as we will see in the next section.

First, however, one final issue pertaining to "How Superman Would End the War" must be addressed. Whatever Siegel's motivation behind the comment, the strip did touch a nerve in the Nazi regime. *Das Schwarze Korps*, the weekly S.S. newspaper, published its retort on April 25, 1940, in a section apparently devoted to amusing or lightweight pieces. It read, in part:

Jerry Siegel, a spiritually as well as physically circumcised man whose head-
quarters is in New York, is the creator of an artistically conceived character
with a healthy appearance, a powerful physique, and red swimming trunks,
who flies through the air. [...] This navigator of the skies, on whom a gen-
erous nature has bestowed overblown musculature in place of much of
an intellect, has been dubbed 'Superman' by the clever Israelite, which is
English for *Übermensch*. [...] There's nothing these Sadducees *[i.e. Jews]*
can't make money from once they get their hands on it!

It concluded with a lamentation: "Pity the poor unfortunate youth of
America who must live in that polluted atmosphere, not even noticing the
poison that they daily swallow."[65]

The US reception of the *Schwarze Korps* piece has always been puz-
zling. When word first trickled back to the USA, journalists there believed
that the Superman story was condemned because the hero's actions were
regarded by the Nazis as "offensively pacifistic."[66] It has resurfaced more
recently, in a disturbing turn of events that illustrates how far the uncritical search for Jewish–comics connections can go. Simcha Weinstein is
the first to reference the article, describing it as having "touched [...] on
the importance" of Siegel and Schuster's Jewish heritage.[67] This "proof"
later appeared in Larry Tye's book, unsourced, but likely inspired by
Weinstein, as an example of an early "recognition" of Superman's "Jewish
roots." When asked in a 2011 BBC broadcast if Superman is Jewish, Marc
DiPaolo (who in his book on superheroes and politics describes Weinstein
as a "Jewish studies scholar") matter-of-factly – and bafflingly – replies:
"Absolutely. [...] Well, actually, Herman Goering knew about Superman
and cited it as Jewish propaganda, replacing the Aryan standard of blond-
haired, blue-eyed beauty with Semitic features."[68] (Chris Gavaler, who
has read Weinstein, but is more interested in unmasking ideologies that
he personally finds distasteful in comics, sidesteps Jewishness entirely and,
after quoting the lamenting closing paragraph, concludes in an almost
woeful tone that "Americans are still swallowing massive doses of that
superhero morality, only now Nazi Germany isn't left to complain."[69])

None of what follows should ever have had to be written, but given
how often this article pops up in the body of Jewish–comics connection
literature, an intervention seems urgently needed. The *Schwarze Korps* did
not touch upon any Jewish heritage of Superman's creators', nor did it
"recognize" any "Jewish roots." The only notion of Jewishness touched
upon in the Nazi-authored article is an ascribed Jewish greed and cultural

parasitism. What is claimed in the piece is that Superman is exerting a corrupting Jewish influence on US culture. Also claimed is that Superman's
Jewish writer is debasing Europe's "latest flowering of manly virtues."
Siegel is imagined by the S.S. writer to have seen this "flowering" and
reacted to it by "smacking his lips, and [...] decid[ing] to appropriate the
idea of manly virtue as an import item, to be distributed among America's
young people in his own way."[70] Jerry Siegel, of course, did none of this.
The Nazis' reading of Superman, of course, has *nothing* to do with Jerry
Siegel the person or with his creation, and everything to do with the anti-
Semitism of Nazi ideology. A Nazi propagandist should, of course, be the
last person anybody looks to for support about what is, and what is not,
Jewish. To present the *Schwarze Korps* article as anything but a vile piece
of anti-Semitic propaganda is to do violence to the past.

SUPERMAN ON THE HOME FRONT

After December 29, 1940, Roosevelt's concerns about events outside the
USA were beyond doubt. In what he said was "not a fireside chat about
war" but a "talk on national security," Roosevelt outlined for Americans
the meaning of the troubles abroad. "If Great Britain goes down, the Axis
powers will control the continents of Europe, Asia, Africa, Australia, and
the high seas – and they will be in a position to bring enormous military
and naval resources against this hemisphere." If that should happen, the
entire Western Hemisphere would be living "at the point of a gun." In
response, military production must increase, and some of its output sent
to the aid of the forces of democracy; this policy, the president said, was
"not directed at war. Its sole purpose is to keep war away from our country
and away from our people." "We must be the great arsenal of democracy,"
Roosevelt said: "For us this is an emergency as serious as war itself. We
must apply ourselves to our task with the same resolution, the same sense
of urgency, the same spirit of patriotism and sacrifice as we would show
were we at war."[71] Military production, which Roosevelt had encouraged
to provide the Allies the tools needed to fight Hitler since January 1939,
was stepped up so that the USA could supply the Allies with war materiel
and ready itself for war, in case it would have to fight.

One aspect of the late 1930s and early 1940s that is closely connected
with both military production for foreign aid and national defense remains
largely unaddressed in extant scholarship on prewar comics. Yanes notes in
passing that the fear of "Nazi agents permeating America was common"

and cites many comic books that are framed in terms of national defense throughout his chapter, but the appearance and critique of Nazis in the comic books equates in his reading only to pro-war sentiment.[72] Wright similarly writes: "As the war in Europe intensified in 1940–41, so did the war in comic books. The United States itself became a battleground, where Nazi spies and saboteurs conspired against American defense build-up."[73] Murray dismisses the fact that early Captain America stories "were based on the homefront [sic] and suggested that there was an army of spies and saboteurs undermining U.S. industrial production" as "complete fantasy," and claims that the intention was "never to accurately depict the situation on the homefront," but to create a sense of urgency and drama to situate US industrial production on the frontline of the war. He concludes from the commonality throughout the superhero genre of concerns about national defense and fears of spies and saboteurs, that it is "obvious that many publishers, editors, writers, and artists adopted an interventionist stance."[74]

The problem with these descriptions and conclusions lies in the fact that, while military production did attain great importance in the prewar USA, and while the paranoiac images of spies and saboteurs were not an accurate depiction of the home front, they were nonetheless a reflection of its mood that was in no way specific to superhero comics. By 1940, a (largely) unfounded fear of the so-called fifth column was widespread in the USA.[75] Many Americans believed that an active phalanx of German and/or Soviet agents really was trying to undermine national defense and rearmament.[76] An August 1940 Gallup poll, for instance, indicated that 48 percent of Americans believed that subversive activities were being undertaken in their own communities, 26 percent were unsure, and only 26 percent were certain that nothing untoward was going on in their neighborhoods.[77]

The fifth column was represented as a dire threat to national security by many influential public figures, including Federal Bureau of Investigation (FBI) director and "folk hero" J. Edgar Hoover and Walter Winchell. Moreover, according to historian Francis MacDonnell, "FDR played a more influential role in shaping attitudes toward the Fifth Column than did any other single individual."[78] Indeed, many of the president's speeches contained at least some mention or allusion to supposed fifth column activities.[79] The mass media played a pivotal role in feeding the fire: newspapers did not underreport the fifth column as they did many other problems during the 1930s and 1940s, and newsreels, pulps, comic books, and many other forms of entertainment tapped into the same fears. After the 1939 *Confessions of a Nazi Spy* became the first cinematic outing to name and attack Hitler's regime, Hollywood increasingly addressed the issue.[80] It is to this discourse and its relationship to superhero comics books that the argument will now turn.

That Siegel and Shuster's Superman approved of Roosevelt designating his country "the arsenal of democracy" is clear. Likely in response to the president's repeated calls for Americans' sacrifice and effort in rearmament and national defense,[81] the hero's creators devoted their character to the cause of democracy and the struggle against the fifth column on the home front throughout 1941. That the opinions of men like Roosevelt, Hoover, and Winchell would be familiar to Superman's creators seems likely: in an earlier comics series, "Federal Men," Siegel and Shuster had capitalized on the then-recently formed FBI's popularity, and that Siegel admired Winchell is suggested not least by the fact that the writer wanted the gossipmonger to announce his second marriage in 1948.[82]

In a *Superman* #8 (January–February 1941) story, titled simply "The Fifth Column," Superman encounters a group of infiltrators plotting to distribute subversive materials: "I've heard enough!," he says. "Now to teach them a little respect for the country they're trying to destroy!" During his one-man raid, Superman secures a list of members, a fact that is soon used against him when he, or rather, his alter ego Clark Kent, is framed for the murder of a US anti-espionage officer. Escaping, Superman discovers an enemy army hidden on US soil, waiting to "strike terror and destruction from the rear when the military forces of the U.S. are attempting to defend the coast against foreign invasion!" Led by a bald and monocled commander, whose appearance conforms to then-rapidly emerging visual stereotypes of Nazis, the army is uniformed in a way that leaves no doubt that they represent the German war machine.[83] Doing what he does best, Superman smashes the army, stating when he gets to its aerial wing that "[t]hese planes will never bomb American cities!"[84] After ensuring that their munitions works explodes, handily killing every last one of the would-be invaders and leaving the USA safe once more, the hero returns to Metropolis and clears his name.[85] Nowhere in the story is anything but a concern with US safety and defense intimated.

After that encounter, every 1941 issue of *Superman* addressed subversive activities in at least one story. In *Superman* #9 (March–April 1941), Superman uncovers a plot to undermine American rearmament and national defense. Part of the plot involves sabotage, which Superman quickly foils. Through that, however, he uncovers another agenda. The "Committee Against Militarism," which is led by a man secretly in the "employ of a warring totalitarian nation," takes a stand in direct opposition to the president's agenda: "No rearmament in the U.S., and no aid to warring democracies!" The spy's duty is "to see that no aid is offered to the democracies, and that the U.S. fails to rearm. Later – when the country I represent takes over America – you will profit!" He goes on, telling his confidantes that "[a]lready the nation I represent is making active efforts to interfere with this country's efforts to re-arm. Only yesterday one of our submarines attacked a supply ship."[86]

This story ties into three aspects of the USA's slow move from isolation to intervention. First, it illustrates the fear that fifth columnists really were trying to prevent American readiness through sabotage. One of the members of the "Committee" is Senator Galsworthy, a well-meaning isolationist who is unaware of the secret agenda. This inclusion reads as if it could have been taken directly from Roosevelt's "Arsenal of Democracy" speech. After warning about the fifth column's plots to sow dissent in America, the president said:

> There are also American citizens, many of then [sic] in high places, who, unwittingly in most cases, are aiding and abetting the work of these agents. I do not charge these American citizens with being foreign agents. But I do charge them with doing exactly the kind of work that the dictators want done in the United States.[87]

Second, it demonstrates the idea, based in part on reality and in part on imagination, that Germany was encouraging American neutrality for its own purposes. Third, it presents an example of what Roosevelt as early as his January 1941 "Four Freedoms" speech had encouraged Americans to do with the "few slackers or troublemakers in our midst." Through his actions, Siegel and Shuster's famous hero shamed his fictional foes and their real-world corollaries by "patriotic example," and thereby followed the president in using the fifth column to discredit and disgrace isolationists, who had fallen out of favor with the turn to military preparedness and national defense production.[88]

The fall from grace of isolationism in large part owed to the fact that some of the leading advocates of neutrality and nonintervention were people like Charles Lindbergh, Fritz Kuhn and his German–American Bund, and the America First Committee, all of whom expressed or were otherwise associated with fascist or pro-Nazi positions.[89] Individuals and organizations such as these were publically opposed in Jewish American circles for the threat they posed to democracy, but few Jewish American organizations would translate opposition to isolation and support of national defense into calls for intervention as long as the nation remained officially neutral.[90] In another story in the same issue, Superman foils a plot "by a foreign agent" determined to get the formula for W-142, a "new substance capable of yielding energy equal to 5,000,000 pounds of coal in a single pound" and, as such, a useful tool for industry and, naturally, war, that should be kept in American hands.[91]

Two stories in *Superman* #10 (May–June 1941) also dealt with subversive elements. The first told about a "sinister spy-ring" striking "at our nation's vital defense secrets!" Superman steps in "[t]o circumvent the subversive activities of a master of espionage." The story revolves around astrology readings used as a front for espionage-through-hypnosis, by which enemy agents get hold of defense secrets. As always, Superman puts an end to the espionage but takes no further action.[92] The second story revolves around the "Dukalia-American Sports Festival," a sporting event that conceals a deal between a foreign arms dealer and an American traitor, who is actually a double agent working a sting. Superman surmises that the event, which bears a striking resemblance to the 1936 Berlin Olympics, is "but the front for unamerican [sic] activities." The hero takes the opportunity to humiliate the racial superiority-rhetoric of the foreign nation's leader, and then to stop their nefarious scheme. But, again, the story goes no further than to suggest that enemy forces have designs against the US.[93]

In *Superman* #11 (July–August 1941), the terrorist "Gold Badge Organization" organizes a terror campaign with the goal of taking over the country only to be stopped by Superman.[94] One story in *Superman* #13 (November–December 1941) begins as a cute yarn about Superman caring for a deserted baby, only to discover that he is watching over the child of an inventor who had been murdered by "agents of a foreign government" for the secret behind his "important wartime invention."[95] Similar to the rest of the 1941 stories, both dealt with subversive activities of saboteurs that are stopped by Superman, without any further repercussions intimated for anyone but the fifth columnists themselves. Indeed, the latter story frames the happy ending in terms of victory over the fifth column. The child's mother tells Lois and Clark: "With your help our government, instead of a foreign power, is in possession of my departed husband's invention."[96]

In *Superman* #12 (September–October 1941), the hero faces the "Grotak Bund," a group that resembles the much-despised German–American Bund, which in the popular imagination was connected with fifth column activities and Nazi Germany. The most notable difference is that fictional Bund is de-Germanized by Siegel's giving their leader an Anglo-Saxon name.[97] Again, fifth column fears are at the center of the narrative, and again the story stops short of advocating any active intervention or retaliation. "Grotak Bund," published only a few months prior to the attack on Pearl Harbor, was introduced in, in hindsight, sadly hyperbolic terms:

> Due to turbulent conditions overseas, it is necessary for the United States to rearm rapidly. Sinister forces, however, seek to impede America's effort to rearm itself so that it will be safe from any attack. But patriot number one, *Superman*, takes upon himself the task of battling the secret foes of our nation – and the resulting battle is one long to be remembered!"[98]

This rhetoric is anchored in the type of national defense rhetoric that Roosevelt had publically promoted and that Jewish American groups had supported. In May 1941, around the time this story would have been written, Roosevelt had spoken about developments in Europe and on the seas, and stressed: "I have said on many occasions that the United States is mustering its men and its resources only for purposes of defense – only to repel attack. I repeat that statement now."[99]

Superman #12 also contained a rare example of Superman leaving US soil to discover a secret submarine refueling base on "Pogo island," belonging to a "foreign power waging war against merchant marine in neutral waters."[100] The plot reads like a comment on the "undeclared naval war in the Atlantic" that raged throughout 1941, in which German submarines sank 650,000 tons of American-made war materiel going to the Allies in April alone. Opinion polls revealed that a majority of Americans were still unwilling to enter the war, and that 70 percent felt that Roosevelt "had already done enough or too much by way of helping Britain." Still, a bare majority supported escorts, perhaps because withholding assistance would in effect mean "feeding Lend-Lease aid to the fishes, would render ABC-1 a mere thinking exercise, and might well leave Britain with no choice but to surrender."[101] Furthermore, Roosevelt had spoken in May about the sinking of transports and advocated patrols to keep the waters of the Western hemisphere free from Nazi ships, and to keep the Nazis from establishing a foothold in any place from which they could launch an attack on the Americas.[102] In light of this public debate, Superman's uncovering and subsequent dismantling of a base from which similar attacks were launched indicates that he served imaginatively as such a patrol and belonged to the faction in favor of convoying, again supporting the government line.

Action Comics introduced a few similar storylines in this period. In issue #36 (May 1941), for example, Superman stops the plots of fifth columnists disguised as anti-rearmament activists attempting to sabotage US infrastructure and poison the water supply in preparation of a foreign invasion.[103] A few months later, in *Action* #41 (October 1941), the superhero squares off against the "ultra-respectable" Ralph Cowan, who has organized widespread sabotage of US industry in return for payments from a "foreign country." When Superman defeats him, Cowan cries out not for an ideal or cause, but simply: "—My opportunity!"[104] Cowan thus embodies the twin threats facing the USA—greed from within and subversion from without—more clearly and more fully than any other foe Superman had faced to date.[105]

While Superman the liberal "champion of the oppressed" was by no means gone, he was in 1941 increasingly introduced in patriotic terms as "Defender of Democracy," a "[f]oe of all interests and activities subversive to this country's best interests."[106] The promotion of rearmament and military production was arguably generally in the interest of Jewish American, whether from the hope that the country would soon come to the aid of European Jewry or the belief that it would ensure the survival of liberal democracy. But in staying as close to Roosevelt's rhetoric as he did in regard to national defense, rearmament, and the fifth column, Siegel and Shuster's Superman also helped keep alive fears that were more at odds with another common Jewish American interest; one of the effects of the fifth column scare was greater popular reluctance toward taking in refugees, for fear that spies might be hiding among them.[107]

When Superman first appeared, until at least as late as 1940, his Jewish publishers would not "allow the character to take even an implicit stand on the subjects of war and fascism."[108] Too many isolationists could keep their children from buying comics, and the German and Italian markets were still open to American business. In 1942, sensing that sending a hero as powerful as Superman to fight would require too much suspension of disbelief (after all, how could he *not* win the war at the drop of a hat?) his writers had Clark classified F-4, unfit for service, in a humorous comic strip: when trying to enlist, excitement causes him to accidentally activate his X-ray vision and read the chart in the next room, thereby failing his eye examination.[109] Thus, even after America entered the war, Superman's presence on the battlefields remained limited to the shipments of comic books that regularly arrived at American bases and his main connection with the overseas war effort consisted of promoting the sale of war bonds and encouraging conservation and scrap metal and paper drives; on the page, he remained stateside.[110]

NOTES

1. Weinstein, *Up, Up, and Oy Vey!*, 21.
2. Weinstein, *Up, Up, and Oy Vey!*, 24, 27–28.
3. Bauer, *History of the Holocaust*, 228–229.
4. *SC2*, 63–64.
5. Wright, *Comic Book Nation*, 35.
6. Yanes, "Graphic Imagery [2009]," 63.
7. Yanes, "Graphic Imagery [2009]," 53–54.
8. Yanes, "Graphic Imagery [2008]," 44.
9. Cf. Shogan, *Prelude to Catastrophe*, esp. 206.
10. On the patriotic fervor and solidarity on the home front, see Putnam 2000, 267–272, passim. That there was much fervor is not to say that the USA was free from turmoil; to the contrary, as Kennedy, *Freedom from Fear*, chap. 21; Takaki, *Double Victory* make clear, the wartime USA was a cauldron of ethnoracial and social tensions.
11. Power, *Problem From Hell*, chap. 3; Kennedy, *Freedom from Fear*, 410–18, 794–97; Takaki, *Double Victory*, chap. 8; Arad, *Rise of Nazism*; Shogan, *Prelude to Catastrophe*; Novick, *Holocaust in American Life*, chap. 3.
12. Cf. Novick, *Holocaust in American Life*, 30–38: "To speak of an entity – American Jewry – is to go awry at the outset." There were many divisions over ideological, theological, and geographical lines, and affinities with European Jews were not always strongly felt after decades of Americanization.
13. Cf. Lipstadt, *Beyond Belief.*
14. Bauer, *History of the Holocaust*, 209–10.
15. Kubert and Carlsson, *Yossel*, np; cf. Novick, *Holocaust in American Life*, 36–38.

16. Kennedy, *Freedom from Fear*, 797; Power, *Problem From Hell*, 33–34.
17. Arad, *Rise of Nazism*, 2; see also Lipstadt, *Beyond Belief*; Shogan, *Prelude to Catastrophe*. Emphasis in original.
18. Arad, *Rise of Nazism*.
19. Yanes, "Graphic Imagery [2008]," 44.
20. On the origin of the slogan, see Dill, "Keep 'Em Flying!" Beyond comics, it could also be heard on radio, seen in cinema (notably the 1941 film *Keep 'Em Flying*), and in newspaper and tabloid advertisements.
21. Cf. Whitson, "Blake Visual Culture."
22. Wright, *Comic Book Nation*, 41; Jones, *Men of Tomorrow*, 187–89.
23. Worcester, "Gleason Family Speaks."
24. Letter from Everett M. "Busy" Arnold to Eisner, dated Feb. 10, 1942. In The Ohio State University Billy Ireland Cartoon Library & Museum, Will Eisner Collection, box WEE 1, folder 9.
25. Gordon, *Comic Strips*, 139–151.
26. Kennedy, *Freedom from Fear*, 386–87.
27. Kennedy, *Freedom from Fear*, 385–86.
28. Herring, *From Colony to Superpower*, 502: "Isolationism has often–and mistakenly–been applied to all of U.S. history. It works best for the 1930s."
29. Quoted in Herring, *From Colony to Superpower*, 503–4.
30. Kennedy, *Freedom from Fear*, 393.
31. Kennedy, *Freedom from Fear*, 393–402; poll in Herring, *From Colony to Superpower*, 503–4; cf. Roosevelt, "European War."
32. Rose, *Myth and the Greatest Generation*, 61.
33. Kennedy, *Freedom from Fear*, 387–88.
34. *SC1*, 14–30; cf. Gordon, *Comic Strips*, 137.
35. According to his testimony in United States Circuit Court of Appeals, "Detective vs. Bruns et al.," 166, Siegel read "The Cleveland News, The Plain Dealer and Press." See also Ricca, *Super Boys*, 156–57.
36. Kennedy, *Freedom from Fear*, 435–36; Shachtman, *Phony War*.
37. *SC3*, 22.
38. Kennedy, *Freedom from Fear*, 434–35.
39. *SC3*, 28–30, 34; cf. *SC1*, 23; cf. Herring, *From Colony to Superpower*, 402–3 on the *Lusitania* and consequences of its sinking.

40. *SC3*, 19.
41. *SC2*, 68, 80.
42. *SC2*, 82.
43. *SC2*, 83.
44. Kahn, Jr., "Why I Don't Believe in Superman"; reprinted in Gilbert, "Comic Crypt." The Sunday comic strip ran a similar story around this time. In that arc, the "small peace-loving European country" Carolia is invaded by "its great sword-rattling totalitarian neighbor, *Bangol!*" The story revolves around Superman, Clark, and Lois working with a Carolian author to gather relief funds for the stricken nation and to foil Bangol spies' violent and exaggerated attempts to stop the fund-raising. See Siegel and Shuster, *Sunday Classics*, 21–32.
45. Siegel and Shuster, "End the War"; also reprinted in Siegel and Shuster, *Sunday Classics*, 187–90.
46. Kennedy, *Freedom from Fear*, 434.
47. Siegel and Shuster, "End the War."
48. Siegel and Shuster, "End the War."
49. DiPaolo, *War, Politics, Superheroes*, 154.
50. Cf. Herring, *From Colony to Superpower*, 450, 494, 506–508.
51. For a discussion on perceptions about similarities between Nazism and Communism, see MacDonnell, *Insidious Foes*, 76–81. See also Alpers, *Dictators*, chaps. 2 and 5, pp. 12, 153.
52. Cf. Lepore, *Wonder Woman*, 184; Welky, *Everything Was Better*, 140–140.
53. Alpers, *Dictators*, 83–93; cf. Murray, *Champions*, 185–86.
54. Gleason, "Americans All," esp. p. 503.
55. Kühl, *The Nazi Connection*, 97–100; Goldstein, *Price of Whiteness*, 192–93, 203–4; Gleason, "Americans All."
56. Burroughs, *Carson of Venus*.
57. Glazer, *Multiculturalists*, 112–14.
58. According to Gleason, "Americans All," 518, cultural pluralism "in all its ambiguities and complexities is the crucial legacy of World War II in respect to American identity." For some warnings about fifth columnist attempts to exacerbate racial and social divisions from around this time, see MacDonnell, *Insidious Foes*, 64–65, 136, 138, 143; cf. Roosevelt, "National Defense"; "Arsenal of Democracy"; Alpers, *Dictators*, 167–69; Jarvis, *Male Body at War*, 50–52; Wright, *Comic Book Nation*, 53.

59. MacDonnell, *Insidious Foes*, 134.
60. E.g. "Is That Necessary?"; "Nazi System"; "Baltimore v. Aryans."
61. Cf. Schlesinger, "This New Man"; Gleason, "Americans All," 505–11.
62. Goldstein, *Price of Whiteness*, 195; Lipstadt, *Beyond Belief*, 127; see Takaki, *Double Victory* for a picture how reality differed from rhetoric. See also Chaps. 7, 8, and 9 in this volume and cf. Welky, *Everything Was Better*, 146: "While justifiably critical of one country's notion of a master race, the Superman comics did nothing to discourage the idea that some people were better than others. It did little more than propose that America's master race was better than anyone else's."
63. Friedländer, *Nazi Germany*, 391.
64. Cf. Arad, *Rise of Nazism*; Lipstadt, *Beyond Belief*; Dollinger, *Quest for Inclusion*, chap. 2; Shogan, *Prelude to Catastrophe*; Medoff, *Blowing the Whistle*; Greenberg, *Troubling the Waters*, 54–59; Power, *Problem From Hell*, chaps. 2–3; Novick, *Holocaust in American Life*, 39–46. As chap. 3 in Novick argues, this applies also to the administration side, hampered by popular opinion, strategic concerns, concerns about image, and realistic assessments of the human cost of, for instance, bombing Auschwitz (strategic bombing was less precise than it was made to appear, and would likely have killed the camp's inmates).
65. Decker, "Reich Strikes Back." Brackets and emphases in original.
66. Gilbert, "Comic Crypt," 43; Decker, "Reich Strikes Back," 30.
67. Weinstein, *Up, Up, and Oy Vey!*, 25–26.
68. Tye, *Superman*, 66; "Surnames." DiPaolo mentions Weinstein in DiPaolo, *War, Politics, Superheroes*, 152–53.
69. Gavaler, *Origin of Superheroes*, 199. See also Bowers, *Superman vs. KKK*, 99–100.
70. Quotes from Decker, "Reich Strikes Back," 29.
71. Roosevelt, "Arsenal of Democracy"; Kennedy, *Freedom from Fear*, 468–69.
72. Yanes, "Graphic Imagery [2009]," 55–59.
73. Wright, *Comic Book Nation*, 40.
74. Murray, *Champions*, 125–26.
75. MacDonnell, *Insidious Foes*, 3; Lipstadt, *Beyond Belief*, 121–27.
76. Fear of Italian or Japanese fifth columns were not as strong. Cf. MacDonnell 1995, 75–76, 82–85.

77. MacDonnell, *Insidious Foes*, 7–8. See Chaps. 9 and 10 in this volume for more.
78. MacDonnell, *Insidious Foes*, 137.
79. Cf. Roosevelt, "National Defense"; "Democratic National Convention"; "Arsenal of Democracy"; "Four Freedoms"; "On Lend Lease"; "Unlimited National Emergency."
80. On pop culture fifth column representations, see MacDonnell, *Insidious Foes*, 133–36.
81. Roosevelt, "National Defense"; "Stab in the Back"; "Democratic National Convention"; "Arsenal of Democracy."
82. Daniels, *Superman*, 25, 37; Ricca, *Super Boys*, 107–11, 234.
83. Cf. Wright, *Comic Book Nation*, 47–48.
84. According to Kennedy, *Freedom from Fear*, 426, 427, passim., air power was a particularly vivid source of American anxiety in these years.
85. *SC5*, 31–43.
86. *SC5*, 108.
87. Roosevelt, "Arsenal of Democracy."
88. Roosevelt, "Four Freedoms"; cf. "Stab in the Back"; "Four Freedoms"; "Unlimited National Emergency."
89. MacDonnell, *Insidious Foes*, passim., but 125–126 and 139–140 in particular.
90. Dollinger, *Quest for Inclusion*, 73–75.
91. *SC5*, 125–37.
92. *SC6*, 30–42.
93. *SC6*, 43–55.
94. *SC6*, 98–110.
95. *SC7*, 113–25.
96. *SC7*, 125.
97. *SC7*, 32–44. On the Bund, see MacDonnell 1995, 43–45, 65–66.
98. *SC7*, 32.
99. Roosevelt, "Unlimited National Emergency."
100. *SC7*, 16.
101. Cf. Kennedy 2001, 469–475, 481–482, 488–493; ABC-1 refers to "America-British Conversation Number 1," a number of secret January 29–March 29, 1940, Anglo-American talks regarding the current international situation.
102. Roosevelt, "Unlimited National Emergency"; see also "Arsenal of Democracy."

103. *SC5*, 180–192.
104. *SC7*, 60–71.
105. The Sunday strip also contained a fifth column strip in 1941. In this arc, the "vicious, anti-American organization" known as the Committee for a New Order tries to install totalitarianism in the USA. Again, Superman defeats the threat, with the help of a "g-man" friend. Siegel and Shuster, *Sunday Classics*, 88–105.
106. *SC7*, 87; *SC6*, 43.
107. Lipstadt, *Beyond Belief*, chap. 6.
108. Jones, *Men of Tomorrow*, 165.
109. The idea for this inspired piece of narrative is credited to Jack Schiff in De Haven 2010, 77. See also Jones 2004, 218; Wright 2001, 43.
110. Gordon, *Comic Strips*, 139–51; "Moral World of Superman," 172–75.

CHAPTER 7

The Hearts and Minds of Supermen

If the sociocultural circumstances surrounding Superman's birth and early years stacked the deck in favor of New Deal liberalism, Americanism, isolationism, and policing the fifth column, the forms in which he was represented were notably in line with the 1930s and early 1940s culture. Playing an increasingly larger role in Americans' lives, radio, which Roosevelt realized early was a potent tool for public opinion-making, "became the electronic equivalent of the New Deal," easing people's minds and shaping the national spirit.[1] The advent of the radio in the 1920s signaled a shift in American society; the medium became "an electronic floodgate through which flowed a one-way tide that began to swamp the values and manners and tastes of once-isolated localities. [...] [It] assaulted the insularity of local communities."[2] Jewish organizations also used the medium to highlight the symmetry between Judaism and American values, in ways that often accommodated "their particularist ethnic agenda to larger currents in American political culture."[3] This effect, of partially supplanting subaltern cultures with a national mass culture, was a feature common to the emerging mass media and mass forms of entertainment and communication, cinema in particular but all others to some degree, from spectator sports to advertising.[4] Even before this effect could be felt, pop culture socialized immigrants and minorities into race consciousness, often representing nonwhites in denigrating ways.[5]

© The Editor(s) (if applicable) and The Author(s) 2016   125
M. Lund, *Re-Constructing the Man of Steel*,
DOI 10.1007/978-3-319-42960-1_7

Jonathan Sarna has remarked that "Jews sometimes like to claim that they created contemporary culture." He cites several such claims before problematizing them:

> Disproportionate as these contributions may be, for years the array of arts in which Jews participated actually bore little relationship to Judaism, and were, in many cases, an effective means of escaping it. Fearing that if their work were "too Jewish" it would remain provincial, the most creative Jews in America hid or sublimated their faith. They changed their names and universalized the products of their creative genius in a bid to attract a wide audience.[6]

In a similar vein, historian Eric A. Goldstein writes that "[f]ew immigrant groups embraced popular music, film, sports, and other forms of mass entertainment as enthusiastically as the Jews, who saw them as major vehicles for claiming their status as white Americans."[7] American Jewry's production and consumption of popular culture, then, seems to have tended largely toward attaining or displaying an American middle-class identity and the whiteness it conferred.[8] As this chapter will argue, this was also the case with Superman.

SUPERMAN'S GENEALOGY

Jerry Siegel liked to give an account of Superman's genesis that has the air of "the kind of apocryphal story you find in juvenile biographies of famous men," a story that seems like a bid on Siegel's part to claim *auteur* status.[9] In Siegel's narrative, he lay awake one hot summer night somewhere between 1931 and 1934 when the ideas started coming: "I hop out of bed and write this down, and then I go back and think some more for about two hours and get up again and write that down. This goes on all night at two hour intervals." Thus, Siegel claimed, in "a simple story of inspiration and belief," Superman was born.[10] The actual story of Superman's creation is far more complex. It has many twists and turns, and new details continue to be uncovered. What can be said with certainty is that Superman was the product of a long process, not a flash of inspiration. Siegel and Shuster had conceived at least two other Supermen, and Siegel created at least one more version with another artist.[11]

Few critics today believe Siegel's story. It is commonly acknowledged that Superman was a hodgepodge of influences and borrowings. What is not agreed upon is what significance this has or, more importantly, which intertexts should be emphasized. We have already discussed the connections drawn to Moses and the golem of Prague and pointed out how tenuous they are. Further, Weinstein also adds Samson to the mix, and comments upon both characters having only one weakness each: Samson has his hair, Superman has Kryptonite.[12] Again, however, metatextual projection creeps in: Kryptonite was another addition to the Superman mythos introduced in the radio show. Siegel did write a story about an alien metal that sapped Superman's strength in 1940, introducing the radioactive alien "K-metal." Had the story been published it would, in Tye's suggestive wording, "have become the once-unstoppable superhero's Achilles heel," but nothing came of it.[13]

However, neither Samson nor Achilles can make a definitive claim to inspiration here: neither is the only hero with a single weakness conceived before Superman and, speaking against their ancestor status, both of their weaknesses are part of their own anatomy rather than external. Nonetheless, Weinstein's reference to Samson is worth dwelling upon. The biblical figure is indeed sometimes explicitly mentioned in the earliest comics.[14] In the aforementioned "Superman Champions Universal Peace!," the hero tears down a pair of pillars to collapse a room in order to speed up peace negotiations, screaming while he does so that "[a] guy named Samson once had the same idea!"[15]

The reference is fleeting, however, and it is the only element that really connects with the biblical judge's narrative. Siegel most likely first encountered Samson in a Jewish setting, but the importance of Samson's inclusion can easily be overstated: Samson, like Moses, would have been "safe" for even the most assimilationist of writers, due to the importance and familiarity with the *Tanakh*, or Hebrew Bible, and its personalities in Christianity and Western culture. For example, non-Jewish writer Lester Dent identified his pulp character (Clark) "Doc" Savage—also known as the "Man of Bronze" and a commonly claimed inspiration for Superman—with Samson as early as 1934.[16] That Samson was a more action-oriented character than Moses might in itself have meant that he was more interesting to Siegel, given the writer's generic tastes, and therefore worthy of explicit mention. Siegel once remarked that the first superman he and Shuster created was a product of reading, locating the biblical figure in a broader and, significantly, popular tradition: "[A]s a science fiction fan, I knew of the various themes in the field. The superman theme has been one of those themes ever since Samson and Hercules; I just sat down and wrote a story of that type."[17] In a 1946 article, Mort Weisinger quotes Siegel characterizing Superman as a "combination of Samson, Hercules, and Atlas plus the moral of Sir Galahad whose mission in life was to smack down the bullies of the world."[18] The mention of Samson here alone makes Superman no more a Jewish character than the other mentions make him a Greek or Arthurian one.

It is, of course, entirely possible that the early Superman comics made biblical references. Although arguably both a stretch of the imagination and a venture into overinterpretation, one could, by way of a thought experiment, connect one of the stories in *Superman* #11 (July–August 1941) with scripture. In the story, Lois and Clark travel to South America in an attempt to find a cure for an epidemic plaguing Metropolis. Forced to travel on foot through forbidding terrain, their party is without water, so Superman burrows deep underground. When the others wake up the next morning to find that their needs have been taken care of, Lois proclaims it a "miracle!" Immediately, however, they are set upon by natives and taken prisoner. Sent to "the *Cave of a Thousand Horrors*," the prisoners are left to fend for themselves amidst a horde of rattlesnakes and scorpions. Here too, Superman steps in and clears the way.[19] Siegel could have borrowed these elements from the Exodus narrative or even from the admonition against letting one's "heart grow haughty and [...] forget the LORD your God – who freed you [the people of Israel] from the land of Egypt, the house of bondage; who led you through the great and terrible wilderness with its seraph serpents and scorpions, a parched land with no water in it, who brought forth water from the flinty rock" (Deut. 8:14–15). It is, after all, an interesting story with exciting imagery. None of this is to suggest an intentional Superman–Moses, or, for that matter, Superman–God connection on Siegel's behalf, but merely to point out that an intertextual relationship with scripture should not be discounted. If such a relationship exists, however, biblical sources appear in a highly transformed and unmarked way.

To some degree, Kaplan, Fingeroth, and Weinstein all acknowledge that other writers on Superman's efforts have been directed at finding intertextual connections outside of Jewish tradition, but neither of the three includes the arguments of others in their own thinking.[20] But the connections are many: actors Harold Lloyd, Kent Taylor, Douglas Fairbanks, Tom Mix, and Johnny Weissmuller have been regarded as models for Superman's behavior and appearance; pulp and film characters like Tarzan, John Carter of Mars, Zorro, the Shadow, and the Scarlet Pimpernel have been claimed as sources; cartoon characters like Popeye are said to have inspired Superman's cartoony take on violence; and comic strip characters like Flash Gordon, whose costume had a similar red, blue, and yellow color scheme and prominent chest insignia, are identified as a further source. Even bodybuilder Bernarr MacFadden is believed to have made his way into the new hero.[21] It is also possible that Superman's designation as a "champion of the oppressed" was lifted from *The Mark of Zorro*, where the titular hero was so described, and that his identity as the "Man of Tomorrow" was swiped from the 1939–1940 New York World's Fair "Democracity" diorama, where that term was used and which Siegel and Shuster had visited.[22] Hugo Danner, the invincible protagonist in Philip Wylie's *Gladiator*, who in adolescence notes that he "can jump higher'n a house […] run fastern's a train […] pull up big trees an' push 'em over," has been very plausibly credited as a source for the young Superman's finding out that he was able to "leap 1/5 of a mile; hurdle a twenty-story building…raise tremendous weights…run faster than an express train."[23]

All of these connections, and many more, have in common that they are supported by an evidentiary base, and are rooted in specifically identifiable and situational sources; they are identified as likely intertexts by critics who take pains to note when and where they appeared, put them in relation to Siegel and Shuster's known cultural tastes and habits, and make an argument for when the creators might have encountered the text. Indeed, whether or not Siegel and Shuster consciously embraced the homogenizing and whitening tendencies of popular culture, they were undoubtedly voracious consumers of its offerings.

In a rare interview where much space was given to Siegel and Shuster's tastes and inspirations, many of which are mentioned above, Siegel said that "I read tremendous amounts of pulps; and Joe and I, we practically lived in movie theaters."[24] As one of the first self-identified fans and creator of the first known "fanzine," Siegel perceived himself as part of the cultural vanguard, and possibly even as being of "a superior order of human."[25] He spent his teens in his bedroom, reading pulp stories or trying to write his own, or at the movies consuming Hollywood's vision of America, although he also found inspiration in a Cleveland newspaper, *The Plain Dealer*, which published little of particular Jewish interest.[26] When success allowed him to buy a house of his own, a fixture in every room was a radio set.[27] Shuster, too, embraced popular culture. According to one biographer, he was "astounded by the comics page" from an early age.[28] The fad of physical culture turned Shuster onto bodybuilding and his physical fitness manuals served as an ersatz portfolio of human anatomy reference material.[29] Some early Superman stories even included tips on how to "Acquire Super-Strength!"[30] Shuster internalized pulp magazine illustrations and learned to draw by tracing newspaper comic strips (some of which he kept throughout his entire life[31]).

Thus, given Siegel and Shuster's well-documented tastes, it is unsurprising that in broad terms, their Superman differs little from contemporary US pop-culture heroes like Tarzan, the Shadow, Buck Rogers, the Phantom, Dick Tracy, Doc Savage, or the Lone Ranger. These and other characters were so similar in recurring basic narrative elements and characters traits in those days that philosopher John Shelton Lawrence and bible scholar Robert Jewett speak of their period of greatest popularity, from 1929 until the proliferation of superheroes in the wake of Superman, as the "axial decade" in the development of the collection of tropes and conventions they name, somewhat grandiosely, "the American Monomyth." This myth, in simplified terms, tells about a harmonious community threatened by an evil which normal authorities fail to contend with, and of a selfless hero who emerges to renounce temptation and carry out the redemptive task before receding back into obscurity.[32] For all the problems with the "Monomyth" thesis, this description fits most of the early Superman stories.

The list of elements in Superman's acknowledged and proposed intertextual mixture could go on. Whatever went into the mix, however, Superman was in the end more than the sum of his separate parts, a specific blend of a variety of figures that were indelibly melded. It is therefore here more rewarding to continue by attempting to see how Superman's characterization employed common representational conventions, tropes, structures, and practices. Proceeding in that direction provides a new angle to Superman's genealogy that can complement previous searches. When Superman is situated in his historical moment, what emerges is very much a typical cultural product of its kind.

POPULAR CULTURE BETWEEN RHETORIC AND REALITY

Superman's creators knew well how hard the times truly were: dire economic straits had been evident in Cleveland since 1927; money was tight after Siegel's father died from heart failure after a robbery in 1932; and in the winter months, Shuster had to draw with gloves on scraps of tissue and wrapping paper on the same bread board that his mother used to bake the Sabbath *challah*, because his family could not afford to buy paper or to heat the apartment.[33] Siegel and Shuster's 1933 "Reign of the Super-Man," a short story about a superhuman villain, begins in a dramatic way, possibly in reference to the inhabitants of the shantytown that existed in Cleveland until 1938: "The breadline! Its row of downcast, disillusioned men; unlucky creatures who have found that life holds nothing but bitterness for them. The breadline! Last resort of the starving vagrant."[34]

Arguably, as Chap. 5 has shown, Siegel and Shuster's later, more lasting and popular superhero also spoke to the uncertain situation of the middle class, the destitute masses of urban working-class unemployed, and the stricken farmers, all of whom were hoping for improvement. He touched upon the lives of those who had suffered through the winter of 1932–1933, the worst in recent memory, who had known hunger intimately, who had experienced recovery only to have it taken away again in the recession of 1937, and who had, through it all, heard promises that things would soon improve. But this Superman was more concerned with the perceived causes of the Depression than he was with its effects; there were many representatives of the uncaring rich, but nary a breadline or "Hooverville" in sight.

Thus, in contrast to their older creation and to more recent popular culture that explicitly addressed the harshness of the times, Siegel and Shuster did not reproduce the proverbial view from out their window when they first created their superheroic Superman. Instead, the comics Superman resembled the press, which for a long time underreported the severity of the Depression, and Hollywood, where "very few feature films depicted the 'hard times' in realistic or penetrating fashion."[35] Superman thus lived in a world both familiar and strange in its own time, connecting with people's fears, channeling and, at least for a moment, neutralizing them, marking a refusal to give in to resignation.[36]

Superman comic books also made frequent use of symbols circulating widely in Depression culture. Siegel had been interested in journalism since high school, he and Shuster had included journalists in a few earlier works, and press movies were in vogue in the late 1920s through the early 1930s; together, these interests likely inspired the decision to make Clark Kent a journalist, a class of people which "Hollywood depicted [...] as defenders of society's right to know, civic virtue and the underdog."[37] Similarly, the recurring critique of tabloids' and sensationalist papers' "yellow journalism" in these stories can be viewed as a response to papers like Robert R. McCormick's "militantly anti-New Deal and obstreperously isolationist" *Chicago Tribune* which, along with his radio station, "trumpeted his trademark prejudices across what he called 'Chicagoland' – the five-state region that stretched from Iowa to Ohio, the very heartland of American isolationism."[38]

In stories and on covers, Superman saves dams, one of the era's most potent social symbols, from destruction.[39] He repeatedly combats gambling and smashes numerous gaming tables which, according to literary critic Sean McCann, were "another central image of Depression literature."[40] Another recurring story structure has Superman caring for underprivileged children, a visible problem during the Depression. Through this care, Superman expresses the then-common belief that providing better environments for what was called "predelinquents" and even institutionalizing runaways could keep them from turning to crime.[41] Further, several stories respond to concerns about organized crime's labor racketeering in connection with "protection" scams and strikes.[42] Superman even worked for better prison conditions in a story criticizing an unjust criminal justice system, recalling for example the 1932 film *I Am A Fugitive From A Chain Gang*.[43]

Similar to many pulp heroes, brains and brawn are often inseparable for Superman, as is evident in Carroll John Daly's Race Williams stories in particular, where "gunfire and rhetorical power are virtually identical forces. ('Yep, it's my gun what speaks,' Race likes to point out)."[44] One introduction in *Superman* #10 trumpets that in the story, "the amazing *Man of Tomorrow* meets fiendish cunning with super-intelligence and offsets scientific destruction with the irresistible force of his superhuman strength!"[45] Later in the same issue, the pretense of wits being divorced from fists vanishes completely: "*Superman* loses no time in going into action when he encounters a menace to American democracy, super-strength clashes with evil super-cunning in another thrilling, dramatic adventure."[46] The struggle between the two types of strength even became the premise of a story, in *Superman* #4 (Spring 1940), when Luthor challenges Superman to a competition of mind versus muscle. To no one's surprise, Superman smashes every device the villain has concocted.[47]

In fighting "evil" and "injustice" and advocating the virtues espoused by New Deal rhetoric, Superman appears almost as a "cartoonified" Roosevelt in a cape: both were patrician saviors displaying a proletarian sense of social justice along with an air of aloofness, heroes who not only offered comforting words but, importantly, transformed them into deeds.[48] By championing isolationism at first and then fighting for democracy's survival against "un-American" ideals and activities feared to be insidiously poisoning the country through the fifth column, Superman patriotically mirrored national sentiment as it shifted toward intervention. In short, Superman was an American. Being American, however, had a cost.

SUPERMAN, AMERICANIZATION, AND POPULAR CULTURE

de Crèvecœur's oft-quoted (and aforementioned) characterization of the American, "this new man," is telling: "He is an American, who leaving behind him all his ancient prejudices and manners, receives new ones from the new mode of life he has embraced, the new government he obeys, and the new rank he holds." Having done so, "[h]e becomes an American by being received in the broad lap of our great *alma mater*. Here individuals of all nations are melted into a new race of men."[49] Just as immigrants were expected to "melt" into de Crèvecœur's America, so too were they admitted into the Great American Melting Pot well into the twentieth century on the condition that they accepted the nation's mores and ideals. Alien cultures and ideas were to be checked at Ellis Island, as it were, and people coming from all over the world were supposed to become a homogeneous whole, a nation of Americans in race, creed, and culture.[50] By conforming to this standard, (some) immigrants could become white. However, by the end of the nineteenth century, as non-Anglo-Saxon Europeans became racialized, the margin for inclusion in the American polity narrowed significantly and the pressure to Americanize increased.[51]

The force of Americanism, even before being revitalized in the New Deal era, "was felt across the entire Jewish ideological, religious, and political spectrum in the United States. It was a campaign waged at the grassroots level, in kitchens and living rooms, in synagogues, public schools, public libraries, and evening classes for adults."[52] Eric Goldstein rightly points out that the Melting Pot proposition was far from an easy one, its acceptance far from complete among American Jews.[53] Even among those who did not buy into the ideal, however, few were comfortable with displaying parochial sentiments at times when the discourse on matters of race and identity became more restrictive.

From around the turn of the century until WWII, when the three major branches of religious American Judaism—Reform, Conservative, and Orthodox—were beginning to formulate themselves ideologically and theologically, most American Jews were more interested in making a life for themselves than in deciding what level of halakhic observance worked for them. According to historian of Judaism Michael Satlow, "[s]truggling to survive financially and to integrate culturally into the melting pot of America, most Jews simply abandoned Jewish affiliations and customs, a fact widely noted at the time by leaders of the nascent movements."[54] About the 1925–1935 "religious depression" in America, which "[s]tatistics suggest [...] affected Judaism more profoundly than other faiths," Jonathan Sarna writes in terms applicable to Siegel and Shuster and their Jewish co-fans all over the country:

> The fear, in Jewish religious circles, was that children like [actor] Al Jolson and [Jolson's character in *The Jazz Singer* (1927)] "Jack Robin" had abandoned God and the synagogue for one of the many "false gods" that preyed upon impressionable young minds: popular culture, atheistic materialism, socialism, communism, and more, each splintered into warring bands of devout followers.[55]

In 1935, three quarters of young Jews surveyed in New York, among whom at least a few of the American comic book pioneers can likely be counted, had not attended religious services at all in the previous year. Although living in Cleveland and raised in an Orthodox home, Siegel was apparently as lax in his religious observance; while probably less accurate in fact than in spirit, his cousin would later claim that "I don't think he ever went to the synagogue in his life."[56] Much to his parents' dismay, Shuster was untraditional enough to develop a liking of non-Jewish women when he started dating.[57] The duo could easily have lived an active Jewish social life if they wanted to. In Cleveland, the mid- to late 1930s provided ample opportunities for Jewish youth activities outside of religious communal life, ranging from Zionism and cultural activities to the Jewish Young Adult Bureau, which offered a comprehensive range of recreational alternatives. By 1940, the Jewish Center in Glenville was the country's largest Conservative congregation, offering sports facilities, Zionist club meetings, Americanization lectures, and more.[58] Siegel and Shuster, however, chose not to take advantage of these opportunities and communities, focusing instead on their creative work.

As quoted earlier, Fingeroth regards Superman as the "embodiment of all those lone immigrants" who came to America from an Old World, to which they could not return, seeking safety and success.[59] There does, however, not appear to have been any desire for Siegel to go back to the place his father had left and from which he had quickly brought over

Jerry's mother and two eldest siblings.[60] Instead, Superman reads like an immigrant success story in a strong Americanizing vein, similar to those Melting Pot stories of immigrants arriving and rapidly assimilating into US society that had dominated American letters for centuries. This in itself was common in comics, and not restricted to comics characters created by Jews. Marston's Wonder Woman, when she first appeared in 1941, similarly came to the USA as a "ready-made patriot."[61] But, although Superman's story was not told as a prolonged immigrant narrative, it may still have betrayed the experience of second-generation immigrants; Jerry's father had rapidly succeeded upon his arrival to the country and quickly been able to afford both to bring over his and his wife's families and to buy a house, an important symbol of achievement, wealth, security, and belonging for immigrants.[62]

If Superman is the "ultimate" expression of the Jewish experience, as Kaplan suggests,[63] coming as he does from another planet, he is also the "ultimate" proof of the USA's equality of opportunity and of successful integration. Tapping into Americans' perception of the nation's past (the idea that "immigrants built this country"), Superman showed that immigrants could not only still fit in but that they could also benefit the country, perhaps more importantly than ever in the Depression. Thus, Fingeroth's identification of Superman as the embodiment of the "Good Immigrant" is in part correct, despite a metatextual projection of the Kents to support the claim.[64] But it misses one of the "Good Immigrant's" qualities: Americanization. As early as 1936, Roosevelt had commended immigrants in no uncertain terms, while also expressing confidence in the success of Americanization:

They [immigrants] have never been—they are not now—half-hearted Americans. In Americanization classes and at night schools they have burned the midnight oil in order to be worthy of their new allegiance.

They were not satisfied merely to find here the realization of the material hopes which had guided them from their native land. They were not satisfied merely to build a material home for themselves and their families.

They were intent also upon building a place for themselves in the ideals of America. They sought an assurance of permanency in the new land for themselves and their children based upon active participation in its civilization and culture.[65]

As noted above, where Superman came from did not play into his early characterization in any significant way; what he did and who his actions made him are thus a testament in the extreme to the country's "regenerative" power.[66] Siegel and Shuster's superhero then appears as an expression of a desire to become more American than Americans, and, with Americanism having by this time been reified "into a fixed pattern of cultural, racial, and other characteristics that were clearly distinguishable from 'alien' ones," to live up to an impossible ideal.[67] In this light, if Superman is an immigrant, he is an immigrant who proves that he, and by extension his creators and those like them, could leave the Old World behind and receive de Crèvecœur's new "prejudices and manners" from the "mode of life" they embraced, "the government they obeyed," and the "rank they held."

NOTES

1. Dickstein, *Dancing in the Dark*, 7–8.
2. Kennedy, *Freedom from Fear*, 227–30; cf. McLuhan, *Understanding Media*, chap. 30.
3. Dollinger, *Quest for Inclusion*, 67–68.
4. Muscio, *Hollywood's New Deal*, 4–11, 21–23, 68–71, 74; Miller, *New World Coming*, 63–64, 333–34; Smith, *Hard-Boiled*, chap. 2; Halter, *Shopping for Identity*, 29–40.
5. Roediger, *Working toward Whiteness*, 180–84.
6. Sarna, *American Judaism*, 330–31.
7. Goldstein, *Price of Whiteness*, 153.
8. Cf. Heinze, *Adapting to Abundance*; Prell, *Fighting to Become Americans*, 92–94.
9. De Haven, *Our Hero*, 62.
10. Jones, *Men of Tomorrow*, 109.
11. Jones, *Men of Tomorrow*, 109–15; De Haven, *Our Hero*, 62–69; Ricca, *Super Boys*, 65–79, 90–102; cf. Fine and Siegel, "Reign of the Super-Man"; Trexler, "Hidden History."
12. Weinstein, *Up, Up, and Oy Vey!*, 26. See also Bowers, *Superman vs. KKK*, 45, in which the writer calls a Samson-reference an example of Siegel letting his "Jewish roots slip out."
13. Tye, *Superman*, 49–50; Ricca, *Super Boys*, 190–92.
14. Cf. *SC1*, 84, 168, 181; *SC2*, 32, 82; *SC3*, 113.
15. *SC2*, 82.
16. Chambliss and Svitavsky, "Pulp to Superhero," 15.
17. Andrae, Blum, and Coddington, "Supermen and Kids," 9.

18. Weisinger's article, "Here Comes Superman!," was published in the July 1946 issue of *Coronet* magazine. Reprinted in Gilbert, "Comic Crypt," 45–46.

19. *SC6*, 123–35.

20. Kaplan, *From Krakow to Krypton*; Fingeroth, *Disguised as Clark Kent*, 41; Weinstein, *Up, Up, and Oy Vey!*, 26.

21. For discussions about the myriad possible contributions to Superman's intertextual mix, see De Haven, *Our Hero*; Ricca, *Super Boys*, esp. chap. 12; Jones, *Men of Tomorrow*; Andrae, Blum, and Coddington, "Supermen and Kids"; Tye, *Superman*, 7–11, 32–35.

22. Conn, *Against the City*, 111; Gavaler, *Origin of Superheroes*, 52; Jones, *Men of Tomorrow*, 179.

23. E.g. Jones, *Men of Tomorrow*, 78–82; De Haven, *Our Hero*, 35; and even Tye, *Superman*, 32–33. Quotes from Wylie, *Gladiator*, 48–49; *SC1*, 4.

24. Andrae, Blum, and Coddington, "Supermen and Kids," 10.

25. Jones, *Men of Tomorrow*, 23–28; Ashley, *Time Machines*, 8; Andrae, Blum, and Coddington, "Supermen and Kids," 7.

26. Jones, *Men of Tomorrow*, 77, passim.; De Haven, *Our Hero*, 69; Rubinstein, *Merging Traditions*, 99.

27. Ricca, *Super Boys*, 169.

28. Ricca, *Super Boys*, 12, 15.

29. Ricca, *Super Boys*, chap. 11; p. 129.

30. *SC1*, 58, 82, 110.

31. Ricca, *Super Boys*, 84.

32. Lawrence and Jewett, *American Superhero*, 36–43, 6.

33. Cf. Jones, *Men of Tomorrow*, 39, 67–68, 71; De Haven, *Our Hero*, 36–37; Daniels, *Superman*, 11, 35; Gartner, *Jews of Cleveland*, 290–91; Ricca, *Super Boys*, 65, 300–306; Andrae, Blum, and Coddington, "Supermen and Kids," 15.

34. Fine and Siegel, "Reign of the Super-Man"; cf. Ricca, *Super Boys*, 67–72; Daniels, *Superman*, 14; Jones, *Men of Tomorrow*, 82–83.

35. Edsforth, *The New Deal*, 39–40, 76–77, 93–94; Jewell, *Golden Age Cinema*, 30; Dickstein, *Dancing in the Dark*, 232.n†.

36. Cf. Dickstein, *Dancing in the Dark*, 8.

37. Most of these films had less-than-savory protagonists, but during the Depression and war years, cinematic journalists became increasingly wholesome. Dickstein, *Dancing in the Dark*, 374; Vaughn and

Evensen, "Democracy's Guardians"; cf. Ricca, *Super Boys*, 30–31, 86, 92; Fine and Siegel, "Reign of the Super-Man."

38. While there are scattered critiques of tabloid journalism throughout, *SC3*, 140–152, is the most focused statement on the issue; cf. Kennedy, *Freedom from Fear*, 404.

39. E.g. *SC1*, 65–67; *SC5*, 85; McCann, *Gumshoe America*, 142; Kennedy, *Freedom from Fear*, 99, 128, 147–49.

40. E.g. *SC2*, 42; *SC5*, 14; *SC6*, 166–68; McCann, *Gumshoe America*, 132.

41. E.g. *SC1*, 89–110; *SC2*, 147–70; *SC4*, 19–31; Appier, "Path to Crime," esp. pp. 197–198.

42. E.g. *SC1*, 181–93; *SC3*, 85–97; cf. Jacobs and Peters, "Labor Racketeering," 229–34; Witwer, "Scandal of Scalise," esp. p. 935. n5; Gabler, *Winchell*, 274–80.

43. *SC4*, 126–38; Dickstein, *Dancing in the Dark*, 57–60.

44. McCann, *Gumshoe America*, 58.

45. *SC6*, 4.

46. *SC6*, 43.

47. *SC3*, 46–58. The challenge is a diversion, which Luthor knows he will lose. The villain has orchestrated the ruse to fool Superman, while he steals an important device, giving the impression that mind has triumphed over matter; this is not the case, and Superman soon smashes his way to ultimate victory.

48. Roosevelt, too, had a dual identity: on the one hand, there was his disabled physical, private body, and, on the other, his dynamic body politic. Cf. Jarvis, *Male Body at War*, 28–35; Muscio, *Hollywood's New Deal*.

49. Crèvecoeur, *Letters*, 43–44.

50. Cf. Lederhendler, *Jewish Responses*, 121–22.

51. Roediger, *Working toward Whiteness*; Brodkin, *How Jews Became White*, 27–34.

52. Lederhendler, *Jewish Responses*, 113; cf. Muscio, *Hollywood's New Deal*, 2; Wenger, *History Lessons*.

53. Goldstein, *Price of Whiteness*; cf. Lederhendler, *Jewish Responses*, 117–19, 124–26.

54. Satlow, *Creating Judaism*, 37.

55. Sarna, *American Judaism*, 226–27; Roediger, *Working toward Whiteness*, 178–79.

56. Sarna, *American Judaism*, 226–27; Siegel's cousin in Jones, *Men of Tomorrow*, 84–85.
57. Ricca, *Super Boys*, 140–42, 170–71; Tye, *Superman*, 53.
58. Rubinstein, *Merging Traditions*, 112; Gartner, *Jews of Cleveland*, 304.
59. Fingeroth, *Disguised as Clark Kent*, 44–45.
60. Ricca, *Super Boys*, 298–99.
61. Smith, "Tyranny of the Melting Pot"; cf. Lepore, *Wonder Woman*, 199–200.
62. Jones, *Men of Tomorrow*, 23–24; Ricca, *Super Boys*, 299–300; Roediger, *Working toward Whiteness*, 158–62.
63. Kaplan, *From Krakow to Krypton*, 14.
64. Fingeroth, *Disguised as Clark Kent*, 46–47.
65. Roosevelt, "Roosevelt Park Address."
66. Lederhendler, *Jewish Responses*, 110–11; cf. Wenger, *History Lessons*, 30–32.
67. Lederhendler, *Jewish Responses*, 109.

CHAPTER 8

Superman and the Displacement of Race

It is impossible to know to what extent Superman's framers internalized the Melting Pot rhetoric. But, judging from what is *not said* and what *does not* appear in their comics—unsensationalized deviations from Americanism's white norm—it seems that, if not necessarily intentionally, they were ready to provide support for its validity. They did so in their character himself, who, like so much of Depression-era cinema, embodied "the typical American virtues" of faith, courage, pragmatism, and individual action, and in the world he inhabited.[1]

People of color appear in many comic books from the period discussed, most often conforming to the then-common racist or racialist representational practices, but are extremely rarely in Superman comics.[2] His world was seemingly only inhabited by whites and a small number of stereotypes.[3] The Glenville area in which Superman was born was more or less a Jewish enclave, in which Siegel and Shuster could potentially go a whole day without encountering non-Jews. As was the case in large parts of white America, contact with people of color was in all likelihood rare, especially in any prolonged or meaningful sense, meaning that any representation would have primarily been based in mediated images.[4] As a consequence, Superman's alien origin highlights the conspicuous lack of diversity in his surroundings. The first nonwhite character to appear in his comic books had to wait two whole years, until *Action* #25 (June 1940). In that story, Superman encountered Medini, an exotified cliché of the turban-clad

© The Editor(s) (if applicable) and The Author(s) 2016
M. Lund, *Re-Constructing the Man of Steel*,
DOI 10.1007/978-3-319-42960-1_8

Eastern mystic, cut from the same popular stereotyped cloth as many other characters in the 1930s culture.[5] Medini was a charlatan who played up his difference for personal gain, using his hypnotic powers to enrich himself; the markers of his ethno-cultural Otherness were thereby employed to cast him as a complete social Other in Superman's USA.

In addition to Medini, there were only three appearances of nonwhites throughout the prewar era, none of which were allowed much in the way of individualism. In *Action* #29 (November 1940), Superman encountered Zolar, a one-dimensional "Arabic" mad scientist, who wanted to destroy the mysterious lost city of Ulonda, whose residents' single-panel appearance provides the story's only example of (pseudo-)individualized "Arabs." Zolar's henchmen, as well as most other "Arabs" encountered in the story, look the same. They are uniformly dressed in long, fluid tunics and keffiyeh. While their similar clothing had basis in reality, everything about them, even their facial hair, is stereotyped and, more importantly, identical. While not as overtly negative as the Hollywood stereotype, since only Zolar's henchmen are deeply, unreflexively evil, their identical appearance constitutes another example of the representational Orientalism common to the day.[6] Similarly, in *Superman* #11 (July–August 1941), Clark and Lois travel to South America to find the Chirroba, an indigenous tribe said to possess the cure to a mysterious disease that has struck Burroughs. The tribe's evil high priest conspires, in cooperation with a white man, to hold the USA ransom under the threat of a pandemic. The reporters and their companions are captured and sent to be tossed into a volcano. Challenging the captors in order to secure the group's freedom, Superman runs a (literal) gauntlet "thru a double-line of witch-doctors," well-armed and indistinguishable from one another, by which he effortlessly proves his superiority.[7] With the high priest defeated, the tribe's rightful chief, Wacouches, who had earlier been saved by Superman and touched by his civilizing hand, ascends to power and gives the travelers the cure they came for.

The final appearance of racial Others also occurs outside the USA, on "Pogo Island," where Lois and Clark are accosted by "superstitious natives" who have been told that the woman who owns a local plantation is a witch. When the uniformly bald and loin-clothed natives speak, it is either in a chorus of their word for witch, "Inga! Inga!," or in pseudo-pidgin English ("Spirit powerful bad medicine"). Misled by a white man disguised as their witch doctor, they capture Lois and her companions, who are again saved at the last moment by Superman.[8] Like the "Arabs" and Native South Americans above, the aboriginal Pogoans are stripped of agency and identity, serving, when it is revealed that the natives have been used to keep outsiders from finding the secret submarine base hidden on the island, only as a plot device in a story ultimately connected to the "undeclared war" in the Atlantic discussed above.

Both Siegel and Shuster were big fans of Tarzan, a series of books, movies, and a comic strip that, along with a powerful fantasy, promoted the vision of Edgar Rice Burroughs, a writer who believed in the "innate virtue of the 'Anglo-Saxon race'." Burroughs' stories told a white supremacist "romantic daydream on the idea that the high-born English baby dropped in the jungle would naturally come to master not only the beasts but black men also."[9] When Superman ventured into Pogo Island, Ulonda, or the South American jungle, these "exotic" places, his escapades also resembled those that filled the pages of "foreign adventure" pulps and, in so doing, reproduced the nativist sentiment they harbored, again chiefly the white supremacist idea that white men could easily master the primitive Other. By following these established conventions, Superman contributed to popular culture's pushing of the national frontier out to distant locations. This, in turn, helped create images of American racial solidarity that drew no explicit lines among "old stock" Americans and "new immigrants," which would have been desirable for his Jewish, racially inbetween, creators.[10] In this way, the early Superman's few ethnoracial Others serve as vehicles for a discourse similar to what author and English-scholar Toni Morrison has called "race talk," negative appraisals and representations of African Americans that can serve as a rite of passage into American culture, "on the backs of blacks."[11]

Arguably, Siegel and Shuster's portrayal of ethnoracial Others also constitutes a form of *symbolic annihilation*. This concept is used to "highlight the erasure of peoples in popular communication." As a concept, symbolic annihilation "points to the way in which poor media treatment can contribute to social disempowerment and in which symbolic absence in the media can erase groups and individuals from public consciousness."[12] Perhaps even more interesting than the above example in this connection is not what appears as mere outlines, but what is fully written out.

In *Superman* #10 (May–June, 1941), the "Dukalia–American Sports Festival," discussed above, takes place in Metropolis. As noted, Superman, who is attending the games as Clark Kent, becomes convinced that they are a front for "unamerican [sic] activities." With Karl Wolff, a Consul of the fictional nation Dukalia who resembles Hitler, about to make a speech,

Superman decides to lend an ear, "[a]nd if I don't like what he says...."
Wolff's racialized speech builds on the fears of Nazi designs on the USA
underlying the fifth column scare: "Present here is the flower of Dukalian
youth! You have seen them perform physical feats which no other human
beings can. Proof, I tell you, that we Dukalians are superior to any other
race or nation! *Proof that we are entitled to be the masters of America!*"[13]

Staying true to his unspoken promise, Superman issues a challenge
to the speaker: "Let's see how superior you *really* are!" Powerfully
putting the lie to the consul's speech, Superman then proceeds to
humiliate the Dukalian athletes and leave Wolff clinging to the top
of a flagpole. Through his actions here, Superman mimics a blow to
Nazi racial ideology delivered at the 1936 Berlin Olympics. There, a
symbolically significant victory was achieved when an African American
athlete, and a fellow Clevelander, named Jesse Owens had won four
gold medals and broke two world records.[14] But, when Owens' accom-
plishment is reconfigured as Superman's humiliation of the "superior"
Dukalians, the man Owens himself, his talent, and people of color as
a social group are all written out, replaced by Siegel and Shuster with
white Americanism.

THE WHITE STREETS OF METROPOLIS

Cleveland's Glenville neighborhood, where Siegel and Shuster lived when
they created Superman, was one of the city's two major Jewish areas of
second settlement; the Kinsman neighborhood was largely working class,
while Glenville, which in Siegel's formative years evinced great Jewish
social mobility, was home to a large cohort of the Americanized Jewish
middle class and a number of more recent immigrant arrivals.[15] The population was mostly of Siegel and Shuster's and their parents' generations,
the latter of which in general did not fight the Americanization of its children, while the former took being Jewish for granted and lived the life
of "average Americans." A common attitude of the day was that religion
was a private matter, when it was regarded as important at all, and Jewish
communal institutions increasingly identified themselves with a middle
class community.[16]

But, while the streets of Glenville did not look too different from
the streets represented on the silver screen or in magazines, they were
lined with Jewish businesses, community centers and organizations, and
synagogues.[17] According to Larry Tye, Siegel's "world" was a "Cleveland

neighborhood that was 70 percent Jewish, where theaters and newspapers were in Yiddish as well as English, and there were two dozen Orthodox synagogues to choose from but only one place – Weinberger's – to buy your favorite pulp fiction."[18] Siegel also experienced the double push and pull of Americanization and Jewishness in his Orthodox home. On the one hand, the Sabbath and high holy days were observed.[19] On the other hand, Siegel's mother was simultaneously very active in Jewish community affairs and "a proud American Jew [...] the kind who learned the language and how to get by, and who put on rouge, lipstick, and a hat to go to the grocer because you never knew who you'd run into – and she couldn't abide people like the Lifshitzes [her neighbors and later in-laws by Jerry] who hadn't adjusted."[20]

According to literary critic Erin A. Smith, language is one of the primary ways through which class, gender, and power hierarchies are (re) produced. The rarity of broken immigrant English or idiomatic working-class speech in Superman stories then similarly furthers a pattern of homogeneous representation by eliding another area of distinction. This also followed the Americanizing pattern of Jewish intergenerational exchange at the time; Yiddish was a language in decline, replaced by English in both home and in Americanizing public schooling, but still audible in the streets and in the Siegel home; Siegel's father had an accent, which apparently embarrassed his son.[21] The world Superman was born in, then, was vastly different from the one in which he lived.

Spatial representation in comics is not a simple matter. As Roland Barthes reminds us, "there is no drawing without style." Drawing is a learned skill, governed by rules and selective in what it represents. It is, in short, a coded practice.[22] Further, comics work through what comics creator and theorist Scott McCloud has called "amplification through simplification," which entails a stripping down of the image to focus on a particular aspect, allowing it to be both more intense and broader in its calls for reader identification.[23] Indeed, as comics scholar Julia Round has noted, "creating a comic is not a way of telling a story with illustrations that replicate the world it is set in, but a creation of that world from scratch."[24] I have argued elsewhere that this means that how a given comic constructs and arranges narrative and visual elements, how it constructs its sense of place, and what and who it includes or excludes are all important factors in how the comic imbues represented space with meaning and offers it to readers. Comics' spatial representation are never merely mimetic of material space, when they claim a real-world model, as

Siegel and Shuster originally did, but always symbolic, selective, and, if not always consciously, ideologically informed.[25]

The average resident of Superman's Cleveland and, later, Metropolis, is unmistakably white. In fact, following a broader pattern in liberal American representation, the USA's great diversity is almost entirely absent from Superman's world.[26] Hair colors come in brown, black, and blond, and there is a little variation in physical build and facial hair style, but little truly distinguishes any one person from another. Lois Lane is similarly largely indistinguishable from several other females: she is slim, beautiful, and toothsome, but remains shy of being overtly sexual; she is not blond, but her skin is fair.[27] Overall, however, the Metropolisian masses are mainly men, with women most often conspicuously absent even in the background. While a number of named minor characters are of a more advanced age and Superman repeatedly helps children, the median age is a diffuse working-age adulthood. A majority is dressed in suits and hats in conservative colors and simple patterns, and Clark Kent is almost compulsively dressed in a blue suit and tie. With fewer "men on the street" wearing jackets and caps, the nonwhite side of the "collar line" is rendered nearly non-visible. The prevalence of blue-collared men among the criminal element thus gives the impression that the city's law-abiding working class is small.[28] Further tying into the civic discourse that marked people as white and nonwhite on the basis of work and legal orientation, occupations are generally undisclosed or indiscernible when not serving narrative purposes, and, lastly, people are almost exclusively of two moral types: they are either upstanding citizens or willingly, even gleefully, involved in the nefarious and more often than not violent schemes that Superman regularly thwarts.[29]

To be sure, there are enough differences between Metropolisians to signify a Melting Pot society, especially in the naming of minor characters, with names originating, or vaguely sounding like they originated in, the Scandinavian (Carol and Emil Carlstrom, Morgan Thorgenson), Dutch (Karl van Breeden), Gaelic (Rufus Carnahan), and Anglo-Saxon (Farnsworth, Nelson, Lassiter) languages, among others. Even so, there are no markers of distinct religious or ethnic identity and few traces of Eastern European "new immigrants," as the sources of names suggests. Aside from a few select villains whose appearances tend toward the simian, visually branding them as degenerates,[30] there is only one truly notable example of divergence: Clark Kent.

Visually inspired by actor Harold Lloyd, but also partly modeled on Siegel and Shuster and on the men they saw in their predominantly Jewish Glenville surroundings, Clark stands out as an everyday-inspired contrast to the White Anglo-Saxon Protestants (WASP) heroes and he-men encountered in pop culture.[31] As will be discussed more in the next chapter, the Kent persona is an effeminate half-man, in a way perpetuating stereotypes about Jews by embodying a decidedly nega-tively positioned *nebbish*-type and deeply ingrained cultural tropes, such as his slouching posture, meek, even cowardly, demeanor, and his glasses, which are otherwise an uncommon accessory in Superman's surroundings.[32]

Conversely, Superman shares many traits with the white majority pro-totype and his alter ego, by being unable to reach the same heights, rein-forces the hero's general conformity to the unspoken norm by contrast. While vaguely ethnic in appearance, rather than conforming so strictly as to become as pure an embodiment of whiteness as the blond and blue-eyed Captain America, Superman has the features of a Hollywood star: broad shoulders, chiseled jaw, and near-perfect posture (as does Clark in the visuals; the physical difference between the two personas is mainly a matter of narration). According to film historian Giuliana Muscio, the Hollywood studio system in the 1930s promoted the mainly WASP stars as role models and downplayed ethnicity in their films to promote and (to a point) define a new national culture.[33] Thus, while possessing amazing powers, Superman manages to fit in with those whom he serves; he is both an everyman and a symbol of inherent human potential realized, with the power to take on the USA's problems.[34]

Smith also writes that hard-boiled detective stories, which Siegel "fiercely read" and emulated in serious and satirical high school writings, "were 'Americanizing' in that they hailed readers as normatively white, implicitly bourgeois, and male."[35] Superman's stories take this underly-ing assumption one step further and makes it part of the comics' world itself: the majority of Metropolis' population is able-bodied, white, male, and, importantly, middle class. Evoking the self-image of the USA as his-torically a country without a strict class order, one reporter stressed at the height of the Depression that "while some became very rich and others very poor, the sovereign authority rested with a great middle class, whom we like to term typical Americans."[36] Some early Superman stories, such as *Action* #3's above-cited mine-owner story, arguably had a working-class bias, but, as noted, this quickly disappeared.

In one of his earliest adventures (*Action #7*, December 1938), Superman indicates that the old myth of individual opportunity, of "pulling yourself up by your bootstraps," is still viable, albeit in a form slightly altered by hard times. A down-on-his luck self-made circus owner, beset by financial troubles caused by poor attendance despite the fact that she show is good, and by the selfish ambitions of a loan shark, concludes that he is about to "lose what it took my entire lifetime to build up!" Taking pity on the "[p]oor, brave old man" who, when "[f]aced with bitter disappointment and certain defeat," still has "the courage to keep up an optimistic front," Superman decides that he "deserves a break... And, by golly, that's just what I'm going to give him!"[37] Putting his allure as strongman at the owner's disposal, Superman quickly becomes the circus' main attraction. Ticket sales soar and the hero ensures the circus' continued security by stopping the loan shark's attempts to sabotage the revived business with potentially lethal "accidents."[38]

Superman's support of the circus speaks to a long-held belief in equal opportunity as inherent in US culture, while the loan shark and those who display similar heartless self-interest show how the individualism this fostered could go too far. In unmistakably New Deal-positive terms, historian Arthur M. Schlesinger, Sr. identified this way of thinking as a recent addition to the "American character" in 1943:

> In the cities the congested living quarters, the growing wretchedness of the poor, and the rise of difficult social problems also created doubts as to the sufficiency of the laissez-faire brand of democracy. Only the rich and the powerful seemed now to profit from the system of unbridled individualism. Though the solid core of ancient habit yielded stubbornly, the average man came gradually to believe that under the altered conditions it was the duty of the government of all to safeguard equal opportunity for all.[39]

Just as the New Deal's programs and policies had tried, Superman intervenes to ensure a level playing field by giving the owner "a break." But in the way he goes about doing this, Superman, like much other Depression culture, highlights the middle-class insecurities more than the destitution of the poor.[40] Siegel had personally known the middle-class life and had seen everything his father had built taken away by society's "lower" elements. The young writer's household had been financially comfortable enough that the Depression was not really felt until his father's death; the youngest Siegel had only rarely had to work in its early years.[41]

By individualizing the Depression's causes and effects and situating them within a middle-class framework, the worst realities of the times and their structural elements could be brushed aside in Superman's stories. Indeed, they would have to be, since class, or at least the deepest recesses of poverty, was also often a question of race. African Americans in particular had endured much lower average life standards long before their poverty was made visible during the Depression.[42] But, as Morris Dickstein notes when writing about representations of the general poverty and want of cotton pickers, which appeared as early as 1934 in John Steinbeck's fictional Californian Torgas Valley, it was "[t]he film version of *The Grapes of Wrath* in 1940 [that] made these living conditions far more widely known. Though the same conditions had affected Mexican and Filipino workers, it was the oppression and dreadful living conditions of *white* workers that would eventually arouse the national conscience."[43]

The near-complete absence of nonwhites and the overall conformity among whites in Superman's comics thus supports an Americanist interpretation: realistic representation of diversity and, with it, difference in class, race, and conditions, would introduce a complexity that could trigger irresolvable ambivalence in a fiction that was marked by a stark social dualism. For all of Shuster's later-claimed nostalgia for his Toronto childhood as a source for his world-building, and unlike severely Depression-struck, two-thirds-immigrant Cleveland, Superman's generically named Metropolis resembles the world created by Hollywood universalism which, as Muscio describes it, is

the trait of Hollywood classical cinema that conceals class and national cultural relations in the name of a cross-class message. Paradoxically, the simultaneous concealing of class and national traits ends up obscuring Americanism through its perfect assimilation in the Hollywood product, so American and so "classical" as to become a geographical abstraction – the nowhere land of dominant ideology.[44]

SUPERMAN AND AMERICAN ANTI-SEMITISM

According to historians Hasia Diner and Tony Michels, scholars of American Judaism have "quite dramatically" avoided the subject of American anti-Semitism, most often treating it within a framework of American exceptionalism that stresses how Jews in the country have overcome anti-Semitic obstacles.[45] The literature on Jews and comics displays a similar tendency;

only after introducing Superman with images of *Kristallnacht* does Weinstein acknowledge that "anti-Semitism was a sad part of American life, too." But his major focus continues to be on Superman as a response to Nazism.[46] Fingeroth, in turn, begins his book by noting that "[t]he creation of a legion of special beings, self-appointed to protect the weak, innocent, and victimized at a time when fascism was dominating the European continent from which the creators of the heroes hailed, seems like a task that Jews were uniquely positioned to take on."[47] In introducing Superman, he idealistically writes that there

> must have been a strange disconnect between the fact that, despite the history of persecution, despite the incontrovertible evidence of what was happening to Jews in Hitler's Germany, and the dread that the Father Coughlins and Charles Lindberghs of the world wanted to do something similar in America, the lives they lived as Jews in America was [sic] relatively free of overt, violent hatred, especially if they stayed within the confines of home and school.[48]

In examples like these, the gaze tends across the Atlantic, too fast dismissing US realities because they were not as overt and, as hindsight has shown, temporary.[49]

At the time of Superman's creation and throughout the period here discussed, however, American Jews were still unstable members of a racial culture dividing the country, further exacerbated by increasing native anti-Semitism from both sides of the "color line."[50] In a Jewish reading of the times, in which anti-Jewish thinking could take such a strong hold in "civilized Germany," it sometimes seemed likely that similar measures might also be enacted in the USA.[51] This was the case even in Cleveland, a city in which anti-Semitism was denounced by a large portion of the populace.[52]

Such fears had basis in reality. By 1924, in part through pressure exerted by a then-resurgent and influential Ku Klux Klan, America's borders had been all but closed to Jewish immigrants who were, by means of a stereotyped conception of Eastern European Jews ("the usual ghetto type"), condemned as "un-American" in the pejorative sense that they were represented as "*primordially unfit to become Americans*: that their physical and mental makeup and social characteristics were *inimical to American values and the American way of life*."[53] The American press sometimes even blamed Nazi anti-Semitic actions on Jews, at least until the belated realization of anti-Semitism's centrality to the ideology.[54] Jim

Crow, a system of racial segregation that was constantly and systematically reinforced in all areas of Southern life, as well as a high number of lynchings of blacks, showed that Americans were capable of radical and violent exclusion.[55] No less important, the 1915 lynching of Leo Frank, a Jewish man wrongfully accused of rape and murder, was a salient reminder that America was perhaps not a *goldene medina* (golden land) for Jews.[56]

According to Larry Tye, Siegel acknowledges in his memoir that his writing was strongly influenced by the anti-Semitism he saw and felt, and the German-American Bund sent threatening letters and picketed outside DC's offices. Naturally, the Nazi denunciation of Superman in 1940, discussed in Chap. 6, likely also affected the duo.[57] While the worst was still on the horizon when Superman was created, with demagogues like Father Coughlin, Fritz Kuhn, and too many others' attacks on imagined undue Jewish influence in the White House, American Jewry's supposed warmongering, or control of finance, growing anti-Semitism had been evident since the twenties and, after 1933, exploded into "unprecedented antisemitic [sic] fervor."[58] In April 1938, the same month that Superman first revealed himself to America, a Gallup poll showed that more than half of Americans believed German Jews to be the cause of their own distress. The month after, 20 percent said they wanted "to drive Jews out of the United States," and almost 25 percent wanted Jewish exclusion from government.[59] Surveys taken between 1940 and 1946 show that Jews were regarded as a greater menace to America's welfare than any other group.[60] For many American Jews, this, along with the harshness and insecurities of the Depression, strengthened the resolve to pursue Americanization over alienation so as to become white, inspiring them to act and express themselves in line with what was perceived as American.[61] After all, one of the privileges of whiteness is invisibility by virtue of belonging to the cultural center; little wonder then, that Siegel and Shuster's Superman gravitated toward it in a time like his present.

The minimal and paradoxically deracializing representation of alien Others and the symbolic annihilation of African Americans and other non-white American minorities in these comics was accompanied by an absence of any evidence of "the period's conventional anti-Semitism."[62] Siegel and Shuster's use of then-common racial tropes and representational strategies in Superman might have been a matter of unreflexive reproduction, but the lack of similar treatment of Jews, and the lack of Jewish representation to any readily apparent extent at all, for that matter, was likely a conscious evasion of anything that could be deleterious to Jewish acculturation or feed American anti-Semitism. It was, in effect, an instance of defensive symbolic annihilation. This evasiveness might signify a Jewish double consciousness on the creators' behalf, a sense of being fully American but not quite full participants in American life, and a practice that was mirrored elsewhere in Jewish American cultural production.[63] Worth noting in this connection is that a comic book that Siegel and Shuster made in 1933 included a strip called "The Pinkbaums," which poked light-hearted fun at a Jewish family at a dinner table; the contrast between that comic and their later Superman suggests that the increase in American anti-Semitism after the ascension of Hitler and the deepening of the economic crisis in the USA since had inspired the duo to be more careful in what they included in their work.[64]

Literary critic and cultural theorist John Michael writes that "identity in the United States has frequently taken shape and shifted in moments of crisis marked by a constitutive conflict between a national promise of justice and those who indicate or embody the injured identities that prove that the nation has failed to make that promise good."[65] Superman's extreme Americanness can be regarded as the result of such a failure, with increasing anti-Semitism starkly contrasting with the promises of the New Deal's "consistently inclusionary ethos." A tragic irony of racism is that, in at least one paradoxical sense, it does not discriminate. Anti-Semitism, especially fervent in the years before WWII, holds that "a Jew is a Jew is a Jew," no matter how the individual perceives of him- or herself. Superman's creators were thus inescapably at risk of being branded as outsiders, even as they were trying to belong.[66] In that capacity, however, they did not sit idly by on the sidelines hoping for inclusion. Rather, they put their patriotism on display and presented an America where they could fit in perfectly.[67]

This was not a new strategy. According to journalist and historian Neal Gabler, the Hollywood moguls were assimilationist Jews who saw in the movies an "ingenious option" to counter nativist resistance to Jewish assimilation: "Within the studios and on the screen, the Jews could simply create a new country – an empire of their own, so to speak – one where they would not only be admitted, but would govern as well."[68] Superman emphasized ideology over ethnicity in his fight for truth, justice, and, as the radio serial would later add, "the American Way." Through this emphasis, Siegel and Shuster could try to dismiss what differences existed between Jewish Americans and the cultural center as insignificant and attempt "normalization" of Jews *in absentia*. In the process, however, they largely removed the option of ethno-culturally marking their work in any explicit way.

NOTES

1. Cf. Muscio, *Hollywood's New Deal*, 2.
2. Cf. Strömberg, *Black Images, Jewish Images, Comic Propaganda*.
3. Cf. Welky, *Everything Was Better*, 142: "Although it showed the lower class more than many publications, the comic offered a world almost exclusively populated by WASPy whites, who not coincidentally accounted for the bulk of comic book sales. Not one African American appeared in the prewar issues of *Superman* or *Action Comics*. Although a few stories included native peoples, they did not have developed personalities and acted chiefly as colorful backdrops for Superman's exploits." One notable exception appears in the Sunday strip, where a stereotypically thick-lipped, Ebonics-speaking, and superstitious server appears in Siegel and Shuster, *Sunday Classics*, 43–44.
4. Cf. Baden, "Residual Neighbors," pt. 1; Jones, *Men of Tomorrow*, 25.
5. *SC3*, 112–25; cf. Dickstein, *Dancing in the Dark*, 282; Jones, *Men of Tomorrow*, 29.
6. *SC4*, 113–26; cf. Shaheen, *Reel Bad Arabs*; Said, *Orientalism*; Michael, *Identity and the Failure of America*, 235–39.
7. *SC6*, 123–35.
8. *SC7*, 6–18.
9. Jones, *Men of Tomorrow*, 70–71, 75–77; De Haven, *Our Hero*, 31, 33–34; Ricca, *Super Boys*, 43–46; Kasson, *Perfect Man*, 157–218; cf. McCann, *Gumshoe America*, 63; Chambliss and Svitavsky, "Pulp to Superhero," 8–11.
10. Cf. McCann, *Gumshoe America*, 64; Wright, *Comic Book Nation*, 36–37.
11. Morrison, "On the Backs of Blacks"; see also Brodkin, *How Jews Became White*, 151–53.
12. Coleman and Yochim, "Symbolic Annihilation."
13. *SC6*, 43–44. Emphasis added.
14. Lipstadt, *Beyond Belief*, 83–84; Ricca, *Super Boys*, 92–93, 183–84.
15. Rubinstein, *Merging Traditions*, 163.

16. Gartner, *Jews of Cleveland*, 294–96; Baden, "Residual Neighbors," 19–20; Neusner, *Judaism in Modern Times*, 207–8; Glazer, *American Judaism*, chap. VI. There were, of course, powerful countercurrents.

17. Cf. Rubinstein, *Merging Traditions*, chap. 4; Tye, *Superman*, 76–77; Ricca, *Super Boys*, 20–21.

18. Tye, *Superman*, 48; cf. Ricca, *Super Boys*, 20–21; Jones, *Men of Tomorrow*, 25–26.

19. Cf. Ricca, *Super Boys*, 59, 92.

20. Tye, *Superman*, 47–48, 77–78; cf. Ricca, *Super Boys*, 199.

21. Cf. Smith, *Hard-Boiled*, 68–71, chap. 5; Roediger, *Working toward Whiteness*, 193–95; Dollinger, "Jewish Identities in 20th-Century America," 148–49; Ricca, *Super Boys*, 53.

22. Barthes, *Image, Music, Text*, 43.

23. McCloud, *Understanding Comics*, 24–59.

24. Round, "Hunting Wippers," 196.

25. Lund, "NY 101"; "'X Marks the Spot.'" I am, of course, writing in these articles about "real" New York spaces represented in comics. Nonetheless, the general principles of what I say are applicable also to the creation of imagined spaces.

26. Cf. Gerstle, "Protean Character," 1068–69.

27. Cf. *SC1*, 25, 37; *SC2*, 113, 120–21, 190; *SC3*, 19.

28. On representations of class and clothing, see Smith, *Hard-Boiled*, chap. 4.

29. Cf. Brodkin, *How Jews Became White*, esp. p. 101.

30. Cf. Chambliss and Svitavsky, "Pulp to Superhero," 9–10.

31. Cf. De Haven, *Our Hero*, 37–38; Tye, *Superman*, 20; Andrae, Blum, and Coddington, "Supermen and Kids," 12.

32. Goldstein, "Unstable Other," 389; Sarna, *American Judaism*, 212, 265; Wenger, *History Lessons*, chap. 3.

33. Muscio, *Hollywood's New Deal*.

34. Cf. Welky, *Everything Was Better*, 134: "Like Steinbeck's Tom Joad or Capra's Jefferson Smith, he [Superman] was an average-looking man who did great things, a vivid expression of the every-day American riled [sic] in support of a just cause."

35. Smith, *Hard-Boiled*, 76; Ricca, *Super Boys*, 33–36, 49–52.

36. Quoted in Dickstein, *Dancing in the Dark*, 218.

37. *SC1*, 86–87.

38. Similar stories reprinted in Siegel and Shuster, *Sunday Classics*, 3–11, 73–87.
39. Schlesinger, "This New Man," 243.
40. Dickstein, *Dancing in the Dark*, xxi.
41. Jones, *Men of Tomorrow*, 38–39; Ricca, *Super Boys*, 21–22.
42. Dickstein, *Dancing in the Dark*, chap. 6; Kennedy, *Freedom from Fear*, 18–19, 168; Takaki, *Different Mirror*, chap. 13.
43. Dickstein, *Dancing in the Dark*, 78–79. Emphasis in original.
44. Muscio, *Hollywood's New Deal*, 67; Polenberg, *One Nation Divisible*, 35.
45. Diner and Michels, "Considering American Jewish History," 9.
46. Weiner, "Review of Up, Up and Oy Vey!," 22.
47. Fingeroth, *Disguised as Clark Kent*, 17.
48. Fingeroth, *Disguised as Clark Kent*, 39–40.
49. Cf. Novick, *Holocaust in American Life*, 41: "In retrospect, it is clear that American anti-Semitism, though broad, was relatively shallow; otherwise, it could not have declined as precipitously as it did after 1945. But this, of course, was unknown to Jews during the war."
50. Goldstein, *Price of Whiteness*, chaps. 7–8; Lester, "Outsiders," esp. p. 76.
51. Goldstein, *Price of Whiteness*, 185; cf. Kennedy, *Freedom from Fear*, 237–38, 255; MacDonnell, *Insidious Foes*, chap. 2.
52. Gartner, *Jews of Cleveland*, 298–303.
53. Lederhendler, *Jewish Responses*, 108–9 (emphasis in original); cf. Arad, *Rise of Nazism*, 62–65; Sarna, *American Judaism*, 214–20; Miller, *New World Coming*, chap. 7; McCann, *Gumshoe America*, chap. 1.
54. Lipstadt, *Beyond Belief*, 1–131, passim.
55. Jim Crow is identified as one of the twentieth century's three "overtly racist regimes" in Fredrickson, *Racism*.
56. Cf. Sarna, *American Judaism*, 216; Levy, "A White Man?"
57. Tye, *Superman*, 67, 78–79.
58. Dinnerstein, *Antisemitism in America*, chap. 6 (quote from p. 105); Lipstadt, *Beyond Belief*, 127; Shogan, *Prelude to Catastrophe*, 108–9.
59. Dollinger, *Quest for Inclusion*, 61.
60. Lipstadt, *Beyond Belief*, 127.

61. Goldstein, *Price of Whiteness*, 146, 189; Arad, *Rise of Nazism*, 70, 193; Lederhendler, *Jewish Responses*, 113.
62. McCann, *Gumshoe America*, 80.
63. Cf. Prell, *Fighting to Become Americans*, 127, 163–65; Brodkin, *How Jews Became White*, esp. 1–2.
64. Ricca, *Super Boys*, 87; Dinnerstein, *Antisemitism in America*, chap. 6.
65. Michael, *Identity and the Failure of America*, 4; Lederhendler, *Jewish Responses*, 116, 121, 128; Arad, *Rise of Nazism*, 222.
66. Cf. Sarna, *American Judaism*, 214–15.
67. An interesting measure of their success: Superman's upper-body centered physique would contribute to the construction of wartime masculinity according to Jarvis, *Male Body at War*, 52–53.
68. Gabler, *Empire of Their Own*, 4–6; cf. Wenger, *History Lessons*; Brodkin, *How Jews Became White*, 155–59.

CHAPTER 9

Of Men and Superman

Superman's heroism, dedication, and appearance were all configured around a widely circulated cultural symbol of the day: the idea of the "Superman."[1] In this case, the "super" can be read as modifying the "man"; it indicates a spectacular, even aggressive, hypertrophied masculinity that is unique to him only insofar as it is made so explicit. Going about his work, Superman does not hesitate to be heavy-handed. Beyond simply landing punches, he tosses and juggles criminals, at one point even using one man as a human javelin.[2] Almost too often to count, he snatches his foes from the ground and carries them either directly to the law or into a dangerous situation where they can be persuaded to confess.[3] Initially, he even killed offenders by commission, for example, tossing them out a window or, once, by throwing an airplane at them [sic!].[4] He also caused deaths by omission, like when he dispassionately watched a war profiteer choke to death on poison gas.[5] After a policy directive banned killing so as to not risk alienating the audience, Superman's lethal streak was generally sublimated into contemplative actions.[6] In a mid-1940 World's Fair comic book, he saves some villains from choking, noting that "the gas doesn't affect me – but I'll have to act quickly to save *them*! They don't deserve saving – but it's better they pay the law's penalty for their crimes!"[7]

Overall, this Superman's imagination is highly physical in orientation: his solution to lacking road safety is to smash offending cars, a solution also applied to the unfair practices of a taxi cartel. Gambling, one of the

© The Editor(s) (if applicable) and The Author(s) 2016
M. Lund, *Re-Constructing the Man of Steel*,
DOI 10.1007/978-3-319-42960-1_9

most "vicious" evils, is remedied in the same way on three occasions, with Superman breaking the slot machines and gaming tables.[8] A verbal viciousness supplements this physical violence: in *Action* #1, Superman instructs a munitions magnate to be on a ship out of the country by the morning or, he says, "I swear I'll follow you to whatever hole you hide in, and tear out your cruel heart with my bare hands," while another war profiteer, reluctant to hand over the stolen formula for a dangerous gas, is told that he should not "quibble" since "[c]racking your head like an egg shell will be a messy job, but if you insist on being stubborn...."[9] Time after time, Superman underscores his seriousness by telling his foes how easy it would be for him to drop them, crush them, or break their necks.[10] In other cases, his speech is more arrogant than vicious, displaying smug superiority instead. After faking his death in front of a firing squad in one early issue, he gets up and lets them try again; as the second harmless barrage of bullets strikes, he quips "[h]o-hum! This is starting to bore me!"[11] Nobody who tries to shoot or harm him in other ways has any luck, and few are spared his ostensible wit.

In Superman's case, the clothes do make the man in a palpable way, since this conduct is only displayed when he is in costume. When not out helping the oppressed, Superman works a day job at a newspaper, sought out for its promise of readily available leads. Under the assumed secret identity of reporter Clark Kent, he affects an attitude of cowardice. This elaborate masquerade is one that Superman clearly does not relish, often reminding readers that it is a façade which, on occasion, he almost forgets to maintain.[12] Kent is Superman's pointed caricature of the unmasculine and, thus, the undesirable. When forced to act without time for a costume change, Superman is afraid that he will be found out. Having uncharacteristically acted courageously as Kent in *Superman* #5 (Summer 1940), he pretends to faint in order to throw Lois Lane and a bystander off. Having "regained consciousness" he asks, with feigned incredulity: "You mean, I – I actually risked my life? I must have been out of my mind!"[13]

Superman's masculinity and its Kentian inverse extend to his relationships with women. When Lois agrees to go out with Clark in order to scoop him on an interview with Superman (*Action* #6, November 1938), she thinks how easily she can twist him around her finger. Pretending to be unaware of her deception, Clark walks away in feigned happiness, thinking in turn "[h]ow easy you are to convince that I'm putty in your hands."[14] In *Action* #9 (February 1939), Lois tells Clark in no uncertain terms how she despises him: "I absolutely *loathe* you! Your contemptible weakling! – Don't you dare even to talk to me any more! [sic]" She then confesses that she is in love with Superman and Clark appears crestfallen. As soon as he is alone, however, the secret Superman displays his true reaction. He is not sad, he is playing a game: "[O]nce the door is shut behind him, an amazing thing occurs – his woeful expression disappears! He clutches his sides and doubles! Then shrieks with – *laughter!*"[15]

Part of the reason for Superman's hypermasculine characterization was undoubtedly the pleasure of so much destruction and action but, as will be discussed below, there was also a personal and an intertextual dimension. So too can the series' framing of desirable gender roles be traced to both autobiographical experience and common tropes in American culture and in Jewish American history.

A SUPERMAN AND HIS PERPETUAL DAMSEL

Most accounts describe Sarah Siegel, Jerry's mother and closest female role model, as a strong woman and matriarch who did not approve of her son's writerly aspirations, all of which might have affected how he wrote female characters.[16] According to literary critic Riv-Ellen Prell, Jewish men's representations of Jewish women in negative ways in twentieth-century USA can be regarded as projections of anxieties about assimilation or an avenue of escape from the Old World and its ethnically marked vestiges. In Prell's strongly worded description of the conflict between generations, "[c]hildren's loathing for their Jewish parents and Jewish women's and men's loathing for one another are some of the legacies of Americanization."[17] Prell also points out that intercultural stereotypes shape intra-cultural ones, which is to say that non-Jewish representations of Jews affect how Jews represent Jews, but the inverse is likely to also occur; Jewish men's stereotypes about Jewish women are likely to have at least some measure of influence on how Jewish men represent non-Jewish women.[18]

The political culture of the New Deal era was not gender-blind, but contained a form of government-sanctioned backlash. The administration attempted to remove women from the workforce and replace them with men. One government slogan aimed at women simply read: "Don't take a job from a man!"[19] Married women, Jewish and non-Jewish, accepted that women worked only out of economic necessity while the man was the wage earner. This was a middle-class norm, desirable for Americanizing Jews.[20] Further, stereotypes about Jewish women had often represented them as garish, too forward, and overly assertive. Stereotyped Jewish women had a wrongful sense of entitlement to the pleasures of freedom and consumption, and a "natural" desire for dominance and power. These traits were often coupled with a pursuit of romance that helped create the stereotype of a young Jewish woman set on success and in search of romance and marriage.[21] While Jewish self-representation between 1935 and 1945 witnessed a sharp decrease in intra-communal gender stereotyping, transposed versions of these stereotypes, along with the New Deal's appeals for female withdrawal, appear to have been filtered in some small way into the character of Lois, who was by no measure a decorous bourgeois woman of the type Siegel's mother represented.[22]

Siegel's representation of women also recalled historical precedent. Feminist scholar Susan Faludi argues that a type of "monomythic" narrative has recurred in the USA "at pivotal moments in our cultural life extending back to the Puritans," responding to crises by reverting to simple masculine hero-narratives that emphasize a discursive potency and mask a substantial impotence. As Faludi explains, Americans restore "our faith in our own invincibility through fables of female peril and the rescue of 'just one young girl'."[23] Presented in the form of both fiction and history, albeit selectively read and amended, strong men save weak women who cannot do so themselves. Because of their tastes in pop-cultural consumption, Siegel and Shuster would have repeatedly received the representations common to the times' majority cultural gender formation. Pop culture had in those days been so willing to adapt the convention that writer Nathaniel West's novel *A Cool Million* (1934), a satire of Horatio Alger that repeatedly sniped at contemporary pop culture, included an over-the-top version of the familiar "pure but endlessly beleaguered maiden of all popular serials, whose repeated rape, abuse, and enslavement [in West's exaggerated version] run parallel to the hero's dismemberment."[24] Of course, neither Lois' actions nor, especially, her outspoken contempt for Clark, endow her with the purity of her sister damsels, which was perhaps a result of her creators' own fears and experiences of rejection, but there can be no doubt that she too is endlessly beleaguered.[25]

The kidnapping of Lois in *Action* #1 that opened this book certainly seems an example of the type of "monomythic" storytelling Faludi writes about: the way it plays out, itself appearing as a throwback to the "captivity narratives" of frontier times,[26] makes the discourse of ambiguous masculinity and the relegation of women into victimhood explicit. Little changed over the years. Lois is brash and superficial, often double-crosses Clark to get a scoop, and repeatedly goes against the "better judgment" of Clark or her superiors, thereby courting disaster. In other cases, if less frequent but equally contrived, Lois is not positioned as the sole cause of her own distress. Whatever the reason, however, she invariably winds up in danger, saved at the last moment by Superman, the cycle of danger and rescue repeating ad nauseam.[27]

Cinema was somewhat different in this regard. Anxiety over masculinity and gender roles in the 1930s fostered what one scholar has dubbed *femmes fortes,* "swaggering gender benders" who often claimed the "prerogatives of men" but always ended up domesticated or lonely in the final reel, as "the less entertaining lesson of their comeuppance."[28] Lois plays both roles, damsel and *femme forte,* throughout the early years of Superman. After (or during) her rescue, Superman always lets Lois know where the fault lies. Commenting on her willfulness with a representative air of superiority and condescension in *New York World's Fair Comics* (1940), Superman glibly asks a bound and gagged Lois: "Haven't I warned you before about your habit of always getting into dangerous scrapes?"[29]

But the most explicit example of Lois being deemed unfit to care for herself appears in *Superman* #10: the first page ends with Clark having "a hunch – and a strong one at that – that Lois is about to engage in her favorite sport...getting into trouble!" Two pages later, Lois indeed finds herself trapped in a laundry basket and about to be drowned. Saving her, again, Superman muses that "[t]he most amazing thing about this whole experience is that, for once, Lois is where she can't venture into further mischief – in this basket! But...it's too good to last." Upon being freed, Lois is told that she "[b]etter be careful! Next time I may not be around when you need me!" Against this, and against what regular readers know to expect, Lois asserts that she is "not so completely helpless as you seem to think!" Immediately afterwards, however, she gets into another pickle: she is hypnotized and sent to kill Clark, her brashness here putting not only herself, but also, potentially, innocent people, in jeopardy.[30]

While Lois is doubtlessly a strong character, she is positioned not as a role model but a plot device, there for Superman to save and to chastise.[31] Because of the contextual and intertextual focus of this study, the discussion of Lois cannot go deeper into how she is, in a sense, written out of the story and into a sort of nonexistence (although such an analysis would be most welcome). This erasure is not surprising since the subject of "universal 'human nature'" has been almost exclusively white, male, and middle class since the Enlightenment, whereas women have only rarely been represented as subjects in their own right.[32] What must be noted, however, is that allowing her subjectivity or, worse, competence independent of the hero, carried the potential of forcing the realization that Superman and many of his readers "belong to the sex that rapes and abuses, that rationalizes its own tendency to violence, that cannot clean up after itself, that whines about any loss of prerogatives, and that *constantly disparages women and any of its own members that are perceived to be womanish.*"[33]

More important to note here is the way in which Lois' femininity is constructed; she is, in a way, marked as nonwhite because of her sense of entitlement and her independence, displays of a lack in "female" temperament. The 1920s had seen the rise of the Jewish Ghetto Girl stereotype, a loud, ostentatious, independent Jewish woman who was perceived to endanger Jewish Americanization because of her flawed understanding of her proper place and of the rules of American life. Thus, Prell writes, "Americanization required that men and women distance themselves from their undesirable former selves. [...] The process seemed to require them to differentiate themselves from some other group or gender of Jews. To distance oneself from a vulgar, noisy Jewish woman was another way to assert one's status as an American."[34]

As anthropologist Karen Brodkin has pointed out, US civic discourse on race has often partly hinged on the idea that different races have different genders and rested on the association of female virtue with heterosexual domestic dependency on a man. "White women were by presumption good women," and either did not work for wages or did so in a way that preserved their femininity and respectability.[35] In this light, Superman's disciplining of Lois can perhaps be regarded as a form of race talk, but even more as a lesson well-learned by her writer, who repeatedly has his hero attempt to whiten her; Lois must be disciplined into her proper social position before she can be accepted as a proper mate.

This is perhaps best illustrated in the unpublished, above-mentioned 1940 "K-metal" story. The script would have caused Superman to reveal himself to Lois and enter into a romantic partnership with her. But this was not the same Lois: she was suddenly sympathetic, "transformed" from a "shallow, shrewish" girl into an "admiring partner."[36] Siegel wrote the script shortly after getting married, so the attempted shift might have been caused by matrimonial bliss or some other reconsideration of femininity. The existing formula worked, however, and the higher-ups probably did not want to risk losing money on a proven success, so the story never appeared, and the status quo ante resumed.[37]

Manifest in Superman's conduct toward Lois is either a streak of misogyny or, at the very least, an air of paternalism toward the "weaker sex" (except for when Superman is left to take care of a baby and she is suddenly needed for her seemingly "natural" expertise[38]). Other women fared no better. In *Superman* #11 (July–August 1941), Superman saves Patricia Randall, heiress to a retail fortune, from being tied down in marriage to a man marked as nonwhite by his un-chivalrous and criminal conduct. "Count" Bergac, her shady suitor (in fact nothing but a "smart convict"), courts Patricia in order to secure the board of her company continued free rein in their "grafting activities." Superman intervenes and secretly transforms the courtship into a comedy of errors. The narrative takes a morbid twist when Bergac replaces Patricia with a doppelganger and arranges to have the real heiress thrown out of an airplane. Superman resolves the issue without undue loss of life (the only people hurt being the kidnappers, who crash to a fiery death that "they brought [...] upon themselves!").[39] It all ends well, then: Patricia takes control of the company and fires the corrupt board. Unlike Lois' troublesome initiative, however, Patricia's ascension and assertiveness are not to be feared; she bears no responsibility for it herself but, as she points out, owes it all to Superman.[40]

Little else should be expected: Superman displays a sense of the "proper" place and conduct of man and woman from the very start. The clearest examples of Superman's adherence to established gender roles can be found in the stories where wealthy socialites whose unruly children have to be set straight enlist his help. In the first case (*Action* #24, May 1940), Superman promises a dying millionaire that he will make a man out of Peter, his "weak-kneed sop and spendthrift" of a son. When Peter is framed for murder, Superman stops him from taking the easy way out by committing suicide and forces him to face his accusers. By the time Peter is exonerated, with Superman's help, he has undergone a transformation; gone is the irresponsible man-child, replaced by a real, responsible, man who wants to "establish a home for wayward underprivileged children," to keep others from walking in his own errant footsteps.[41]

In the second story (*Action* #40, September 1941), billionaire Morgan Thorgenson asks Superman to "straighten out" his daughter Nancy, who also embodies vestigial traits of the Ghetto Girl: "The girl's stubborn, foolhardy – spends money like it was water, gets into countless scrapes," Thorgenson says.[42] She is desire-driven and autonomous, completely lacking in bourgeois femininity. Despite attempts by Superman to "handle" Nancy, she finally comes around of her own accord. When a flood strikes,

Superman rushes off to dig a ditch to divert the water. Upon returning to the Thorgenson mansion, he finds Nancy caring for flood victims until she passes out from exhaustion, a real (white) woman at last.[43] Both these stories have the same basic structure, the same main conflict, and resolutions that tap into New Deal collectivism with their conversions from self-indulgence to selflessness. They are also undeniably "traditional" in the assignation of gender roles that were common aspirations among Jewish Americans: Peter becomes a provider while Nancy becomes a nurturer, devoting herself to aiding unfortunates. "I've learned that there are more important things in life than night clubs and selfish living," she says, affirming the gendered political and pop cultures of the day.[44]

SUPER-MASCULINITIES

In *Superman* #5 (Summer 1940), when the *Daily Planet* becomes embroiled in a street war with a competing newspaper owned by a corrupt politician, Clark fails to stand up to an aggressive rival. Meekly, he tries to explain why, as he slinks after his partner: "But, Lois – he was twice my size! Surely you didn't expect me to...[sic]." Before he can finish, Lois cuts in: "[B]ehave like a normal, red-blooded he-man? You? *NO!!*"[45] Nonetheless, the editor values Clark above Lois. She, the willful employee who has repeatedly shown initiative (if in hindsight always, inevitably, misguided) is told to stay in the office, since "it's too dangerous!" Clark, notwithstanding his proven cowardice, is sent back on the streets to get some "*red hot news.*" He responds predictably: "*Me,* go out on the – the streets, *NOW?* – (Gulp!) – okay!" Out of the others' sight, however, the tune changes: narration tells us that "[i]n a deserted spot near the *Planet* building, the meek reporter doffs his outer garments, transforming himself into daring *SUPERMAN!*" The hero stresses the rightness of his way, saying that "[t]he *Planet's* too conservative a newspaper to hire thugs to fight back, – so there's nothing left but for me to appoint myself its defender!"[46]

Superman here represents two conflicting visions of manhood: an activist, masculine, physical man, and a passive, feminized, cowardly man. Elsewhere, this distinction is on occasion made fully explicit: during an air raid in *Action* #22 (March 1940), narration emphasizes that "[a]dhering to his false attitude of cowardliness, Clark dives for cover under a nearby table." After changing identities, the hero unequivocally spells out the difference between Superman and his alter ego, by actually screaming that

"*Superman acts!*"[47] This was a feature present from the start: faced with Butch Matson in *Action* #1, the feebly protesting Clark, reluctant to act, gets pushed aside and is emasculated by Lois, who calls him "a spineless, unbearable *COWARD!*"[48] Superman, on the other hand, shakes the kidnappers' car like a man possessed and hunts them down as they flee. The panel in which this happened was featured in a blown-up version on the cover of the issue, and Brad Ricca suggests that it was a reason for its selling so well: "In the strongman world, muscle men had been trying to lift cars for years; it was the ultimate expression of man resisting the onslaught of modern machinery. But no one could do it," before Superman.[49]

By the time of the New Deal, masculinity was in crisis. Faced with deskilling, mechanization, and urbanization, white male privilege seemed fast eroding, and many men could not live up to their "traditional" roles as providers. Pride kept many from accepting charity or asking for help during the Depression and many fathers left their families, either in search of a wage or for more selfish reasons.[50] Personally, from his father's death, Siegel knew well what terrible price failing strength could exact from a man and what want could bring another to do; Ricca even suggests that Superman is Siegel's working-through of his father's inability to handle the robbery and a psychological ghost perpetually resurrected by the son.[51]

Hard-boiled fiction and other pulps overcompensated to the "crisis" with "anxiously overdone manliness."[52] Siegel and Shuster's Superman arguably also carries out his mission in an "overdone" manner, but he also conforms to the New Deal's masculine ideal of the "selfless public servant whose 'satisfaction derived from sinking individual effort into the community itself, the common goal and the common end'," and who was, as he says himself, "not interested in glory."[53] His characterization also contains more than a kernel of the "man controlling his environment," anticipating what Faludi regards as the prevailing postwar image of masculinity, according to which a man is supposed to prove himself, "not by being part of society but by being untouched by it, soaring above it [...] travel[ing] unfettered, beyond society's clutches, alone–making or breaking whatever or whoever crosses his path. [...] He's a man because he won't be stopped."[54] Superman acts like a "normal, red-blooded heman" while his alter ego is something other, less than a "real" man, and a critique of the "weakness" ostensibly so widespread among men in the 1930s.[55] As has been seen throughout this book, transforming from one to the other allows Superman to defy "the full technological power of the modern world [...] organized crime, governmental corruption, greedy businessmen, and enemy armies: everything that could make a man feel powerless in the mid-twentieth century."[56]

However, Superman's dual identity has also been said to stem from his creators' Jewishness and to serve as a means of negotiating supposedly conflicting identities. In Larry Tye's stereotyped description, "Clark and Superman lived the way most newly arrived Jews did, torn between their Old and New World identities and their mild exteriors and rock-solid cores. That split personality was the only way he could survive, yet it gave him *perpetual angst. You can't get more Jewish than that.*"[57] Further, Harry Brod has claimed that

> [t]he ridiculed personality that Clark Kent sheds when he casts off his street clothes is a gendered stereotype of Jewish inferiority. Superman exists to counter the notion that strength or manliness and Jewishness are incompatible. [...] It is the combination of Superman's invincibleness and the nebbish-like characterization of Clark Kent that makes Superman such a Jewish character. [...] In the Old Country of Eastern Europe [sic], the gentle ideal of Jewish masculinity came into being in the same breath as its opposing counterpart. [...] Clark's Jewish-seeming nerdiness and Superman's non-Jewish-seeming hypermasculinity are two sides of the same coin, the accentuated Jewish male stereotype and its exaggerated stereotypical [hypermasculine non-Jewish] counterpart.[58]

Brod also writes that "Superman sees 'mortal men' as the world sees Clark, which is essentially how the anti-Semitic world sees Jewish men. His [Superman's] wish for Lois to fall in love with Clark is then the revenge of the Jewish nerd for the world's anti-Semitism."[59] This last judgment of Brod's, however, is based in part on an overinterpretation of Siegel's claim to have fantasized that if he were "real terrific," the girls he had crushes on might notice him, and in part on a partial and Judeocentrically overdetermined reading of Jules Feiffer, that stops short of mentioning that Feiffer regarded Clark as "a control for Superman [...] marking the difference between a sissy and a man."[60]

It is here important to consider the Clark/Superman duality's genderedness and its bully dynamic, not least since Siegel's above-quoted claim traces the origin of the trope to experiences in a largely Jewish student body.[61] As Yiddishist and Jewish studies scholar Eddy Portnoy points out in his review of Brod's book, "[t]hat Jews were often historical victims isn't particularly relevant to Siegel and Shuster's own victimhood:

their social haplessness occurred within a mostly Jewish world."[62] That there is a personal basis for Siegel and Shuster's representation is evident from the full discussion that Brod quotes in part, which continues with Siegel saying that "the concept came to me that Superman could have a dual identity, and that in one of his identities he could be meek and mild, as I was, and wear glasses, the way I do."[63] According to Tye's own earlier summary of Siegel's autobiographical self-description, he was awkward and shy for most of his youth, a loner who felt victimized by bullies from an early age and had a "giant sized inferiority complex"; Shuster was even more "sheepish and sweet".[64]

Siegel has summarized his thinking about his creation's dual identity: "Secretly, I kind of enjoyed the thought that women, who just didn't care at all about somebody like Clark Kent, would go ape over Superman. I enjoyed the fact that he wasn't at all affected by their admiration. When you come down to it, some of the greatest lovers of all time simply aren't that crazy about women: It's the women who are crazy about them."[65] English scholar Eric Berlatsky is worth quoting at length here, about the Superman/Clark/Lois love triangle:

> Kent is in love with Lois (or claims to be) and perpetually wishes, at the very least, to take her on a date, while Lois, of course, falls for Superman, the "he-man" that appears to be everything Clark is not. Just as Lois rebuffs all of Clark's advances, however, Superman rejects hers, taking a kind of perverse pleasure in revenge for her mistreatment of his "other self" and laughing at her behind her back. [...] There is a kind of "perverse" pleasure achieved through Superman's perpetual scorning of Lois (and Lois' of Clark).

Tying these ideas to the Siegel interview quoted above, Berlatsky further notes that, if Superman was "wish-fulfillment" for Siegel and for those readers who were "similarly frustrated," "the 'wish' that seems to be granted is the assertion of power over women, in which they become a toy to be played with, mocked, and manipulated, as 'revenge' for failing to notice the 'super' qualities hidden underneath the modest, weak, and introverted exterior (qualities which, of course, may not exist for Superman's real-life readers and counterparts)."[66]

Brod and Tye both locate the origins of the dual identity in an Eastern Europe that Siegel and Shuster never knew, and neither considers that a reconfiguration could have occurred within America's borders. A new ideal of Jewish masculinity was indeed being promoted in the USA at this time, one that adopted key traits of American manhood and reached back in Jewish history for male role models. As Beth Wenger summarizes, in a way that fits Superman, the new Jewish American man was discursively constructed as having been "remade by America's freedoms," and was "not only physically strong and capable, unlike his European forebears, but also fiercely loyal to his adopted homeland and willing to defend it."[67] Further, Jewish American veterans and athletes – boxers in particular – had since the late 1800s helped promote images of strong, fighting American Jews as a means of combating anti-Semitism and the image of the weak, effeminate Jew as an easy victim. Jews were "the dominant ethnic group" in boxing in the first half of the twentieth century, and Jewish boxers earned 30 world championships between 1910 and 1940.[68] There were also Jewish strongmen like Siegmund Breitbart and Joseph Greenstein touring the country in the 1920s and 1930s, putting the lie to the idea that Jews were "milquetoasts," to use Tye's word; Shuster, as an aspiring bodybuilder, knew of, admired, and was inspired by these men.[69]

Indeed, Superman's masculinities appear to also owe much to pop culture. Clark is certainly a caricature, but one more similar to the alter egos of the Scarlet Pimpernel, Zorro, and the Shadow, all of whom Siegel is known to have encountered. Siegel himself has said that Zorro and other popular characters "definitely" influenced the secret identity motif, although he "didn't much care for" the 1934 *Pimpernel* film.[70] To this can be added that the stereotype of the unmanly Jew also appeared in American vaudeville and burlesque until the end of the 1920s and continued its existence on the radio and other media, and so would be relatively easily recognized. As American studies scholar Lawrence Mintz describes the Vaudeville stage, Jews were often represented as "canny [...], that is, they are smart in the sense of too clever, manipulative, dishonest – but they are also portrayed, perhaps surprisingly as dumb, especially as lacking in 'street smarts', and potential suckers. Jewish men are also particularly weak, cowardly, the victims of bullies (including Jewish women)."[71] The latter part of that description certainly applies to Clark Kent. In its own time, however, the stereotype was not necessarily regarded as aggressively anti-Semitic. Comedian Jack Benny wrote in his autobiography that "[b]ad as you may think this kind of humor was, I think it was a way that America heated up the national groups and the ethnic groups in a melting pot and made one people out of us – or tried to do so."[72]

Thus, the elements for an alternative interpretation of Superman's dual identities in terms of subversive humor, gendered and perhaps ethnic, are present in the character and his creative context. Siegel was by all accounts a self-styled humorist; among his first work was *Goober the Mighty*, a Tarzan parody, and, in one of his early bids for fame and fortune, he tried to launch a mail-order school of humor with Shuster's brother.[73] It should not be forgotten that Superman himself was an occasional comedian. Rather than a source of "perpetual angst," the alter ego was a tool for Superman's practical jokes, representing a sense of superiority over both the weak outsider he plays and the society in which he moves. This is evident not least in the example of his game with Lois, cited in this chapter's introduction.

If one adds rising US anti-Semitism to the equation, Superman's dual identity perhaps serves a dual purpose: by disarming and discrediting the effeminate half-man and the stereotyped Jew, and playing a joke on a supposedly superior mainstream of tormentors that does not recognize him as human, Superman's subversive behavior represents a "nerdy" power fantasy of the once-bullied that empowers through its promotion of hidden "superness" and Americanized Jewish masculinity. Significant in this respect is that Clark is all surface, this feigned inferiority in effect appearing as a vehicle for Siegel's saying to girls, bullies, and, perhaps, anti-Semites that "anything you can do, I can do better." In this reading, the effete, bespectacled weakling is a veneer that does not really exist; nonideological difference is cast as illusory, or at least as inconsequential. What matters, it says, is not how you look, but how you act.

Perhaps, then, when read in ethnoracial terms, Clark is not so much a "Jewish nerd's" revenge against anti-Semites as a response to it: the Jewish Other as it is constructed through stereotypes similarly does not exist, and underneath that assigned identity rests a true American. Superman, the hypermasculine and patriotic true self that emerges out of the affected stereotype, is the type of man that can rescue Lois time and time again and can do what is needed to "banish fear" in America, the type of man that many were increasingly being told that they should be, and that many, including Siegel and Shuster, wished they were.[74]

NOTES

1. Cf. Ricca, *Super Boys*, 129–30; Jones, *Men of Tomorrow*, 80–81, for an indication of how widespread the "superman" idea was at the time; Alpers, *Dictators*, 26–27, even shows how President-elect Roosevelt was called a vigorous superman.

2. For some extreme examples, see *SC1*, 27, 102, 106, 187; *SC2*, 19, 94, 128; *SC3*, 30, 43; *SC4*, 17, 57, 70, 72, 145, 146; *SC5*, 12, 51–52, 94, 182; *SC6*, 55, 130, 169; *SC7*, 17, 50, 83. On one occasion, Superman even tortures a man whose only crime was to react a little too strongly on finding Superman, a stranger, in his office (*SC4*, 161–162).

3. E.g. *SC1*, 11–12, 15–16, 29, 81–151, 177, 200; *SC2*, 11, 15–16, 114–115; *SC3*, 78, 83–84, 97, 107, 139, 152; *SC4*, 17, 56–57, 70, 94–5–138, 158–159; *SC5*, 16, 55, 106–107; *SC6*, 16, 27–29, 42, 72, 167, 30, 31, 41–43, 95–56, 118, 125, 165, 166.

4. E.g. *SC1*, 19, 193; *SC2*, 145; *SC3*, 19, 38, 84, 125, 165; *SC4*, 66, 192; *SC5*, 83, 124; *SC7*, 122.

5. E.g. *SC1*, 184–85; *SC2*, 80–81; *SC3*, 63, 76; *SC4*, 65; *SC6*, 110.

6. Daniels, *Superman*, 41–42; a few late examples of reluctance to save villains in *SC6*, 64, 80.

7. *SC3*, 188. Incidentally, "the law's penalty" is often swiftly executed death sentences, as in for example *SC2*, 84–85; *SC3*, 108.

8. *SC5*, 4; cited examples and more in *SC1*, 108–10, 151–52, 161–62; *SC2*, 111, 133; *SC3*, 11, 42, 174; *SC6*, 16.

9. *SC1*, 19; *SC2*, 69.

10. E.g. *SC1*, 15–16, 96, 101–102; *SC2*, 30, 39, 40, 41, 42, 43, 71, 96, 97, 101; *SC3*, 36, 75, 83, 89–90, 146, 148; *SC4*, 80, 164; *SC5*, 168, 172; *SC6*, 13, 73, 146–147, 161, 188; *SC7*, 76. Cf. Cf. Siegel and Shuster, *Sunday Classics*, 25.

11. *SC2*, 19, 55, 75; also e.g. *SC3*, 24, 119, 134; *SC4*, 27–28, 39–41, 79, 179; *SC6*, 51. Cf. Siegel and Shuster, *Sunday Classics*, 44, 98.

12. E.g. *SC1*, 84, 113; *SC2*, 122; *SC3*, 128–29; *SC5*, 8, 45, 75, 94, 113, 138, 140, 150, 153, 180; *SC6*, 60–69, 77–78, 85, 96, 101, 124; *SC7*, 7, 18, 22, 33–34, 48, 66–67, 92–93, 160.

13. *SC3*, 129; also *SC4*, 5–6, 35, 36.

14. *SC1*, 73.

15. *SC1*, 113–14; cf. *SC6*, 36, for a later example of Superman sadistically getting "some amusement" from playing with human emotions.

16. Cf. Jones, *Men of Tomorrow*, 14, passim.; Ricca, *Super Boys*, passim.; Tye, *Superman*, 13, passim.

17. Prell, *Fighting to Become Americans*, 9.

18. Prell, *Fighting to Become Americans*, 18.

19. Alpers, *Dictators*, 43.

20. Prell, *Fighting to Become Americans*, 104–7.
21. Prell, *Fighting to Become Americans*, chap. 1–2 passim., p. 87.
22. Jewish self-representation between 1935 and 1945 in Prell, *Fighting to Become Americans*, chap. 4.
23. Faludi, *Terror Dream*, 200, 212–13.
24. Dickstein, *Dancing in the Dark*, 283.
25. An explicit example of teenage rejection in *SC1*, 46–58; Siegel's own rejection discussed in Ricca, *Super Boys*, 38–39, 136–44.
26. Faludi, *Terror Dream* discusses the significance of captivity narratives in promoting gendered hero myth.
27. E.g. *SC1*, 59–82, 93–96, 174–76; *SC2*, 163–78; *SC3*, 126–53; *SC4*, 23–26, 29–30, 84, 93, 108–109, 111–112, 115–117, 146, 174–79, 185; *SC5*, 9–13, 21–30, 62–64, 82–83, 144–149, 160–163, 165–78, 191–92; *SC6*, 30–34, 87–88, 107–110, 115, 122, 135, 14–15, 38–41, 44, 55–56, 70, 109–112, 124–125, 151–152, 161–162, 165–166.
28. See Rubin, "New Deal in Entertainment," 97–98.
29. *SC3*, 189; cf. more condescending remarks in *SC4*, 26, 117; *SC7*, 39, 41, 112. Also Siegel and Shuster, *Sunday Classics*, 61.
30. *SC6*, 30–38; cf. esp. *SC7*, 100–112.
31. Cf. Berlatsky, "Between Supermen": "Far from a queen on the chessboard of these comics, she [Lois] is a pawn manipulated by the two men who are actually one. In all of this, the early Superman stories both acknowledge and illustrate the shifting position of women in American society and attempt to recuperate male power by suggesting that newfound female agency is carried out as a result of (Super)man's largesse and power, not in spite of it." See also Welky, *Everything Was Better*, 143.
32. Hollinger, "Feminist Theory and Sci-Fi," 125–26.
33. Attebery, *Decoding Gender*, 7 (emphasis added); cf. Faludi, *Backlash*.
34. Prell, *Fighting to Become Americans*, 52–53.
35. Brodkin, *How Jews Became White*, 100–101.
36. Jones, *Men of Tomorrow*, 182.
37. Tye, *Superman*, 49–50; Jones, *Men of Tomorrow*, 181–83.
38. *SC7*, 116.
39. The same phrasing used in Siegel and Shuster, *Sunday Classics*, 28.
40. *SC6*, 138–48; see *SC3*, 85–97 for a similar plot. See also n31 to this chapter above.

41. *SC3*, 99–111.
42. *SC6*, 165.
43. *SC6*, 163–75.
44. *SC6*, 175; cf. Prell, *Fighting to Become Americans*, Hark, "Introduction," 11–12.
45. This type of condescension can also be found in Siegel and Shuster, *Sunday Classics*, 11, 24, 27, 49.
46. *SC3*, 142.
47. *SC3*, 23. This characterization also appears in Siegel and Shuster, *Sunday Classics*, 16.
48. *SC1*, 10.
49. *Super Boys*, 153.
50. Alpers, *Dictators*, 43; Jarvis, *Male Body at War*, chap. 1; Prell, *Fighting to Become Americans*, 104–7. This phenomenon is directly addressed, if briefly, in Siegel and Shuster, *Sunday Classics*, 11.
51. Ricca, *Super Boys*, 306–10.
52. Cf. Smith, *Hard-Boiled*, 26–32, 38–39, 44, 150–152, 162, 165.
53. Faludi, *Stiffed*, 20; *SC6*, 179.
54. Faludi, *Stiffed*, 20.
55. Cf. Smith, *Hard-Boiled*, 28.
56. Chambliss and Svitavsky, "Pulp to Superhero," 22–23.
57. Tye, *Superman*, 66.
58. Brod, *Superman Is Jewish?*, 10–11; cf. Boyarin, *Unheroic Conduct*.
59. Brod, *Superman Is Jewish?*, 8.
60. Siegel quoted in Brod, *Superman Is Jewish?*, 8. Elsewhere, Brod quotes Feiffer's discussion about two "schools" of comics appreciation: the "Superman school" and the "Batman school." According to Brod (p.11), Feiffer "capture[s] the difference between the two, particularly as it relates to his own Jewish psyche". There is nothing in the Feiffer quote which follows that references Jewishness; rather, Feiffer clearly bases his choice to favor Superman on individual preference and personal experiences, including his being "lousy at science" (*Comic Book Heroes*, 25–27).
61. Jones, *Men of Tomorrow*, 26, 63–67; Gartner, *Jews of Cleveland*, 296–97; Rubinstein, *Merging Traditions*, 134–36; Ricca, *Super Boys*, 27.
62. Portnoy, "Superman Is a Glatt Goy."
63. Andrae, Blum, and Coddington, "Supermen and Kids," 11.
64. Tye, *Superman*, 3–4, 17, 17, 21; cf. Ricca, *Super Boys*, 28.

65. Andrae, Blum, and Coddington, "Supermen and Kids," 12.
66. Berlatsky, "Between Supermen." The full quote Berlatsky is refer-
    encing reads: "If you're interested in what made *Superman* what it
    is, here's one of the keys to what made it universally acceptable. Joe
    and I had certain inhibitions...which led to wish-fulfillment which
    we expressed through our interest in science fiction and our comic
    strip. That's where the dual-identity concept came from, and Clark
    Kent's problems with Lois. I imagine there are a lot of people in
    this world who are similarly frustrated. Joe and I both felt that way
    in high school, and he was able to put the feeling into sketches."
    From Andrae, Blum, and Coddington, "Supermen and Kids," 19,
    ellipsis in original.
67. Wenger, *History Lessons*, 105–6.
68. Norwood, "American Jewish Muscle"; Bodner, *Jewish Sport.*
69. Ricca, *Super Boys*, 122–24; "milquetoast" in Tye, *Superman*, 73.
70. According to Jones, *Men of Tomorrow*, 27–28, 73–75, Siegel was a
    big fan of Douglas Fairbanks' Zorro since childhood and of the
    Shadow from its introduction; Siegel quotes from Andrae, Blum,
    and Coddington, "Supermen and Kids," 11–12.
71. Mintz, "Humor and Ethnic Stereotypes," 21.
72. Benny, *Sunday Nights at Seven*, 108.
73. Cf. Ricca, *Super Boys*, 29–30, 44–46, 84–87; Tye, *Superman*, 18,
    77–78. Siegel and Shuster's lasting interest in humor can be seen
    in their later character Funnyman, reprinted in Siegel and Shuster,
    Siegel and Shuster's Funnyman.
74. Smith, *Hard-Boiled*, 58–73; Daniels, *Superman*, 12; De Haven,
    Our Hero, 34–35; Jones, *Men of Tomorrow*, 26–27, 28–29.

CHAPTER 10

Forgotten and Remembered Supermen

A Superman of His Time

Superman's early years are arguably escapist, poorly drawn, and filled with ham-fisted dialogue and on-the-nose exposition, repetitive plots, and puerile gags, displaying as loose a grip on consistency as they do on physics. They were also extremely popular and, like so much of the era's cinematic, musical, and literary output, testify to the way people felt about the world or at least display potboiler sensitivity to reigning cultural concerns. By no means a simple character, Superman embodied America's long-cherished, but in the 1930s declining, ideal of rugged individualism *along with* New Deal collectivism, expressed both fear *and* security, and exposed the tension between private initiative and public planning that was at the heart of the New Deal.[1] In his day, he was the right man at the right time, a character configured in relation and response to a pressing situation.

In many ways, the so-called Roaring Twenties had seemed like a period of the American Dream realized.[2] This could not last, and when it all crashed – and crashed hard – blame had to be placed somewhere: for Roosevelt, the most immediate targets became "the rulers of the exchange of mankind's goods." As a hero, Superman also needed villains, and, for the most part, he fought the same people that Roosevelt had targeted. In this sense, Superman was in touch with Roosevelt's disenfranchised "forgotten man," the "one-third of a nation ill-housed, ill-clad, ill-nourished," fighting

© The Editor(s) (if applicable) and The Author(s) 2016
M. Lund, *Re-Constructing the Man of Steel*,
DOI 10.1007/978-3-319-42960-1_10

an otherwise seemingly untouchable enemy.[3] His physical activism and unilateral action on behalf of others, and only *his*, authorized, unilateral action,
as his repeated opposition to mob violence suggests,[4] was a symbol of the
"good state" envisioned by the New Deal. This Superman served as a populist "prophet of direct action" in a cultic revolution in American civil religion, as the New Deal heralded the entry of federal government and welfare
into people's lives on a scale and to a degree theretofore unknown.[5]

Comics scholar Jeffrey Brown has remarked that "[a]t its core, the
superhero genre is about boundaries. [...] Specific plots are almost irrele-
vant, what the superheroes repeatedly enact for readers is a symbolic policing of the borders between key cultural concepts: good and evil, right and
wrong, us and them."[6] Superman shows that this has been part and parcel
of the genre since its beginning. By embodying American virtues as *pro-
totypes*, characteristics believed to describe in-group members, Superman
and his world seem like an attempted redefinition of who "fits in." The
line was drawn through what social psychologist Peter Herriot calls the
meta-contrast principle, by which differences between members of the in-
group are minimized while the differences between the in-group and the
out-group are maximized.[7] In Superman's case, difference resonated with
the dualism evident in contemporary populist rhetoric, which placed the
blame for all social ills and current injustices on the moneyed powers.[8]

Leaving no room for parochial thinking, and accounting for the low-
contrast Jewish/non-Jewish border in representation, this division pitted
"real Americans" against a generalized Other, made "un-American" by
not serving the "greater good." Through formulaic and simplified representations of the New Deal's rhetoric and the Melting Pot idea as social
realities, Superman helped propagate and popularize a hegemonic image
of a homogeneous USA worth fighting for, paralleling the shift in the
USA's identity-climate that would significantly whiten the country's "new
immigrant" peoples by the time WWII ended.[9] To be one of "Us" was to
be law-abiding and hardworking, to contribute to what made the country
great; conversely, "They" chose power over community and wealth over
humanity, worked only for their own good and profit, did not care for
their neighbor, and had no respect for the rule of law. It was an effective
move. As a child psychologist reported shortly after the war, a young girl's
response to a boy saying "[l]ook out! I'm Superman, and I'll hurt you" is
telling: "You can't frighten me, [...] Superman never hurts *good* people."[10]

Being a product of his time, however, Superman juxtaposed this high-
minded rhetoric of security and inclusion with repeated failures to live up

to the same: on the one hand, he spoke to the better angels of Americans' natures, echoing the New Deal's aspiration not only for economic recovery but for structural reform, aimed at creating "a better life for all Americans, and a better America to live it in"; on the other hand, he spoke to old fears of and anxieties about the Other, deeply ingrained in the national culture.[11] In its theoretical reconfiguration of America toward slightly greater inclusion, Superman's potential gain came at the cost of a number of failures of identity: his propagation of fifth column fears fed into a hysteria that made Americans less inclined to open their borders to European refugees, his close identification with middle class concerns led to the erasure of people of color, and his heroic hypermasculinity depended on the denigration of women.[12]

It can be objected, and rightly so, that the values Superman embodied, particularly social justice and patriotism, are also cherished Jewish American values. It is entirely possible that his creators saw socially conscious ethical monotheism or Prophetic Judaism reflected in the New Deal and created their character as a vicarious expression of that belief, but there is no way to link this textually.[13] Superman's patriotism is likely an expression of a Jewish sense of pride and belonging in the USA. Conversely, perhaps Superman became so American because Siegel and Shuster worried that events in Germany were building toward something bigger, but did not dare to speak up for fear of exacerbating US anti-Semitism, hoping instead, like so many of their fellows, to "gain acceptance at the height of rejection."[14] But if it is true, as John Michael argues, that people often see themselves in terms of whichever of their allegiances is most under attack, and that the result of such attacks is the emergence of identity and a desire for vindication or justice, Superman is interesting indeed.[15] If he was intended as a Jewish reaction to the push of anti-Semitism, whether Nazi or, more likely, of the native variety, it was a reaction couched overwhelmingly in terms of America's pull and promise.

According to most descriptions, Jerry Siegel, the anchor of early Superman production, spent most of his teens in front of his typewriter, looking up at the silver screen, or reclining with a pulp magazine in his hands. In Gerard Jones' portrait of the writer as a young man, he "immersed himself in ink" and identified, "to the point of obnoxiousness," with his own storytelling abilities.[16] Similarly, Siegel's description of his younger self leaves no doubt about his goals: "I definitely wanted to be a science fiction writer."[17] Given that Siegel and Shuster lived in Glenville, more or less a Jewish enclave, albeit with a strong sense of Americanization, the creative process likely involved a conscious effort to not reproduce Jewish difference or specificity so as to fit an American market.

Ultimately, however, whether Superman was inspired by Moses or Jesus, or lifted more from the pages of Yudl Rosenberg's *Niflo'es Maharal* than from Philip Gordon Wylie's *Gladiator* is inconsequential, as far as his initial characterization and success is concerned. Arguing that Superman "is" a take on one figure or another confuses the part with the whole. If Superman were a Moses figure, he arrived not in unfriendly Egypt but in the American Promised Land, and if he were a golem, he was a defender not of Jews but of American democracy and capitalism. Superman, as he appears in his early comic books, is an unabashedly American character: he is the Man of Steel, a hero for hard times; he is the Man of Tomorrow, champion of a brighter American future; he is a red-blooded American he-man, configured in line with common conventions communicated by the New Deal, Americanism, and pop culture, doing what he believes is best for his country. Superman is possibly also, as has so often been suggested, the hero that every young man, including his creators, wished they could be, hiding within the Clark Kent they feared they were.

Over the half-century preceding Superman's creation, Jewish American leaders and cultural producers had argued that Jewish and American culture share the same core beliefs and values and consciously created— "virtually from whole cloth," as Beth Wenger reminds us—and disseminated the idea of an American Jewish heritage.[18] Furthermore, many Jewish leaders and organizations of the day stressed the convergence of Jewish and American interests, and American Jews were looking forward to a future in the USA. Perhaps Superman was an exaggerated attempt to do the same, wherein the blend Jewishness and Americanness in which some assertion of Jewish specificity was otherwise common amounted, when filtered through the simplifying language of populism and comics, to a sort of hyper-Americanism and super-patriotism.[19]

However, it is here worth highlighting that Siegel and Shuster's Superman included a few Yiddishisms. For example, when Superman jumps through the skies on his way to "stop the war" that Hitler and Stalin have just started, one German pilot can be seen asking, with a clear Yiddish inflection, "[v]os is diss?" And in a multilevel joke, the background of the opening panel to the second "Toran–Galonian" war story features a sign in a Toran city that names the street as "Plotzen Platz." The scene includes a triple pun on the Yiddish word "platsn," which can mean "to split" or "crack," but also "to faint" or "to explode": in the foreground,

Clark Kent is shown running from an exploding Galonian shell, with an unconscious woman in his arms, while a brick that has been violently dislodged by the shelling hits the wall just above the sign and cracks it.[20] These Yiddishisms alone do not make Superman Jewish by any stretch of the imagination, but they illustrate Siegel and Shuster's willingness to "sign" their work, in all its overdone Americanness, as the creation of two young Jewish men from Cleveland; this incorporation signifies an existential identification with the character as both Americans and as Jews. If that is the case, Superman ties into the discourse of Jewish American heritage creation as a Jewish American practice in the present, connecting with a Jewish American past, and working toward a Jewish American future.[21] In this sense, Siegel and Shuster's early Superman is an existentially authentic Jewish American character.

JUDAIZING SUPERMAN

In the introduction to his Superman book, Larry Tye flatly states about the character that "[h]e is Jewish."[22] The evidence given later, in a three-page laundry list of familiar tropes like the "Hebrew" reading of Kal-El, the Moses "parallel," the *tikkun olam* reading of Superman's activism, the *Schwarze Korps* article, and a few others, is cobbled together, mostly, from Simcha Weinstein, Danny Fingeroth, and Arie Kaplan's books, and presented as fact. Indeed, after the listing, as noted earlier, Tye bemoans how the "evidence that he was a Jew did not stop other faiths from claiming Superman as theirs."[23]

Tye also opened a 2013 event at New York's Center for Jewish History by repeating the same tropes, followed by several others that made many of the remaining claims that have been addressed in this book.[24] S. Brent Plate, in his Superman article discussed in Chap. 2, similarly references Weinstein and Harry Brod to close on a note about the "secret connections between the Jewish creators and superheroes," and about considering the Jewish roots of messiahs "as we await the messianic Man of Steel in theaters this summer [2013]."[25] In 2012, Rick Bowers ticked off another laundry list of where Siegel and Shuster's Jewish heritage supposedly "deeply influenced" Superman's creation, lifted from Weinstein.[26] In 2016, the Israeli newspaper *Haaretz* published an article that quoted Weinstein, Fingeroth, and Kaplan, and reiterated the Kal-El trope, the Moses parallel, and the golem claim, as well as the Nazi condemnation of Superman, and cited Chabon as a revealer of history.[27]

Perhaps the most explicit example of how the popular literature has become consecrated comes in the bibliography to 2013's *Superman: The Unauthorized Biography*. There, the writer, Glen Weldon, says that, as he "clicked to order" Weinstein's book on Amazon, he realized that he "wouldn't have much to add by spending a lot of time rehashing Superman's Jewish roots." In Weldon's opinion, *Up, Up, and Oy Vey*, along with Fingeroth's book, already "does a great job of" this.[28] Here, and in all the examples above, is evidence that interpretive sedimentation in relation to Superman and the Jewish–comics connection has come a long way in popular, journalistic, and academic realms.[29]

The argument for reading Superman in Judeocentric terms today finds much fertile ground, perhaps somewhat paradoxically, because of American Jewry's successful assimilation into American culture. More important, perhaps, is the fact that the Judeocentric interpretive lens, so labeled by Fingeroth who erroneously calls it relatively new, is readily available.[30] Jonathan Sarna has already been quoted as listing and dismissing several claims that Jews "created contemporary culture," and journalist Adam Garfinkle has written a passable survey of "Jewcentricity," or "why the Jews are praised, blamed, and used to explain just about everything."[31] It is interesting, then, to note that the most frequently recurring tropes enlisted in Judaizing Superman are Moses, the Holocaust, the golem, and *tikkun olam*, all of which serve at present as important signifiers, tied deeply to conceptions of Jewishness and Jewish authenticity in the contemporary Western imagination. The inclusion and treatment of these terms and tropes in the literature bears a striking resemblance to the hegemonic understanding of Christianity argued by Douglas E. Cowan to be at work in Christological eisegeses of the 1951 movie *The Day the Earth Stood Still*: these are "understandings largely divorced from or ignorant of the historical, theological, and ideological realities" of—in our case—Judaism as it has developed around the world.[32] On this basis, the writers discussed in this book construct an imagined community, onto which they can project similarities between historical formations of Judaism and Jewishness and their own time, even as they create them.[33]

However, in making its critically unfiltered claims, this celebratory literature not only dismisses the subtle complexities of history and effaces almost all traces of non-Jews from comics history; it also depersonalizes the Jewish creators, removing any variation in biographical or intertextual experience. Weinstein's creators are presented as scripturally learned beyond what can reasonably be expected; Fingeroth's creators read like nostalgically sepia-toned immigrants from the Lower East Side or the Jewish Bronx, no matter what neighborhood, borough, or city they came from or lived in[34]; and Kaplan's creators are situated primarily as Jews contributing to civilization as Jews, in a chain of tradition that was supposedly passed from one comics-making generation to the next.[35]

The framing of the Jewish–comics connection as a "tradition," which is most explicit in Kaplan's book but is present to some degree in all the others, confers several benefits: it helps, for example, to strengthen several other Jewish "traditions" of recent invention, most notably the social justice interpretation of *tikkun olam* and the Jewish quasi-essentialism in some golem readings, likely because they have already taken such strong hold on the Jewish and non-Jewish imagination.[36] All of this helps create a bonding cultural memory that works in favor of an imagined community, in a time when American Judaism seems to some increasingly fractured and diverse and when, as historian David Roskies has written, "all of Jewry is [...] divided along ideological lines, and each ideology has carved out a different piece of the past."[37] Over the past century, there have been "multiple and competing pasthoods [...] brought into every Jewish home." The authors of the popular Jewish–comics connection literature have all attempted to maneuver this efflorescence of pasthoods and have, to some extent, contributed to it.[38]

Overinterpretation of mainstream superhero comics and the recent production of self-consciously Jewish comics have most likely played into each other. But remembering always implies forgetting; the search for a "usable past" in comics history happens to the detriment of the thriving present, or so it often seems. Perhaps, then, if one should probe Michael Chabon's influential novel for terminology or comparisons, it is better to look toward the middle, where he writes: "One of the sturdiest precepts of the study of human delusion is that every golden age is either past or in the offing [i. e. on the horizon, about to happen]." Writing about an exception, Chabon coins the nonce word *aetataureate* to describe something "of or pertaining to a golden age," noting how on rare occasions people can feel about their own time "that strange blend of optimism and nostalgia which is the usual hallmark of the aetataureate delusion."[39] The description—although certainly not a proof of anything in itself—is nonetheless apt for the situation described in this book. Eddy Portnoy writes in his review of Brod's book that "*Superman is Jewish?* is symptomatic of an ongoing and particularistic American-Jewish search for cultural avatars. As it is, the 'Jewish imagination' has produced enough of significance without having to stake claims to things it didn't."[40] As suggested above, the books by Weinstein, Fingeroth, and Kaplan are endemic of the same process.

But, as Portnoy writes, when it comes to comics, there is certainly enough material of significance to grab hold of. Art Spiegelman, Ben Katchor, and James Sturm's works have already been mentioned, but they are only a small part of a rapidly growing roster of explicitly and proudly Jewish comics. A list that only scratches the surface of such materials published around the time the above-discussed books about Jews and comics were starting to appear can include such diverse titles as the already-mentioned didactic superhero comic *Jewish Hero Corps* (2003) and the propagandistic superhero *Captain Israel* (2011), and Joe Kubert's *Jew Gangster* (2004) and *Yossel* (2005).[41] In addition, it is worth noting that many of Will Eisner's latter-day long-form comics contained some measure of Jewish signification, and that his final work, *The Plot* (2005), was an attack on the anti-Semitic forgery known as the *Protocols of the Elders of Zion*, unambiguously placed in a Jewish discursive tradition.[42] Other examples include Harvey Pekar's *Yiddishkeit* and the posthumously published *Not the Israel My Parents Promised Me* (2012), Stan Mack's *Story of the Jews* (2001), Sarah Glidden's *How to Understand Israel in 60 Days or Less* (2010), and Liana Finck's *A Bintel Brief: Love and Longing in Old New York* (2014).[43]

These comics are important to note. While assertions that, for example, Siegel and Shuster's Superman was a Moses figure do not pass critical muster, the meditations on identity in, for example, Neil Kleid's *The Big Kahn* (2009) or the bustling immigrant Lower East Side in Leela Corman's *Unterzakhn* (2012), or in any of the just-listed comics and graphic novels, are—though not exclusively nor simplistically so—undeniably and self-consciously Jewish.[44] The "Golden Age of Jewish comics" might be happening right now, but recent works like the ones mentioned above go largely unremarked in the Jewish–comics connection literature discussed above, addressed when they appear almost exclusively in terms of what they hopefully promise about the future. Regrettably, in the rush to Judaize Superman and his contemporaries, the current flourishing of a vivid and interesting comics literature, which is certainly worthy of celebration and the most fully realized manifestation of a Jewish–comics connection by any measure, is largely forgotten. This is particularly the case of Jewish women cartoonists who, until literary scholar Tahneer Oksman's excellent *"How Come*

Boys Get to Keep Their Noses?": Women and Jewish American Identity in Contemporary Graphic Memoirs, had flown almost completely under the critical radar.[45]

Ultimately, it is likely that there is a "tightly woven and indelible relation between Jewish identity and the genesis of the superhero," as the editors of *The Jewish Graphic Novel* claim,[46] and it is probable that it extends far beyond the bygone Golden Age that Superman helped usher in. It is also true that this possibility has long remained understudied, with studies of Superman and his costumed cohorts focusing more on their Americanness and on their connections with US majority culture.[47] A corrective to this sometimes-myopic, Americentric focus that critically considers and seriously entertains the possibility of a Jewish–comics connection is sorely needed in comics scholarship; however, that connection will not be found in a novel written more than six decades after the fact, or in a notion of a "transplanted" or essentialized culture. Every time a new book or article appears that references Chabon or the celebratory literature as if they were historical scholarship, or that makes a grand and textually unmoored claim based on them, the argument for that relationship does not become stronger. In fact, it might in the long run even come to seem less critically viable.

Again, it is helpful to here consider Cowan: the thrust of this argument is not to suggest that consumers do not have a right to read Superman in these ways, but to understand what it is they bring to the text and what that tells us about the relationship between audience and text. Without debate and alternatives, it is possible that the celebratory readings discussed throughout this book become widely accepted as "The Meaning" of Superman, "as though other meanings, other interpretations, other readings, other eisegeses, are by definition bounded out."[48]

Such boundary-making calls are already being made. Tye is quoted in that vein at the beginning of this section. Arnaudo claims that Superman's "profound Jewish roots" are "recodified" and "insisted on to the point of preachiness" when the hero is Christologized in the 1978 Superman film (which, as noted earlier, was a narrative and symbolic turn made by a Jewish American script doctor).[49] Brod, in turn, claims that Superman is drifting away from his supposed "original Jewish sensibility." Brod then connects this drift with his own project of Jewish "reclamation" that is, as Portnoy suggests, unreasonably, linked to the Holocaust.[50] The quoted writers all strike an almost strident, and implicitly accusatory, tone against interpretations that do not match their own, ahistorical ones, and claim, without offering much textual support, that non-Jewish readings of Superman amount to a de-Judaization of the character. It is worth noting that the last two, most negative judgments, are made by academics; their work, as noted, is highly speculative, but is lent an imprimatur of scholarship by virtue of their authors' academic titles and their publishers' links to universities. Such forceful eisegesis can only be harmful in the long run.

As this book has argued, few of the claims made in the celebratory or pseudo-scholarly Jewish–comics connection literature hold up under historically, contextually, textually, and biographically sensitive examination. The primary purpose of the popular books is not scholarship, but naming and claiming Jews who have made contributions to US culture, engaging in Jewish religio-cultural edification, and strengthening Jewish identity and community, in a time when they seem to become ever more fractioned and diverse. As such, there is no reason why they should hold up to a scholarly gaze. And Chabon's novel, no matter how well-written, is still fiction. They are nonetheless excellent, in that they ask questions and prompt their readers to do the same. Their recurrent use in writing is evidence that they serve as a gateway into the Jewish–comics connection and an invitation to its further investigation. My own path to studying the intersections of Jewish American history and comics started with Chabon and Weinstein.

However, since the books tend toward cultural myth and memory, rather than history, they do not provide the historian with answers. Answers cannot be found in a nostalgic Lower East Side, through a reifying gaze across the Atlantic to the Old World, or in Talmudic treatises, because this is not where Jewish-created characters like Superman were born. The past decade's myth-making has left a complex, exciting, and sometimes disturbing history by the wayside, and replaced it with grand claims that themselves often end up having unintended and counter-productive logical consequences. Instead of reiterating the same themes time and again—no matter how enjoyable reading they might make for—what is needed now is basic research that brings new perspectives to the material, that takes seriously the lives of the creators, and that critically considers their work as having been shaped in the meeting between Jewishness and Americanness, between Judaism and Americanism, and that rigorously considers the cultural, ethnoracial, gendered, and classed politics of their time, hard, grueling, and, perhaps, occasionally disappointing or disconcerting work though it may be.

Notes

1. Cf. Dickstein, *Dancing in the Dark*, 227.
2. For a good narrative history of the USA's 1920s, see Miller, *New World Coming*. This section builds in part on Lund, "American Golem," 90.
3. Roosevelt, "Second Inaugural"; cf. Dickstein, *Dancing in the Dark*, 525–26.
4. *SC1*, 197–98; *SC4*, 16–17, 105–6; *SC6*, 116.
5. Phrase from Dickstein, *Dancing in the Dark*, 352. There can be no doubt that the New Deal-era was revolutionary: at the 1929 stock market crash, the US Government was small and generally hands-off; by the end of the New Deal, "[a]nd ever after, Americans assumed that the federal government had not merely a role, but a major responsibility, in ensuring the health of the economy and the welfare of citizens" (Kennedy, *Freedom from Fear*, 55, 377; cf. Patterson, *Grand Expectations*, 55–56).
6. Brown, "Supermoms?," 78.
7. Herriot, *Fundamentalism*, 33–34.
8. Dickstein, *Dancing in the Dark*, 489; Alpers, *Dictators*, 8–9.
9. Brodkin, *How Jews Became White*, 26–37; Roediger, *Working toward Whiteness*, (esp. pp. 235–244).
10. Gilbert, "Comic Crypt," 46.
11. Quote from Kennedy, *Freedom from Fear*, 244; cf. MacDonnell, *Insidious Foes*, 4; Michael, *Identity and the Failure of America*. Note also Smith, "Tyranny of the Melting Pot," 132: "Comic books have [...] served as vehicles for promoting conservative values, but in the process have contributed to the normalization of certain prejudices." Cf. Berlatsky, "Between Supermen": "Opposing himself to unfair power, however, he [Superman] also ironically becomes that which he opposes. More than balancing the scales, he becomes irresistible, forcing others to accede to his will, even as he represents the power-less whose will is subjugated."
12. To borrow a pointed phrasing from Welky, *Everything Was Better*, 146, "while Superman spoke of the greatness of democracy and the American system, his actions indicated that these things applied only to a chosen few. His definition of Americanism no longer included those who fell through the cracks; the American Way of Life no longer stood for a commitment to aiding the increasingly

unseen underclass. Nor did democracy imply tolerance and diversity."

13. This conception had developed parallel to the Social Gospel—its Christian counterpart which significantly shaped the political culture of the New Deal—and a larger national trend towards social progressivism from the late 1800s. Cf. Kennedy, *Freedom from Fear*, 145–46; Sarna, *American Judaism*, 194–95.

14. Cf. Arad, *Rise of Nazism*, 222.

15. Michael, *Identity and the Failure of America*, 32.

16. Jones, *Men of Tomorrow*, 77.

17. Andrae, Blum, and Coddington, "Supermen and Kids," 8.

18. Wenger, *History Lessons*, 15–29.

19. Cf. Wenger, *History Lessons*, 40–41; Sarna, "Cult of Synthesis." See also Chabon, *Kavalier & Clay*, 32; Patterson, *Grand Expectations*, 180; Muscio, *Hollywood's New Deal*, 43.

20. Siegel and Shuster, "End the War"; Siegel et al., *SC3*, 32. Thanks to Niklas Olniansky for talking with me about the "platsn" joke. It is worth noting, parenthetically, that one Sunday strip also has an Ontario Street sign, marking it as a product of Cleveland. In Siegel and Shuster, *Sunday Classics*, 65.

21. Cf. Charmé, "Varieties of Authenticity."

22. Tye, *Superman*, x.

23. Tye, *Superman*, 65–67.

24. Leon, "Superman at 75."

25. Plate, "Superheroes Get Religion."

26. Bowers, *Superman vs. KKK*, 28–29.

27. Anderman, "Supermensches."

28. Weldon, *Superman*, 337.

29. Cowan, "Seeing the Saviour."

30. Fingeroth, *Disguised as Clark Kent*, 25.

31. Sarna, *American Judaism*; Garfinkle, *Jewcentricity*, 330–31.

32. Cf. Cowan, "Seeing the Saviour," np.

33. Cf. Anderson, *Imagined Communities*.

34. Fingeroth, *Disguised as Clark Kent*, 20. Writes Fingeroth, in a book that is named after Clark Kent, the creation of two Clevelanders: "The personal point of entry into this book [...] is the realization as an adult that the creators of the comics I enjoyed [...] were cut from the same cloth as my own relatives. These were

the same children of Eastern European Jewish immigrants who were my parents, aunts, and uncles, down to their growing up on the Lower East Side or in the Jewish Bronx."

35. Kaplan, *From Krakow to Krypton*, xiv–xv.
36. The Prague tourist industry does a brisk trade in all things golem-related, and the figure has appeared in everything from fantasy literature to *The Simpsons*, while such visible non-Jewish figures as Bill Clinton and Cornell West have spoken about *tikkun olam*. See Jacobs, "History of 'Tikkun'."
37. Roskies, *Usable Past*, 14.
38. Cf. Roskies, *Usable Past* (quote from p. 12).
39. Chabon, *Kavalier & Clay*, 340.
40. Portnoy, "Superman Is a Glatt Goy."
41. Oirich and Randall, *The Amnesia Count-Down*; Schumer, *A Superhero for Our Time*; *The Venomous BDS!*; Kubert, *Jew Gangster*; *Yossel*.
42. Eisner, *The Plot*. Other examples include *A Contract with God* (1978), *A Life Force* (1988), *To the Heart of the Storm* (1991), *Dropsie Avenue* (1995), *Minor Miracles* (2000), *The Name of the Game* (2001), and *Fagin the Jew* (2003). These are reprinted in Eisner, *Contract Trilogy*; *Eisner's New York*; *Life*; *Fagin the Jew*; *Minor Miracles*.
43. Pekar, Buhle, and Hartman, *Yiddishkeit*; Pekar and Waldman, *Not the Israel*; Mack, *Story of the Jews*; Glidden, *Understand Israel*; Finck, *Bintel Brief*.
44. Kleid and Cinquegrani, *The Big Kahn*; Corman, *Unterzakhn*.
45. Oksman, *Keep Their Noses?* Moreover, as Oksman notes on p. 18: "[Jewish American women] remain woefully absent or misrepresented in the history of the superhero genre, not to mention other modes of Jewish American representation. In a sense, their autobiographical comics can be seen as a kind of antidote to that superheroic tradition, which presumes that only the all-powerful, assimilating male and his counterparts, however much they are fantasies, deserve to be seen and heard."
46. Baskind and Omer-Sherman, "Introduction," xxiii.
47. E.g. Wright, *Comic Book Nation*; Coogan, *Superhero*; Lawrence and Jewett, *American Superhero*.
48. Cowan, "Seeing the Saviour," np. Emphatic capital "T" in original.
49. Arnaudo, *Myth of the Superhero*, 47.

50. Brod, *Superman Is Jewish?*, 14–16, xxvi; Portnoy, "Superman Is a Glatt Goy": "A thousand years of European Jewish culture is comparable to the juvenile fantasies of two kids from Cleveland? 'Jewish' superheroes being assimilated into mainstream culture (huh?) is a Holocaust?"

BIBLIOGRAPHY

Alpers, Benjamin L. 2003. *Dictators, democracy, and American public culture: Envisioning the totalitarian enemy, 1920s–1950s.* Chapel Hill: University of North Carolina Press.

Andelman, Bob. 2005. *Will Eisner, a spirited life.* Milwaukie: M Press.

Anderman, Nirit. 2016. Supermensches: Comic books' secret Jewish history. *Haartetz*, January 24. http://www.haaretz.com/israel-news/culture/1.698619

Anderson, Benedict. 2006 [1982]. *Imagined communities: Reflections on the origin and spread of nationalism.* Rev. ed. London: Verso.

Andrae, Thomas. 1987. From Menace to Messiah: The history and historicity of Superman. In *American media and mass culture: Left perspectives*, ed. Donald Lazere, 124–138. Berkeley/Los Angeles: University of California Press.

Andrae, Thomas. 2010a. Funnyman, Jewish masculinity, and the decline of the superhero. In *Siegel and Shuster's Funnyman: The first Jewish superhero, from the creators of Superman*, ed. Thomas Andrae and Mel Gordon, 49–83. Port Townsend: Feral House.

Andrae, Thomas. 2010b. The Jewish superhero. In *Siegel and Shuster's Funnyman: The first Jewish superhero, from the creators of Superman*, ed. Thomas Andrae and Mel Gordon, 38–47. Port Townsend: Feral House.

Andrae, Thomas, Geoffrey Blum, and Gary Coddington. 1983. Of Supermen and kids with dreams. *Nemo*, August.

Appier, Janis. 2005. 'We're blocking youth's path to crime' The Los Angeles Coordinating Councils during the Great Depression. *Journal of Urban History* 31(2): 190–218.

Arad, Gulie Ne'eman. 2000. *America, its Jews, and the rise of Nazism.* Bloomington: Indiana University Press.

© The Editor(s) (if applicable) and The Author(s) 2016
M. Lund, *Re-Constructing the Man of Steel*,
DOI 10.1007/978-3-319-42960-1

Arnaudo, Marco. 2013. *The myth of the superhero*. Trans. Jamie Richards. Baltimore: Johns Hopkins University Press.

Asad, Talal. 1986. *The idea of an anthropology of Islam*. Washington, DC: Center for Contemporary Arab Studies.

Ashley, Michael. 2000. *The time machines: The story of the science-fiction pulp magazines from the beginning to 1950*. Liverpool: Liverpool University Press.

Assmann, Jan. 2006. *Religion and cultural memory*. Trans. Rodney Livingstone. Stanford: Stanford University Press.

Attebery, Brian. 2002. *Decoding gender in science fiction*. London/New York: Routledge.

Baden, John K. 2011. *Residual Neighbors: Jewish-African American interactions in Cleveland from 1900 to 1970*. Master's thesis, Case Western Reserve University.

Baltimore v. Aryans. *Time* 32(5), August 1938, p. 11.

Barthes, Roland. 1977. *Image, music, text*. Trans. Stephen Heath. London: Fontana Press.

Barthes, Roland. 2009. *Mythologies*. London: Vintage.

Baskind, Samantha, and Ranen Omer-Sherman. 2010. Introduction. In *The Jewish graphic novel: Critical approaches*, ed. Samantha Baskind and Ranen Omer-Sherman, xv–xxvii. New Brunswick: Rutgers University Press.

Bauer, Yehuda. 2001. *A history of the Holocaust*. New York: Franklin Watts.

Beaty, Bart. 2012. *Comics versus art: Comics in the art world*. Toronto: University of Toronto Press.

Bellow, Saul. 2005. Starting out in Chicago. In *Who we are: On being (and not being) a Jewish American writer*, ed. Derek Rubin, 3–11. New York: Schocken Books.

Benny, Jack. 1990. *Sunday nights at seven: The Jack Benny story*. New York: Warner Books.

Berlatsky, Eric. 2013. Between Supermen: Homosociality, misogyny, and triangular desire in the earliest Superman stories. *Comics Forum*, April 11. https://comicsforum.org/2013/04/11/between-supermen-homosociality-misogyny-and-triangular-desire-in-the-the-earliest-superman-stories-by-eric-berlatsky/

Blecher, Arthur. 2007. *The New American Judaism: The way forward on challenging issues from intermarriage to Jewish identity*. New York/London: Palgrave Macmillan.

Bodner, Allen. 1997. *When boxing was a Jewish sport*. Westport: Praeger.

Boese, Carl, and Paul Wegener. 1920. *The golem*.

Bowers, Rick. 2012. *Superman versus the Ku Klux Klan: The true story of how the iconic superhero battled the men of hate*. Washington, DC: National Geographic.

Boyarin, Daniel. 1997. *Unheroic conduct: The rise of heterosexuality and the invention of the Jewish man*. Berkeley: University of California Press.

Brahm Levey, Geoffrey. 1995. Toward a theory of disproportionate American Jewish liberalism. In *Values, interests, and identity: Jews and politics in a changing world*, ed. Peter Y. Medding, 64–85. Oxford: Oxford University Press.

Brenner, Michael. 2010. *Prophets of the past: Interpreters of Jewish history*. Princeton: Princeton University Press.

Brevoort, Tom, and Stan Lee. The Jewish thing: Transcript. Interview by Brooke Gladstone and Bob Garfield. http://www.onthemedia.org/2002/aug/02/the-jewish-thing/transcript/?utm_source=sharedUrl&utm_media=metatag&utm_campaign=sharedUrl. Accessed 2 Jan 2013.

Brewer, H. Michael. 2004. *Who needs a superhero?: Finding virtue, vice, and what's holy in the comics*. Grand Rapids: Baker Books.

Brinkley, Alan. 1983. *Voices of protest: Huey Long, Father Coughlin, & the Great Depression*. New York: Vintage.

Brod, Harry. 1996. Did you know Superman is Jewish? *Davka*.

Brod, Harry. 2012. *Superman is Jewish? How comic book superheroes came to serve truth, justice, and the Jewish-American way*. New York: Free Press.

Brodkin, Karen. 1998. *How Jews became white folks and what that says about race in America*. New Brunswick: Rutgers University Press.

Brown, Jeffrey A. 2011. Supermoms? Maternity and the monstrous-feminine in superhero comics. *Journal of Graphic Novels and Comics* 2(1): 77–87.

Burroughs, Edgar Rice. 1939. *Carson of Venus*. Tarzana: Edgar Rice Burroughs, Inc. http://gutenberg.net.au/ebooks03/0300181h.html#chap9

Byrne, John, Terry Austin, and Keith Williams. 1987. The Secret Revealed! In *Superman*, vol. 2. New York: DC Comics.

Cannato, Vincent J. 2009. *American passage: The history of Ellis Island*. New York: Harper Collins.

Chabon, Michael. 2005. *The amazing adventures of Kavalier & Clay*. London/New York/Toronto/Sydney: Harper Perennial.

Chambliss, Julian, and William Svitavsky. 2008. From pulp hero to superhero: Culture, race, and identity in American popular culture, 1900–1940. Faculty Publications, October 1. http://scholarship.rollins.edu/as_facpub/2

Charmé, Stuart Z. 2000. Varieties of authenticity in contemporary Jewish identity. *Jewish Social Studies* 6(2): 133–155.

Charmé, Stuart Z., Bethamie Horowitz, Tali Hyman, and Jeffrey S. Kress. 2008. Jewish identities in action: An exploration of models, metaphors, and methods. *Journal of Jewish Education* 74(2): 115–143.

Cohen, Anthony P. 1989. *The symbolic construction of community*. London/New York: Routledge.

Coleman, Robin R. Means, and Emily Chivers Yochim. 2008. Symbolic annihilation. In *The international encyclopedia of communication*, ed. Wolfgang Donsbach, vol. 11, 4922–4924. Malden: Blackwell. http://go.galegroup.com/ps/i.do?id=GALE%7CCCX1329701247&v=2.1&u=nysl_me_cuny&it=r&p=GVRL&sw=w&asid=cb2ac16aa6373030e50ff265c4e50abf

Conn, Steven. 2014. *Americans against the city: Anti-urbanism in the twentieth century.* Oxford: Oxford University Press.

Conzen, Kathleen Neils, and David A. Gerber. 1992. The invention of ethnicity: A perspective from the U.S.A. *Journal of American Ethnic History* 12(1): 3.

Coogan, Peter. 2006. *Superhero: The secret origin of a genre.* Austin: MonkeyBrain Books.

Cooke, Jon B. 2001. Comic Book Artist Magazine #13 – Roy Thomas Interview. March 8. http://www.twomorrows.com/comicbookartist/articles/13thomas.html

Cooper, Levi. 2013. The Tikkun Olam Catch-All. *Jewish Educational Leadership* 11(1): 46–53.

Corman, Leela. 2012. *Unterzakhn.* New York: Schocken Books.

Costello, Matthew J. 2009. *Secret identity crisis: Comic books and the unmasking of Cold War America.* New York: Continuum.

Cowan, Douglas E. 2009. Seeing the Saviour in the Stars: Religion, conformity, and The Day the Earth Stood Still. *Journal of Religion and Popular Culture* 21(1): 3.

Crèvecoeur, J. Hector St John de. 2009. *Letters from an American farmer.* Oxford: Oxford University Press.

Culler, Jonathan. 1992. In defense of overinterpretation. In *Interpretation and overinterpretation*, ed. Stefan Collini, 109–123. Cambridge: Cambridge University Press.

Dan, Joseph. 2007. *Kabbalah: A very short introduction.* Oxford: Oxford University Press.

Daniels, Les. 2004. *Superman: The complete history.* San Francisco: Chronicle Books.

Darowski, Joseph J. (ed.). 2012. *The ages of Superman: Essays on the man of steel in changing times.* Jefferson: McFarland & Co.

Dauber, Jeremy. 2006. Comic books, tragic stories: Will Eisner's American Jewish history. *AJS Review* 30(2): 277–304.

De Haven, Tom. 2010. *Our hero: Superman on earth.* New Haven: Yale University Press.

Decker, Dwight R. 2008. The Reich strikes back: A close look at the Nazis Vs. Superman in 1940. *Alter Ego* 3(79): 25–31.

Dershowitz, Alan M. 1998. *The vanishing American Jew: In search of Jewish identity for the next century.* New York: Simon & Schuster.

Dickstein, Morris. 2010. *Dancing in the dark: A cultural history of The Great Depression.* New York: W.W. Norton.

Dill, Harry F. 2001. Keep 'Em Flying! *Air Power History* 48(2): 36.

Diner, Hasia, and Tony Michels. 2007. Considering American Jewish History. *OAH Newsletter* 35(4): 9, 18.

Diner, Hasia R., Jeffrey Shandler, and Beth S. Wenger (eds.). 2000. *Remembering the Lower East Side: American Jewish reflections.* Bloomington: Indiana University Press.

Dinnerstein, Leonard. 1994. *Antisemitism in America.* Oxford: Oxford University Press.

DiPaolo, Marc. 2011. *War, politics and superheroes: Ethics and propaganda in comics and film.* Jefferson: McFarland & Co.

Dollinger, Marc. 2000. *Quest for inclusion: Jews and liberalism in modern America.* Princeton: Princeton University Press.

Dollinger, Marc. 2003. Jewish identities in 20th-century America. *Contemporary Jewry* 24: 9–28.

Donner, Richard. 1978. *Superman: The movie.* Burbank: Warner Home Video.

Dyer, Richard. 1997. *White.* London/New York: Routledge.

Eco, Umberto. 1979. *The role of the reader: Explorations in the semiotics of texts.* Bloomington: Indiana University Press.

Edsforth, Ronald. 2000. *The New Deal: America's response to the Great Depression.* Malden: Blackwell Publishers.

Eisner, Will. 1994. *The Christmas spirit.* Northampton: Kitchen Sink Press.

Eisner, Will. 2003. *Fagin the Jew.* New York: Doubleday.

Eisner, Will. 2006a. *The contract with God trilogy: Life on Dropsie Avenue.* New York: W.W. Norton.

Eisner, Will. 2006b. *The plot: The secret story of the Protocols of the Elders of Zion.* New York: W.W. Norton.

Eisner, Will. 2006c. *Will Eisner's New York: Life in the big city.* New York: W.W. Norton.

Eisner, Will. 2007. *Life, in pictures: Autobiographical stories.* New York: W.W. Norton.

Eisner, Will. 2009. *Minor miracles: Long ago and once upon a time back when uncles were heroic, cousins were clever, and miracles happened on every block.* New York: W. W. Norton.

Eisner, Will, and Frank Miller. 2005. In *Eisner/Miller: A one-on-one interview*, ed. Charles Brownstein. Milwaukie: Dark Horse Books.

Elkin, Michael. 2006. Super ... Mensch? *The Jewish Exponent*, July 6. http://www.jewishexponent.com/super-mensch

Engle, Gary. 1987. What makes Superman so darned American? In *Superman at fifty! The persistence of a legend*, ed. Dennis Dooley and Gary Engle, 79–87. Cleveland: Octavia Press.

Evanier, Mark. 2008. *Kirby: King of comics.* New York: Abrams.

Faludi, Susan. 1992. *Backlash: The undeclared war against women.* London: Vintage Books.

Faludi, Susan. 1999. *Stiffed: The betrayal of the modern man.* London: Chatto & Windus.

Faludi, Susan. 2007. *The terror dream: Fear and fantasy in post-9 11 America.* New York: Metropolitan Books.

Fanning, Charles. 2013. George McManus and Irish America. *ImageTexT: Interdisciplinary Comics Studies* 7(2). http://www.english.ufl.edu/imagetext/archives/v7_2/fanning/

Feiffer, Jules. 1999. The Minsk theory of Krypton. In *The American values reader*, ed. Harvey S. Wiener and Nora Eisenberg, 696–700. Boston: Allyn and Bacon.

Feiffer, Jules. 2003 [1965]. *The great comic book heroes*. Seattle: Fantagraphics Books.

Finck, Liana. 2014. *A bintel brief: Love and longing in old New York*. New York: Ecco.

Fine, Lawrence. 1995. The art of metoscopy: A study in Isaac Luria's charismatic knowledge. In *Essential papers on Kabbalah*, ed. Lawrence Fine, 315–337. New York: New York University Press.

Fine, Herbert S., and Jerry Siegel. 1933. Reign of the Super-Man. In *Science fiction – The advance guard of future civilization*, vol. 3, 4–14. Cleveland: Self-published. http://ufdc.ufl.edu/UF00077088/00001

Fingeroth, Danny. 2007. *Disguised as Clark Kent: Jews, comics, and the creation of the superhero*. New York: Continuum.

Flanzbaum, Hilene (ed.). 1999. *The Americanization of the Holocaust*. Baltimore: Johns Hopkins University Press.

Fleming, Robert Loren, Keith Giffen, and Pat Broderick. 1991. The Folktale. *Ragman*, vol. 2 #3. New York: DC Comics.

Fredrickson, George M. 2002. *Racism: A short history*. Princeton: Princeton University Press.

Friedländer, Saul. 2009. *Nazi Germany and the Jews, 1933–1945*. New York: Harper Perennial.

Frye Jacobson, Matthew. 2008. *Roots too: White ethnic revival in post-civil rights America*. Cambridge: Harvard University Press.

Gabilliet, Jean-Paul. 2010. *Of comics and men: A cultural history of American comic books*. Trans. Bart Beaty and Nick Nguyen. Jackson: University Press of Mississippi.

Gabler, Neal. 1989. *An empire of their own: How the Jews invented Hollywood*. New York: Anchor.

Gabler, Neal. 1995. *Winchell: Gossip, power and the culture of celebrity*. New York: Vintage.

Gage, Christos N. 2010. *Ragman: Suit of souls*. New York: DC Comics.

Galchinsky, Michael. 2008. *Jews and human rights: Dancing at three weddings*. Lanham: Rowman & Littlefield.

Gans, Herbert J. 1979. Symbolic ethnicity: The future of ethnic groups and cultures in America. In *On the making of Americans: Essays in honor of David Riesman*, ed. Herbert J. Gans, Nathan Glazer, Joseph R. Gusfield, and Christopher Jencks, 193–220. Philadelphia: University of Pennsylvania Press.

Garfinkle, Adam M. 2009. *Jewcentricity: Why the Jews are praised, blamed, and used to explain just about everything*. Hoboken: Wiley.

Garrett, Greg. 2005. *Holy superheroes!: Exploring faith & spirituality in comic books*. Colorado Springs: Piñon Press.

Gartner, Lloyd P. 1978. *History of the Jews of Cleveland*. Cleveland: Western Reserve Historical Society.

Gavaler, Chris. 2015. *On the origin of superheroes: From the big bang to Action Comics no. 1*. Iowa City: University of Iowa Press.

Geis, Deborah R. (ed.). 2003. *Considering Maus: Approaches to Art Spiegelman's "Survivor's tale" of the Holocaust*. Tuscaloosa: University of Alabama Press.

Gelbin, Cathy S. 2011. *The golem returns: From German romantic literature to global Jewish culture, 1808–2008*. Ann Arbor: University of Michigan Press.

Gerstle, Gary. 1994. The protean character of American liberalism. *The American Historical Review* 4: 1043–1073.

Gilbert, Michael T. 2000. Mr. Monster's Comic Crypt!! *Alter Ego*.

Glazer, Nathan. 1989. *American Judaism*. Chicago: University of Chicago Press.

Glazer, Nathan. 1997. *We are all multiculturalists now*. Cambridge: Harvard University Press.

Gleason, Philip. 1981. Americans all: World War II and the shaping of American identity. *The Review of Politics* 43(4): 483–518.

Glenn, Susan A. 2002. In the blood? Consent, descent, and the ironies of Jewish identity. *Jewish Social Studies* 2/3: 139–152.

Glidden, Sarah. 2010. *How to understand Israel in 60 days or less*. New York: Vertigo.

Goldstein, Eric L. 2001. The unstable other: Locating the Jew in progressive-era American racial discourse. *American Jewish History* 89(4): 383–409.

Goldstein, Eric L. 2006. *The price of whiteness*. Princeton: Princeton University Press.

Goodwin, George M. 2001. More than a laughing matter: Cartoons and Jews. *Modern Judaism* 21(2): 146–174.

Gordon, Ian. 1998. *Comic strips and consumer culture, 1890–1945*. Washington, DC: Smithsonian Institution Press.

Gordon, Ian. 2015. The moral world of Superman and the American war in Vietnam. *Journal of Graphic Novels & Comics* 6(2): 172–181.

Greenberg, Cheryl Lynn. 2006. *Troubling the waters: Black-Jewish relations in the American century*. Princeton: Princeton University Press.

Gross, Max. 2002. It's a Jewish thing: Comic hero comes out of a cultural closet. *The Forward*, July 26. http://www.highbeam.com/doc/1P1-79272336.html

Hajdu, David. 2008. *The ten-cent plague: The great comic-book scare and how it changed America*. New York: Farrar, Straus and Giroux.

Halter, Marilyn. 2000. *Shopping for identity: The marketing of ethnicity*. New York: Schocken Books.

Hark, Ina Rae. 2007. Introduction. In *American cinema of the 1930s: Themes and variations*, ed. Ina Rae Hark, 1–24. New Brunswick: Rutgers University Press.

Heinze, Andrew R. 1990. *Adapting to abundance: Jewish immigrants, mass consumption, and the search for American identity.* New York: Columbia University Press.

Herring, George C. 2008. *From colony to superpower: U.S. foreign relations since 1776.* Oxford: Oxford University Press.

Herriot, Peter. 2007. *Religious fundamentalism and social identity.* London/New York: Routledge.

Hertzberg, Arthur. 1989. *The Jews in America: Four centuries of an uneasy encounter.* New York: Simon & Schuster.

Hobsbawm, Eric. 1992. Introduction: Inventing traditions. In *The invention of tradition,* ed. Eric Hobsbawm and Terrence Ranger. Cambridge: Cambridge University Press.

Hollinger, Veronica. 2003. Feminist theory and science fiction. In *The Cambridge companion to science fiction,* ed. Edward James and Farah Mendelsohn, 125–163. Cambridge: Cambridge University Press.

Idel, Moshe. 1990. *Golem: Jewish magical and mystical traditions on the artificial anthropoid.* Albany: SUNY Press.

Ignatiev, Noel. 2009 [1995]. *How the Irish became white.* London/New York: Routledge.

Is that necessary? *Time* 27(16), April 20, 1936, p. 26.

Jacobs, Jill. 2007. The history of 'Tikkun Olam.' *Zeek: A Jewish Journal of Thought and Culture,* June. http://www.zeek.net/706tohu/

Jacobs, James B., and Ellen Peters. 2003. Labor Racketeering: The Mafia and the Unions. *Crime and Justice* 30: 229–282.

James, Bruce. 1982. ZAP! POW! BAM! OY! *Baltimore Jewish Times,* April 30.

Jarvis, Christina S. 2004. *The male body at war: American masculinity during World War II.* DeKalb: Northern Illinois University Press.

Jewell, Richard. 2007. *The golden age of cinema: Hollywood, 1929–1945.* Malden: Blackwell Publishers.

Jones, Gerard. 2004. *Men of tomorrow: The true story of the birth of the superhero.* London: Arrow Books.

Kahn, Jr., E. J. 1940. Why I don't believe in Superman. *The New Yorker,* June 29.

Kane, Bob. 1989. *Batman and me.* Forestville: Eclipse Books.

Kanigher, Robert. 1976. 75-25 or die! *Ragman,* vol. 1 #2. New York: DC Comics.

Kaplan, Dana Evan. 2005. *The Cambridge companion to American Judaism.* Cambridge: Cambridge University Press.

Kaplan, Arie. 2008. *From Krakow to Krypton: Jews and comic books.* Philadelphia: The Jewish Publication Society.

Kaplan, Dana Evan. 2009. *Contemporary American Judaism: Transformation and renewal.* New York: Columbia University Press.

Kaplan, Dana Evan, and Alan Mittelman. 2005. Judaism and democracy in America. In *The Cambridge companion to American Judaism,* ed. Dana Evan Kaplan, 299–313. Cambridge: Cambridge University Press.

Kasson, John F. 2002. *Houdini, Tarzan, and the perfect man: The white male body and the challenge of modernity in America*. New York: Hill and Wang.

Katchor, Ben. 1998. *The Jew of New York*. New York: Pantheon Books.

Kavadlo, Jesse. 2009. X-istential X-men: Jews, Supermen, and the literature of struggle. In *X-men and philosophy*, ed. Rebecca Housel and Jeremy Wisnewski, 38–49. Hoboken: Wiley.

Kennedy, David M. 2001. *Freedom from fear: The American people in depression and war, 1929–1945*. Oxford: Oxford University Press.

Kennedy, Robert C. 2014. On this day: May 8, 1875. http://www.nytimes.com/learning/general/onthisday/harp/0508.html. Accessed 29 Oct 2014.

Kleid, Neil, and Nicolas Cinquegrani. 2009. *The big Kahn: A sequential Drama*. New York: NBM.

Kronenberg, Michael. 2011. Auteur theory. In *Will Eisner: Conversations*, ed. M. Thomas Inge, 220–230. Jackson: University Press of Mississippi.

Kubert, Joe. 2004. *The adventures of Yaakov & Isaac*. Jerusalem: Mahrwood Press.

Kubert, Joe. 2005. *Jew gangster*. New York: DC Comics.

Kubert, Joe, and Pete Carlsson. 2011. *Yossel: April 19, 1943*. New York: DC Comics.

Kühl, Stefan. 1994. *The Nazi connection: Eugenics, American racism, and German National Socialism*. Oxford: Oxford University Press.

Kurtzman, Harvey. 1988. *My life as a cartoonist – The story of one of the legendary creators of MAD magazine*. New York: Pocket Books.

Lawrence, John Shelton, and Robert Jewett. 2007. *The myth of the American superhero*. Grand Rapids: W.B. Eerdmans.

Lederhendler, Eli. 1994. *Jewish responses to modernity: New voices in America and Eastern Europe*. New York: New York University Press.

Lee, Stan, and George Mair. 2002. *Excelsior! The amazing life of Stan Lee*. New York: Simon & Schuster.

Leon, Masha. 2013. 'Superman at 75' unmasks the superhero as a Jew from the planet Krypton. *The Forward*, February 15. http://forward.com/articles/171301/superman-at-75-unmasks-the-superhero-as-a-jew-from/

Lepore, Jill. 2014. *The secret history of wonder woman*. New York: Alfred A. Knopf.

Lester, Julius. 1995. The outsiders: Blacks and Jews and the American soul. *Transition* 68: 66–88.

Leviant, Curt. 2007. Introduction. In *The golem and the wondrous deeds of the Maharal of Prague*, ed. Yudl Rosenberg, xiii–xxxv. New Haven: Yale University Press.

Levy, Eugene. 1974. 'Is the Jew a white man?': Press reaction to the Leo Frank Case, 1913–1915. *Phylon* 35(2): 212–222.

Lipstadt, Deborah E. 1986. *Beyond belief: The American press and the coming of the Holocaust, 1933–1945*. New York: Free Press.

Loeb, Jeph, and Tim Sale. 2002. *Superman for all seasons*. New York: DC Comics.

Lowenthal, David. 1998. Fabricating heritage. *History & Memory* 10(1): 5–25.

Lund, Martin. 2012. American golem – Reading America through super new-dealers and the 'melting pot'. In *Comic books and American cultural history*, ed. Matthew J. Pustz, 79–93. New York: Continuum.

Lund, Martin. 2015a. 'NY 101': New York city according to Brian Wood. *International Journal of Comic Art* 17(2): 1–33.

Lund, Martin. 2015b. The mutant problem: X-men, confirmation bias, and the methodology of comics and identity. *European Journal of American Studies* 10(2). http://ejas.revues.org/10890

Lund, Martin. 2015c. 'X marks the spot': Urban dystopia, slum voyeurism and failures of identity in district X. *Journal of Urban Cultural Studies* 2(1–2): 34–56.

MacDonnell, Francis. 1995. *Insidious foes: The Axis Fifth Column and the American home front*. New York: Oxford University Press.

Mack, Stanley. 1998. *The story of the Jews: A 4,000-year adventure*. New York: Villard.

Malcolm, Cheryl Alexander. 2010. Witness, trauma, and remembrance: Holocaust representation and X-men comics. In *The Jewish graphic novel: Critical approaches*, ed. Samantha Baskind and Ranen Omer-Sherman, 144–160. New Brunswick: Rutgers University Press.

Maney, Patrick J. 2000. They sang for Roosevelt: Songs of the people in the age of FDR. *Journal of American & Comparative Cultures* 23(1): 85.

Mantlo, Bill, and John Buscema. 1981. *"Power in the Promised Land"*. *The Incredible Hulk #256*. New York: Marvel Comics Group.

Mazlish, Bruce. 1982. *Crevecoeur's new world*, 140–147. Autumn: The Wilson Quarterly.

Mazur, Eric Michael. 2004. *The Americanization of religious minorities: Confronting the constitutional order*. Baltimore: The Johns Hopkins University Press.

McCann, Sean. 2000. *Gumshoe America: Hard-boiled crime fiction and the rise and fall of New Deal liberalism*. Durham: Duke University Press Books.

McCloud, Scott. 1993. *Understanding comics: The invisible art*. New York: Harper Paperbacks.

McIntosh, Peggy. 1988. White privilege and male privilege: A personal account of coming to see correspondences through women's studies. Working Paper No. 189.

McLuhan, Marshall. 2001 [1964]. *Understanding media*. London/New York: Routledge.

Medoff, Rafael. 2009. *Blowing the whistle on genocide: Josiah E. Dubois, Jr., and the struggle for a U.S. response to the Holocaust*. West Lafayette: Purdue University.

Michael, John. 2008. *Identity and the failure of America: From Thomas Jefferson to the war on terror*. Minneapolis: University of Minnesota Press.

Mietkiewicz, Henry. 1996. Great Krypton! Superman was the Star's Ace Reporter (Joe Shuster's final interview). *The Joe Shuster Awards*, April 26. http://

joeshusterawards.com/hof/hall-of-fame-joe-shuster/superman-at-the-star-joe-shusters-last-interview/

Millar, Mark, Chris Bachalo, Tim Townsend, Andy Owens, and Aaron Sowd. 2003. *Ultimate X-Men vol. 5: Ultimate War*. New York: Marvel Comics.

Miller, Nathan. 2004. *New world coming: The 1920s and the making of modern America*. Cambridge, MA: Da Capo Press.

Mintz, Lawrence E. 1996. Humor and ethnic stereotypes in Vaudeville and Burlesque. *MELUS* 21(4): 19–28.

Morrison, Toni. 1993. On the backs of blacks. *Time*, p. 57.

Morrison, Grant, and Frank Quitely. 2007. *All-star Superman, vol. 1*. New York: DC Comics.

Most, Andrea. 2006. Re-imagining the Jew's body: From self-loathing to 'grepts'. In *You should see yourself: Jewish identity in postmodern American culture*, ed. Vincent Brook, 19–36. New Brunswick: Rutgers University Press.

Murray, Christopher. 2011. *Champions of the oppressed? Superhero comics, popular culture, and propaganda in America during World War II*. Cresskill: Hampton Press.

Muscio, Giuliana. 1997. *Hollywood's new deal*. Philadelphia: Temple University Press.

Nazi System. *Time* 31(23), May 30, 1938, p. 28.

Neusner, Jacob. 1995. *Judaism in modern times: An introduction and reader*. Cambridge: Blackwell.

Nigosian, S.A. 2004. *From ancient writings to sacred texts: The Old Testament and Apocrypha*. Baltimore: Johns Hopkins University Press.

Norwood, Stephen A. 2009. 'American Jewish Muscle': Forging a new masculinity in the streets and in the ring, 1890–1940. *Modern Judaism* 29(2): 167–193.

Novick, Peter. 2000. *The Holocaust in American life*. Boston: Houghton Mifflin Harcourt.

Nutter, David. 2001. Pilot. *Smallville*.

Nyberg, Amy Kiste. 1998. *Seal of approval: The history of the comics code*. Jackson: University Press of Mississippi.

O'Rourke, Daniel J., and Morgan B. O'Rourke. 2012. 'It's morning again in America': John Byrne's re-imaging of the Man of Steel. In *The ages of Superman: Essays on the man of steel in changing times*, ed. Joseph J. Darowski, 115–124. Jefferson: McFarland & Co.

Oirich, Alan, and Ron Randall. 2003. *"The Amnesia Count-Down"*. *The Jewish Hero Corps #1*. New York: Shayach Comics/Judaica Press.

Omi, Michael, and Howard Winant. 1994. *Racial formation in the United States: From the 1960s to the 1990s*, 2nd ed. London/New York: Routledge.

Oppenheimer, Deborah, Scott Chamberlin, Gretchen Skidmore, and David Cesarani. 2007. Kindertransport. In *Encyclopaedia Judaica*, ed. Michael Berenbaum and Fred Skolnik, vol. 12, 2nd ed, 160–161. Detroit: Macmillan Reference. http://go.galegroup.com/ps/i.do?id=GALE%7CCX2587511136&v=2.1&u=lununi&it=r&p=GVRL&sw=w

Pak, Greg, and Carmine Di Giandomenico. 2009. *X-Men: Magneto testament*. New York: Marvel Comics.

Parker, Bill, and C. C. Beck. 1940a. Untitled Captain Marvel Story #1. In *Whiz Comics*, vol. 1. #2. Louisville: Fawcett Publications, Inc.

Parker, Bill, and C. C. Beck. 1940b. Untitled Captain Marvel Story #2. In *Whiz Comics*, vol. 1. #3. Louisville: Fawcett Publications, Inc.

Parker, Bill, and C. C. Beck. 1940c. Untitled Captain Marvel Story #3. In *Whiz Comics*, vol. 1. #4 [Cover numbered 3]. Louisville: Fawcett Publications, Inc.

Patterson, James T. 1997. *Grand expectations: The United States, 1945–1974*. Oxford: Oxford University Press.

Pekar, Harvey, and J.T. Waldman. 2012. *Not the Israel my parents promised me*. New York: Hill and Wang.

Pekar, Harvey, Paul Buhle, and Hershl Hartman (eds.). 2011. *Yiddishkeit: Jewish Vernacular & the New Land*. New York: Abrams ComicArts.

Plate, S. Brent. 2013. Superheroes get religion, or the other way around? *Huffington Post*, July 4. http://www.huffingtonpost.com/s-brent-plate/superheroes-get-religion-or-the-other-way-around_b_3009310.html

Polenberg, Richard. 1980. *One nation divisible: Class, race, and ethnicity in the United States since 1938*. New York: Viking Press.

Portnoy, Eddy. 2013. Superman is a Glatt Goy. *The Marginalia Review of Books*, October 16. http://marginalia.lareviewofbooks.org/archives/3987

Power, Samantha. 2002. *"A problem from hell": America and the age of genocide*. New York: Basic Books.

Prell, Riv-Ellen. 1999. *Fighting to become Americans: Jews, gender, and the anxiety of assimilation*. Boston: Beacon Press.

Putnam, Robert D. 2000. *Bowling alone: The collapse and revival of American community*. New York: Simon & Schuster.

Reynolds, Richard. 1992. *Super heroes: A modern mythology*. Jackson: University Press of Mississippi.

Ricca, Brad. 2013. *Super Boys: The amazing adventures of Jerry Siegel and Joe Shuster – The creators of Superman*. New York: St. Martin's Press.

Rimmon-Kenan, Shlomith. 2002. *Narrative fiction: Contemporary poetics*, 2nd ed. London/New York: Routledge.

Rising to the Moment. *The Kindertransport Organization*. http://www.kindertransport.org/history03_rising.htm. Accessed 30 June 2013.

Roediger, David R. 1999. *The wages of whiteness: Race and the making of the American working class*. London/New York: Verso.

Roediger, David R. 2005. *Working toward whiteness: How America's immigrants became white. The strange journey from Ellis Island to the suburbs*. New York: Basic Books.

Roosevelt, Franklin D. 1932. The forgotten man. *New Deal Network*, April 7. http://newdeal.feri.org/speeches/1932c.htm

Roosevelt, Franklin D. 1933a. Fireside Chat 1: On the Banking Crisis. *Miller Center of Public Affairs*, March 12. http://millercenter.org/scripps/archive/speeches/detail/3298

Roosevelt, Franklin D. 1933b. First inaugural address. *Miller Center of Public Affairs*, March 4. http://millercenter.org/president/speeches/speech-3280

Roosevelt, Franklin D. 1935. Fireside Chat 7: On the Works Relief Program and Social Security Act. *Miller Center of Public Affairs*, April 28. http://millercenter.org/president/speeches/detail/3304

Roosevelt, Franklin D. 1936a. Address at Madison Square Garden, New York City. *The American Presidency Project*, October 31. http://www.presidency.ucsb.edu/ws/index.php?pid=15219#axzz1KFXk5ybE

Roosevelt, Franklin D. 1936b. Address at Roosevelt Park, New York City. *The American Presidency Project*, October 28. http://www.presidency.ucsb.edu/ws/index.php?pid=15211#axzz1x7PweJmV

Roosevelt, Franklin D. 1937. Second inaugural address. *Miller Center of Public Affairs*, January 20. http://millercenter.org/president/speeches/detail/3308

Roosevelt, Franklin D. 1939. Fireside Chat 14: On the European War. *Miller Center of Public Affairs*, September 3. http://millercenter.org/president/speeches/detail/3315

Roosevelt, Franklin D. 1940a. Democratic National Convention. *Miller Center of Public Affairs*, June 19. http://millercenter.org/president/speeches/detail/3318

Roosevelt, Franklin D. 1940b. Fireside Chat 15: On National Defense. *Miller Center of Public Affairs*, May 26. http://millercenter.org/president/speeches/detail/3316

Roosevelt, Franklin D. 1940c. Fireside Chat 16: On the 'Arsenal of Democracy.' *Miller Center of Public Affairs*, December 29. http://millercenter.org/president/speeches/detail/3319

Roosevelt, Franklin D. 1940d. 'Stab in the back' speech. *Miller Center of Public Affairs*, June 10. http://millercenter.org/president/speeches/detail/3317

Roosevelt, Franklin D. 1941a. Fireside Chat 17: On an Unlimited National Emergency. *Miller Center of Public Affairs*, May 27. http://millercenter.org/president/speeches/detail/3814

Roosevelt, Franklin D. 1941b. On Lend Lease. *Miller Center of Public Affairs*, March 15. http://millercenter.org/president/speeches/detail/3322

Roosevelt, Franklin D. 1941c. State of the Union (four freedoms). *Miller Center of Public Affairs*, January 6. http://millercenter.org/scripps/archive/speeches/detail/3320

Rose, Kenneth D. 2008. *Myth and the greatest generation: A social history of Americans in World War II.* London/New York: Routledge.

Rosenberg, Yudl. 2007. *The golem and the wondrous deeds of the Maharal of Prague.* Trans. Curt Leviant. New Haven: Yale University Press.

Rosenfeld, Alvin H. 2011. *The end of the Holocaust*. Bloomington: Indiana University Press.

Rosenthal, Gilbert S. 2005. Tikkun Ha-Olam: The metamorphosis of a concept. *Journal of Religion* 85(2): 214–240.

Roskies, David. 1999. *The Jewish search for a usable past*. Bloomington: Indiana University Press.

Rossen, Jake. 2008. *Superman Vs. Hollywood: How fiendish producers, devious directors, and warring writers grounded an American icon*. Chicago: Chicago Review Press.

Roth, Laurence. 2010. Contemporary American Jewish comic books: Abject pasts, heroic futures. In *The Jewish Graphic Novel: Critical Approaches*, ed. Samantha Baskind and Ranen Omer-Sherman, 3–21. New Brunswick/London: Rutgers University Press.

Round, Julia. 2010. 'Be vewy, vewy quiet. We're hunting wippers': A Barthesian analysis of the construction of fact and fiction in Alan Moore and Eddie Campbell's From Hell. In *The rise and reason of comics and graphic literature: Critical essays on the form*, ed. Joyce Goggin and Dan Hassler-Forest, 188–201. Jefferson: McFarland & Co.

Royal, Derek Parker. 2009. Native Noir: Genre and politics of indigenous representation in recent American comics. *ImageTexT: Interdisciplinary Comics Studies* 5(3). http://www.english.ufl.edu/imagetext/archives/v5_2/wegner/

Royal, Derek Parker. 2011. Jewish comics; or, visualizing current Jewish narrative. *Shofar: An Interdisciplinary Journal of Jewish Studies* 29(2): 1–12.

Royal, Derek Parker. 2013a. Review of the Jewish graphic novel: Critical approaches, ed. Samantha Baskin and Ranen Omer Sherman; Yiddishkeit: The Jewish Vernacular and the New Land, ed. Harvey Pekar and Paul Buhle; Jewish images in comics: A visual history, ed. Frederick Strömberg; and Superman is Jewish?: How comic book superheroes came to serve truth, justice, and the Jewish-American way, ed. Harry Brod. *MELUS* 38(2): 247–252.

Royal, Derek Parker. 2013b. Siegel and Shuster's Funnyman: The first Jewish superhero, from the creators of Superman, ed. Thomas Andrae and Mel Gordon. Port Townsend: Feral House, 2010, X + 183 pp., US$24.95 (Paperback), ISBN 987-1-9325-9578-9. *Journal of Graphic Novels and Comics* 4(2): 363–366.

Rubin, Derek. 2005. Introduction. In *Who we are: On being (and not being) a Jewish American writer*, ed. Derek Rubin, ix–xix. New York: Schocken Books.

Rubin, Martin. 2007. Movies and the new deal in entertainment. In *American cinema of the 1930s: Themes and variations*, ed. Ina Rae Hark, 92–116. New Brunswick: Rutgers University Press.

Rubinstein, Judah. 2004. *Merging traditions: Jewish life in Cleveland*. Kent: Kent State University Press.

Rushkoff, Douglas. 2003. *Nothing sacred: The truth about Judaism*. New York: Crown Publishers.

Sabin, Roger. 2001. *Comics, comix & graphic novels: A history of graphic novels.* London/New York: Phaidon Press.

Said, Edward W. 2003 [1978]. *Orientalism.* London: Penguin.

Sanderson, Peter. 1982. Interview with Chris Claremont (part two). In *X-Men Companion II*, ed. Peter Sanderson, 18–51. Stamford: Fantagraphics Books, Inc.

Sanderson, Peter. 2006. Comics in context #125: Miller, front and center. *IGN. com*, March 20. http://au.comics.ign.com/articles/696/696965p1.html

Sarna, Jonathan D. 2004. *American Judaism: A new history.* New Haven: Yale University Press.

Sarna, Jonathan D. 1999/1998. The cult of synthesis in American Jewish culture. *Jewish Social Studies* 5(1/2): 52–79.

Satlow, Michael L. 2006. *Creating Judaism: History, tradition, practice.* New York: Columbia University Press.

Schlam, Helena Frenkil. 2001. Contemporary scribes: Jewish American cartoonists. *Shofar: An Interdisciplinary Journal of Jewish Studies* 20(1): 94–112.

Schlesinger, Arthur M. 1943. What then is the American, this New Man? *The American Historical Review* 48(2): 225–244.

Schulman, Bruce J. 2002. *The seventies: The great shift in American culture, society, and politics.* Cambridge: Da Capo.

Schumacher, Michael. 2010. *Will Eisner: A dreamer's life in comics.* New York: Bloomsbury.

Schumer, Arlen. 2011a. A superhero for our time. *Captain Israel* #1. Los Angeles: StandWithUs.

Schumer, Arlen. 2011b. The venomous BDS! *Captain Israel* #2. Los Angeles: StandWithUs.

Schwartz, Julius. 2000. *Man of two worlds: My life in science fiction and comics.* New York: HarperEntertainment.

Shachtman, Tom. 1982. *The phony war: 1939–1940.* New York: Harper & Row.

Shaheen, Jack G. 2009. *Reel bad Arabs: How Hollywood vilifies a people.* Northampton: Interlink.

Shogan, Robert. 2010. *Prelude to catastrophe: FDR's Jews and the menace of Nazism.* Chicago: Ivan R. Dee.

Siegel, Jerry. 1975. Re: THE VICTIMIZATION SUPERMAN'S ORIGINATORS, JERRY SIEGEL AND JOE SHUSTER (Facsimile). *The Comics Journal.* http://archives.tcj.com/275/siegel1975.pdf

Siegel, Jerry, and Joe Shuster. 1940. How Superman would end the war. *Look Magazine*, February 27. http://ia700300.us.archive.org/0/items/HowSupermanWouldEndTheWar/look.pdf

Siegel, Jerry, and Joe Shuster. 2006. *Superman Sunday classics 1939–1943.* New York: Sterling.

Siegel, Jerry, and Joe Shuster. 2010. *Siegel and Shuster's Funnyman: The first Jewish superhero, from the creators of Superman.* Port Townsend: Feral House.

Siegel, Jerry, Wayne Boring, and Stan Kaye. 2006. Superman's return to Krypton. In *Showcase presents: Superman*, vol. 2, 360–386. New York: DC Comics.

Siegel, Jerry, Joe Shuster, et al. 2006–2009. *Superman chronicles*, vols. 1–9. New York: DC Comics.

Singer, Bryan. 2006. *Superman returns*. Burbank: Warner Bros. Pictures.

Skelton, Stephen. 2006. *The Gospel according to the world's greatest superhero*. Eugene: Harvest House Publishers.

Smith, Erin A. 2000. *Hard-boiled: Working-class readers and pulp magazines*. Philadelphia: Temple University Press.

Smith, Matthew J. 2001. The Tyranny of the melting pot metaphor: Wonder woman as the Americanized immigrant. In *Comics & ideology*, ed. Matthew P. McAllister, Edward H. Sewell, Jr., and Ian Gordon, 129–50. New York: P. Lang.

Spiegelman, Art. 1986. *Maus: A survivor's tale*. New York: Pantheon Books.

Strömberg, Fredrik. 2010. *Comic art propaganda: A graphic history*. New York: St. Martin's Griffin.

Strömberg, Fredrik. 2012a. *Black images in the comics: A visual history*, 2nd ed. Seattle: Fantagraphics.

Strömberg, Fredrik. 2012b. *Jewish images in the comics: A visual history*. Seattle: Fantagraphics.

Sturm, James. 2001. *The golem's mighty swing*. Montreal: Drawn and Quarterly.

Surnames – War, politics and comic strip superheroes. *Thinking Allowed*. BBC 4, August 16, 2011. http://www.bbc.co.uk/programmes/b015cnnt

Sutton, Philip. 2013. Why your family name was not changed at Ellis Island (and one that was). *The New York Public Library*, July 2. http://www.nypl.org/blog/2013/07/02/name-changes-ellis-island

Tabachnick, Stephen E. 2014. *The Quest for Jewish belief and identity in the graphic novel*. Tuscaloosa: University of Alabama Press.

Takaki, Ronald T. 2000. *Double victory: A multicultural history of America in World War II*. Boston: Little, Brown and Co.

Takaki, Ronald T. 2008. *A different mirror: A history of multicultural America*. New York: Back Bay Books/Little, Brown, and Co.

Thurber, James. 1999. *The Thurber carnival*. New York: Perennial Classics.

Trexler, Jeff. 2008. Superman's Hidden History: The Other 'First' Artist. *Newsarama*, August 20. http://www.newsarama.com/comics/080820-SupermanKeaton.html

Tye, Larry. 2012. *Superman: The high-flying history of America's most enduring hero*. New York: Random House.

United States Circuit Court of Appeals. 1939. Detective Comics, Inc. against Bruns Publications, Inc., Kable News Company, and Interborough News Co., November 10.

United States Holocaust Memorial Museum. "Kindertransport, 1938–1940." *Holocaust Encyclopedia.* http://www.ushmm.org/wlc/en/?ModuleId= 10005143. Accessed 30 June 2013.

Vaughn, Stephen, and Bruce Evensen. 1991. Democracy's guardians: Hollywood's portrait of Reporters, 1930–1945. *Journalism & Mass Communication Quarterly* 68(4): 829–838.

Walzer, Michael. 1995. Liberalism and the Jews: Historical affinities, contemporary necessities. In *Values, interests, and identity: Jews and politics in a changing world,* ed. Peter Y. Medding, 3–10. Oxford: Oxford University Press.

Weiner, Robert G. 2007. Up, up and Oy Vey!: How Jewish history, culture, and values shaped the comic book superhero. Simcha Weinstein. Baltimore: Leviathan Press, 2006. 150 Pages. $19.95 Paper. *MELUS* 32(3): 315–318.

Weiner, Robert G. 2011. Marvel comics and the golem legend. *Shofar: An Interdisciplinary Journal of Jewish Studies* 29(2): 50–72.

Weinstein, Simcha. 2006. *Up, up, and Oy Vey!: How Jewish history, culture, and values shaped the comic book superhero.* Baltimore: Leviathan Press.

Weiss, Jeffrey. 2002. Comic superhero, thing, revealed as a Jew. *The Dallas Morning News.* September 14, 2002.

Weiss, Michael. 1995. Secret identities: The real-life faces behind the masks of comic books' greatest super-heroes, June 13, 1995. http://www.hoboes.com/pub/Comics/About%20Comics/Essays/Secret%20Identities/

Weldon, Glen. 2013. *Superman: The unauthorized biography.* Hoboken: Wiley.

Welky, David. 2008. *Everything was better in America: Print culture in the great depression.* Baltimore: University of Illinois Press.

Wenger, Beth S. 2010a. *History lessons: The creation of American Jewish heritage.* Princeton: Princeton University Press.

Wenger, Beth S. 2010b. Inventing American Jewry. *Journal of Jewish Communal Service* 86(1/2): 3–9.

Whitfield, Stephen J. 1999. *In search of American Jewish culture.* Hanover/London: Brandeis University Press.

Whitfield, Stephen J. 2008. The Paradoxes of American Jewish culture. In *American Jewish identity politics,* ed. Deborah Dash Moore, 243–265. Ann Arbor: University of Michigan Press.

Whitson, Roger. 2007. Introduction, 'William Blake and Visual Culture.' *ImageText: Interdisciplinary Comics Studies* 3(2). http://www.english.ufl.edu/imagetext/archives/v3_2/introduction.shtml

Wilson, Woodrow. 1915. Address to naturalized citizens at Conventiona Hall, Philadelphia. *The American Presidency Project.* http://www.presidency.ucsb.edu/ws/?pid=65388

Witwer, David. 2003. The Scandal of George Scalise: A case study in the rise of labor racketeering in the 1930s. *Journal of Social History* 36(4): 917–940.

Wolkin, David. 2012. Internal monologue reviews: Ragman. *Wolkin's House of Chicken and Waffles (and Comics!)*. Accessed 9 Jan 2012. http://wolkin.com/2010/12/1454/internal-monologue-reviews-ragman/

Worcester, Kent. 2010. Lev Gleason: The family speaks! *The Comics Journal*. http://classic.tcj.com/history/lev-gleason-the-family-speaks/

Wright, Bradford. 2001. *Comic book nation: The transformation of youth culture in America*. Baltimore: Johns Hopkins University Press.

Wylie, Philip. 2004 [1930]. *Gladiator*. Lincoln: University of Nebraska Press.

Yanes, Nicholas. 2008. Graphic imagery – Jewish American comic book creators' depictions of class, race, and patriotism. Florida State University. http://etd.lib.fsu.edu/theses_1/available/etd-04052008-172103/unrestricted/YanesNSpring2008.pdf.

Yanes, Nicholas. 2009. Graphic imagery: Jewish American comic book creators' depictions of class, race, patriotism and the birth of the good captain. In *Captain America and the struggle of the superhero: Critical essays*, ed. Robert G. Weiner, 53–65. Jefferson: McFarland & Co.

Yanes, Nicholas. 2016. Joseph J. Darowski on his comics scholar career and the ages of Iron Man. *Sequart Organization*. Accessed 9 May 2016. http://sequart.org/magazine/61502/editor-darowski-on-the-ages-of-iron-man/

Yerushalmi, Yosef Hayim. 1996. *Zakhor: Jewish history and Jewish memory*. Seattle: University of Washington Press.

Index

Note: Page numbers followed by "n" denote notes.

© The Editor(s) (if applicable) and The Author(s) 2016
M. Lund, *Re-Constructing the Man of Steel*,
DOI 10.1007/978-3-319-42960-1

Printed by Books on Demand, Germany